BRITANNIA
ROYAL NAVAL COLLEGE

DARTMOUTH

Lord High Admiral's Divisions

From a painting by Mandy Shepherd

IT.IS:ON.THE:NAVY
UNDER:THE:GOOD:PROVIDENCE
OF:GOD:THAT.OUR WEALTH:PROSPERITY:AND
PEACE:DEPEND

BRITANNIA
ROYAL NAVAL COLLEGE

DARTMOUTH

An Illustrated History

Dr Jane Harrold and Dr Richard Porter

Richard Webb

PUBLISHER'S ACKNOWLEDGEMENT

Full and grateful acknowledgement is given to the Commodore and staff of the Britannia Royal Naval College and to the Chairman and Trustees of the Britannia Association for their support and involvement in the publication of this book.

First published in the United Kingdom in 2005 by Richard Webb, Publisher
First edition April 2005
Second edition October 2007
Third edition April 2012

Text copyright © 2005 Dr Jane Harrold and Dr Richard Porter

Illustrations © 2005 Britannia Royal Naval College (unless otherwise credited)

Design and typography © 2005 Richard Webb, Publisher

The right of Dr Jane Harrold and Dr Richard Porter to be identified as the authors of this work have been asserted by them in accordance with the Copyright, Designs and Patents Act, 1988

Edited and indexed by Michael Forder

Designed by Laurence Daeche, Anon Design Co., Christchurch, Dorset

A CIP catalogue record for this book is available from the British Library

ISBN 978-0-9568464-3-3

Typeset in Bembo 12/14

Printed and bound in China
Lion Production Ltd / Hanway Press Ltd

Richard Webb, Publisher
Dartmouth, England
www.dartmouthbooks.co.uk

THIS BOOK IS DEDICATED TO THE

MEMORY OF THE OFFICERS, CADETS AND STAFF OF

BRITANNIA ROYAL NAVAL COLLEGE

WHO GAVE THEIR LIVES IN THE

SERVICE OF THEIR COUNTRY.

FOREWORD

BUCKINGHAM PALACE.

It hardly needs to be said that the training of young officers for the services is absolutely crucial to their effectiveness. For years, if not centuries, the Navy relied on an 'apprenticeship' system where the young learn by precept and example from their seniors. Considering the quality of leaders produced by this system in the struggles against Spain and France over three centuries, it must have been successful. However, the art and technology of sail and the primitive weapons of those days made no great intellectual demands on the officers.

Come the age of steam, rifled cannons, improvements in fire control, communications and navigation, the need for some system to prepare young officers to cope with these developments became vital. The Britannia Royal Naval College, and its preparatory college at Osborne, were the Navy's answer to the problem. This detailed and fascinating book tells the story of the College and how it evolved to meet the needs of a world-wide fleet at a time of very rapid modernisation and of the challenges of two great wars.

The senior officers, who were responsible for the structure and content of the training system, knew what would be demanded of the young officers when they went to sea, and they devised a system of indoctrination, discipline and instruction that would ensure that young officers joining the fleet would be sufficiently knowledgeable to be useful in an unfamiliar environment.

This book is a worthy memorial to the young men who were trained at Dartmouth and who lost their lives in the service of their country while serving in the Royal Navy.

PREFACE

Admiral Sir Mark Stanhope GCB OBE ADC

First Sea Lord and Chief of Naval Staff

The United Kingdom is first and foremost a maritime nation whose fortunes are, as they always have been, inextricably linked with the sea. A sea that sustains, moulds and inspires us. Consequently, man's close relationship with the maritime endures.

For those of us directly involved in protecting our island nation's interests – by which I mean the security of its people, its economic well-being, our freedoms and our values – through service as an officer in the Royal Navy, that relationship between man and maritime is nurtured first at Dartmouth. Next year, 2013, will see the 150th anniversary of Royal Navy officers' training being based on the River Dart, initially on board HMS *Britannia* before eventually moving ashore in 1905 to the College that we recognise with such affection today. This celebrated book, now in its third edition, tells that story in a highly readable and authoritative way.

Just as the College has evolved over the years, so of course has the world around it. Ours is an increasingly complex, multi-dimensional and uncertain world. A world which, largely as a result of globalisation, will lead to the United Kingdom's and other nations' economic, political and security interests being affected both more rapidly and more unpredictably by global events. Thus, as an outward-looking nation, with global responsibilities and global ambitions, engagement with such a world brings risk and reward in equal measure. Accordingly, the Royal Navy, more particularly those who lead and serve in it, continues to play its part in protecting our nation's interests in an uncertain world.

So as the Royal Navy educates today its leaders of tomorrow, Britannia Royal Naval College importantly provides our officers, as well as those representing other Navies from around the world, with the skills necessary to lead with clarity, confidence and conviction. To grow leaders with the ability to apply logic, emotion, purpose and compromise according to the nuance of the moment. To produce leaders who, in embracing our increasingly ambiguous world, intuitively understand maritime doctrine and can apply it flexibly and appropriately across the joint and multinational environments. But, above all, the College equips leaders with courage. The courage to believe in themselves, their endeavours and their people, because ultimately it is courage that enables leaders to inspire others to aspire.

To inspire the sailors and marines upon which the Royal Navy of the 21st Century depends. And to inspire people who are committed and confident operating in the maritime environment.

This fine book records how such noble legacies have been taught, encouraged and developed at Dartmouth. Legacies that have been faithfully captured by Jane Harrold and Richard Porter in this latest edition. I am delighted therefore that this updated and refreshingly presented account of the College's rich heritage is published in Her Majesty The Queen's Diamond Jubilee year. The book serves not only as a celebration and witness to the Royal Household's long and dedicated connection with the College but of course more widely with the Royal Navy. In doing so, it echoes the broader connection between the nation and its Navy.

I have every confidence that the enduring ethos of the Royal Navy and spirit of the College will – just as the sea does – continue to sustain, mould and inspire all those who serve in the years ahead.

Introduction

The story of officer training and education in the Royal Navy is the story of Britain over the past century. One hundred years ago Britain was apparently at the height of her power. The Empire was at its full extent and its people confident that Britannia would continue to rule the waves well into the next century. However, beneath the veneer of Imperial power and prosperity the seeds of Britain's decline were already sown. Other empires and economies were beginning to grow and looked jealously towards Britain. In order to keep these new, aspiring powers at bay Britain would once again have to turn to the Royal Navy to provide her security. In two world wars the Navy managed to ensure that Britain was able to survive until victory, but by the second of these conflicts Britain's power was all but exhausted. Nevertheless, despite being overtaken by the two new superpowers of the Cold War, Britain and the Royal Navy continued to function as an essential bulwark against communism and totalitarianism. Since the end of that conflict the Royal Navy has once again emerged as an important tool of national interests. Throughout this period of change in Britain's fortunes, coupled with the massive technological changes that have taken place over the last century, so the means and methods of preparing young men and women to be the future officers of the Royal Navy have also evolved. This is the story of that process.

The town of Dartmouth has been associated with initial officer training for 150 years, since the old *Britannia* sailed into the Dart on 30th September 1863. The early period of training on the river in *Britannia* was recorded in a book by Commander E P Statham, published in 1904; this remains one of the most important records of those early years and as such has been widely drawn from in subsequent histories. It was to be almost fifty years before E A Hughes, Second Master on the academic staff, published the first history of the College ashore in 1950. This was followed in 1966 by Captain S W C Pack's account of *Britannia at Dartmouth*. As onetime Deputy Director of the Naval Education Service at the Admiralty he was well placed to chronicle the momentous changes that took place in the mid-twentieth century, when the College changed from being a naval public school to a college of initial officer training. For the College's seventy-fifth anniversary in 1980 two of the academic staff, Eric Grove and Evan Davies published a history of the college, entitled *The Royal Naval College Dartmouth, Seventy-five Years in Pictures*. Since 1980 awareness has grown within the Navy of the importance of its own heritage. The expansion of the archive and the opening of the Britannia Museum in 1999 have reflected this at the College. Subsequently more material has become available through donations of photographs and historical material to the College. In addition the thirty-year rule has meant that much more official material has become available from the Public Record Office that was not accessible to the authors of previous studies. As the College celebrates its centenary year it is therefore timely for a completely new and definitive history of officer training at Dartmouth.

Inevitably any such history, while primarily concentrating on the last one hundred years and the shore based college, would be incomplete without reference to the old ships HMS *Britannia* and *Hindostan* moored in the river or indeed to the history of training that preceded the ships location at Dartmouth. It is the history of Royal Naval officer training prior to Dartmouth that is introduced in the first chapter before a description of life on the old ships and an examination of training at that time. By the end of the nineteenth century, however, it was becoming clear that if Britain was to maintain her position the Royal Navy would have to reform. This would require not only technological advances in ships and armaments but also a radical reworking of the way in which the Navy trained and educated its officers of the future. The old hulks were clearly no longer the appropriate venue for teaching the naval officers of the twentieth century. Consequently in 1898 the foundations were laid for a modern, shore-based College.

With the inspiration of royal architect Sir Aston Webb the new college was clearly built to impress, in bricks and mortar, that the Royal Navy remained confident in its task, as carved in stone on the front of the building, to promote Britain's 'wealth, prosperity and peace.' The second chapter of the book therefore examines the building itself and how it relates as a piece of classic Edwardian architecture.

Naval education and training is critically examined in two chapters, the first covering the early years up to 1945 and the importance of the Selborne-Fisher Scheme. This new scheme of naval education, introduced by First Lord of the Admiralty Lord Selborne, and inspired by Second Sea Lord Admiral Fisher, was revolutionary by the standards of the day, emphasising the importance of practical engineering, science, history and modern languages. It aimed to provide the Navy with a common entry of twelve to thirteen year old boys for all executive, engineer and marine officers. In particular it was an attempt to break the traditional barriers, largely class based, between the executive and engineering branches, which was becoming increasingly anachronistic as the engine room became the heart of the modern warship. Although the Selborne scheme was to fail both to encompass Royal Marine officers and remove the stigma of the engineering branch it was, in modified form, to provide basis for the most common route for officers joining the Royal Navy until after the Second World War.

A further chapter of education focuses on the major changes introduced after the Second World War, and an era of almost continuous change that has permeated BRNC's second half century. With a new Socialist government in power the apparently elitist system of entry at thirteen, which was seen to benefit public school boys for whom thirteen was the natural age of progression from preparatory to senior school, was ceased. A new scheme was introduced based upon a sixteen-year-old entry and all fees were abolished. However, before this system had even produced its first Lieutenant for the fleet it was judged to be failing and a further review was initiated. The findings of this review actually found in favour of a return to the thirteen-year-old entry, but this was clearly unfeasible in the political climate of the time. Instead it was decided to turn to an all eighteen-year-old entry. Eighteen year olds had been entering the Navy since the Special Entry scheme was introduced by Winston Churchill in 1913 but the introduction of an all eighteen entry in 1955 was to lead to a complete transformation of the College. No longer was Dartmouth a public school, with a headmaster, masters and schoolboys, but a tertiary college, with a director of studies, lecturers and students of university age.

Both World Wars had a dramatic effect on the College, the first conflict seeing early mobilisation of the whole of College. On August 1st 1914 the Captain received a telegram from Plymouth ordering the immediate mobilisation of the College. Before the day was out all the ship's company and all the cadets, some just fifteen years old, were sent off to their billets in Plymouth, Portsmouth and Chatham. Amongst those boys sent away from the College that day were thirteen cadets who were to be among the fatalities on board HMS *Cressy, Aboukir* and *Hogue* in September 1914. Throughout the rest of the Great War, the College's student population was to fluctuate according to the manning requirements of the fleet. A national debate had surrounded the issue of cadets at sea during wartime, the Admiralty finally conceding to reimburse the parents of midshipmen killed in action, a proportion of their annual fees.

The outbreak of the Second World War in September 1939 failed to break the daily routine to the same extent as the First. However, in September 1942 the war came to Dartmouth when six Focke-Wulf aircraft dropped their payload over the College, two bombs hitting their target in opposite corners of the quarterdeck. Fortunately, the attack had taken place one week before the start of term, consequently casualties were light although there was one fatality. Nevertheless, the damage sustained had rendered the building unfit for its intended task, requiring the College – students and staff – to seek refuge at Eaton Hall in Cheshire, where the Royal Naval College remained until repairs at Dartmouth were complete in September 1946. Meanwhile the College buildings themselves were put to use as a base first for Combined Operations and later by the United States Navy, as a training establishment in the run up to the D-Day landings in June 1944.

The College has had a long connection with the Royal family, dating back to the 1870s, when the Prince of Wales decided to send his two sons, Albert Victor and George, to be educated at Dartmouth on board *Britannia*. George V was to send his own three sons, Edward, Albert and George to Dartmouth, between 1909 and 1920. In 1939, Prince Philip of Greece joined the Special Entry at Dartmouth, when legend would speculate that he and the future Queen first met. More recently both Prince Charles and Prince Andrew have passed through the College.

Although this is generally a historical survey commemorating 150 years of officer training at Dartmouth, the College continues to deliver the same core aims and objectives that it has always done. Despite the many changes, not only to the College but also to the Royal Navy and indeed the nation, its mission remains the same: to train and educate naval officers for the demanding challenges of the front line. The book therefore concludes with a look at College life in the twenty-first century and its vision for the future.

Dr Jane Harrold
Dr Richard Porter
Dartmouth 2012

Contents

HMS Britannia *and HMS* Hindostan *in the River Dart, from a watercolour painted in 1900 by Colonel Charles William Fothergill (1838-1903). C.W. Fothergill studied at the Royal Naval Academy, Portsmouth in 1855. In 1868 he was appointed Instructor of Military Drawing and Surveying at The Royal Military Academy, Sandhurst, and rose to the rank of Honorary Lieutenant Colonel in February 1881, when he retired at his own request.*

CHAPTER 1

Life on Board
HMS Britannia *and* Hindostan

Officer Training before Dartmouth

Prior to the end of the seventeenth century officers had usually entered the Navy by private arrangement between their parents and the Captain of a ship. This system was known as the 'Captain's Servant Entry' and the young boy would learn his skills while under the supervision of the Captain to whom he was assigned as a servant. The Admiralty had no control over this system whatsoever: it was left to Samuel Pepys, when secretary to the Admiralty, to introduce another scheme of entry where young gentlemen, sponsored by the Admiralty, were sent to sea as 'Volunteers-per-Order' or as they were sometimes known, 'King's Letter Boys.'

In 1729 the Admiralty decided to build a Naval Academy in Portsmouth Dockyard. This opened four years later in 1733 'for the better education and training' of these 'Volunteers' and continued until 1837. The 'Volunteer' scheme ran in addition to those parents who still thought that the future lay in sending their sons to sea with a good Captain. In 1837 the Royal Naval College in Portsmouth was abandoned in favour of sending all 'Volunteers' to sea. In the twenty years that followed the Admiralty gradually gained control of the training of young cadets and in 1857 it decided that all cadets should have a period in a moored ship prior to going to sea. The ship chosen was the two-decker HMS *Illustrious*, to be replaced by the larger HMS *Britannia* in 1859.

Britannia before Dartmouth

The *Britannia* that first came to Dartmouth in 1863 was the fourth ship to bear the name, she was a first rate of 120 guns, with three decks and weighing 2616 tons, launched at Plymouth in 1820. She had been the flagship in the Mediterranean after 1840 and again from 1852 to 1855 flying the flags of Admiral Sir William Parker. As such she had seen active service in the Crimea, where in 1854 she assisted in the bombardment of Sevastopol. However, this second stint as flagship might not have been the case but for a last minute diplomatic decision, calculated to avoid offending Britain's French allies, as Admiral Parker recalled in his memoirs:

'The 120-gun ship *Waterloo* had been selected as our flag-ship on the station, and it had been completely fitted out for that duty, when suddenly, at the last moment, the Government, in surely a weak spirit for Englishmen, apparently fearing lest the name should give offence to the new ruler of France, Louis Napoleon, requested the Admiralty to keep back the *Waterloo* and substitute some ship with another name. The choice was the *Britannia*. It was, indeed good for the *Britannia's* fame that she went to the Mediterranean just then, for she was thus able to take part as Commander-in-Chief's flag-ship at the bombardment of Sevastopol.'

On her return from the Black Sea *Britannia* was laid up until chosen as the cadet training ship in 1859. Following the necessary alterations she was moored in Haslar Creek in Portsmouth Harbour. However, the proximity of the town of Portsmouth was considered to be an unsuitable environment for young gentlemen, and consequently she sailed to Portland in February 1862, accompanied on the somewhat hazardous journey by a steam two-decker *Trafalgar* for support. She sailed with the cadets embarked but there were only a few 'bluejackets' and dockyard riggers on board to act as an experienced crew. This was to be the last time that the old ship would be seen under full sail.

It was also in 1862, when the *Britannia* was under the command of Captain R A Powell, that the Admiralty decided to introduce corporal punishment for serious breaches of conduct amongst cadets. It is not known why it was introduced at this time but no doubt it had come to the attention of their Lordships misdemeanours were being perpetrated that required some cadets to be made examples of as a deterrent to the others. The first use of the birch as a punishment on board for a cadet was witnessed by all the cadets while the culprit was lashed in true 'man o' war' fashion, on the side of the deck facing a port. However, Statham (1904) states that the birchings were not common, at least under the command of Captain Powell. It was Captain Powell that persuaded the Admiralty that Portland was not ideal as the ship was there exposed to strong winds and there was little ashore for the cadets. It was almost certainly Powell that suggested Dartmouth to their Lordships, so in 1863 HMS *Britannia* sailed to Dartmouth, where there was a sheltered harbour and facilities ashore. The journey was again made with the cadets on board, but this time it was considered to be too much of a risk under sail, even though the ship was at that time still fully rigged.

She set sail for Dartmouth at 0745 on 29th September with 108 cadets on board, about half the full number, the others being sent on leave. Two vessels were provided to tow the *Britannia*, the first an old paddle sloop called the *Geyser*, with an Admiralty tug called the *Prospero* leading. *Britannia's* sails were available if required, but alas they were not. Dartmouth was reached later that day but the ship spent the night outside the harbour. Thus it was that the *Britannia* entered Dartmouth harbour at 0900 on the morning of September 30th 1863; the town has served as the 'Cradle of the Navy' ever since.

Britannia at Dartmouth 1863 – 1869[1]

Many of the townspeople turned out to welcome and cheer the arrival of the ship and church bells were rung to herald the new era of cadet training in the town. She was to be moored off Sandquay, the site having been previously surveyed by Captain Powell and visited by the Lords of the Admiralty. A working party from Devonport had prepared the site by sinking four five-ton anchors in five fathoms of water, each with seventy fathoms of cable, which would have been

1 Much of the information pertaining to life on board HMS *Britannia* and *Hindostan* is taken from Statham's book *The Story of Britannia* (1904). Captain Pack also drew heavily from Statham for his history of the College in 1966.

HMS Britannia *under sail en route from Portland to Dartmouth on 29th September 1863. From a painting by Charles Dixon.*

sufficient to anchor the vessel with two anchors at both bow and stern making her secure. However, as the months to follow there was much work to be done ashore, where landings and secure berthing for the boats was required. A cricket ground was laid out in the grounds of the Raleigh Estate and paths constructed leading to it, to avoid the town, most of the work being carried out by the ship's company.

When *Britannia* arrived at Dartmouth she had about 230 cadets on her books. However, this number was to prove insufficient to provide the Navy with the number of lieutenants needed, the answer was to considerably increase the number of cadets entering the ship and after only a few terms the number had increased to 306. This led to overcrowding on the sleeping decks and the studies, and caused problems in the mess room and catering areas. Overcrowding would prove to be a problem at Dartmouth on numerous occasions in the future. Captain Powell was to make many representations to the Admiralty before they finally decided in 1864 to supplement the accommodation with another ship.

HMS *Hindostan* 1864-1905

An old two-decker of seventy-four guns, HMS *Hindostan* was selected for the purpose of supplementing *Britannia's* accommodation and she arrived from Devonport in 1864. The *Hindostan* was one of a number of ships built in India of locally supplied teak for the Royal Navy and given names associated with the country. She was built in Bombay and launched in 1841. When she arrived at Dartmouth she was moored ahead of the *Britannia* and the two vessels were connected by a covered gangway. In addition to being used as a passageway the gangway was also used as a paper store, reflecting the shortage of available space on board the two ships. As the space was limited, a special size of paper was manufactured so that it could be stored in the confined space, known as 'gangway

An oil painting (artist unknown) showing HMS Britannia *and HMS* Trafalgar *at Portland circa 1862. Also depicted are cadets boarding the steam paddle tender ready to go ashore.*

paper' and it was still possible to order such 'gangway paper' from the HM Stationery Office as late as the 1950s. Although the *Britannia* arrived at Dartmouth fully rigged, she was to lose her main and mizzen masts in the years to follow, to allow space for structures to be erected on the upper deck, as a watercolour of her in the college collection, painted in 1868 by John Mogford, testifies.

There were two major innovations introduced in the latter half of the 1860s, once life aboard the *Britannia* and *Hindostan* had settled into some sort of routine. The first of these was the arrival at Dartmouth of HMS *Bristol*, a steam frigate that had been recommissioned as a sea-going training ship for cadets. They would spend a year in her after leaving the *Britannia*. In the 1980s a more modern HMS *Bristol* would again take cadets to sea as part of the Dartmouth Training Squadron. The second innovation was the proposal in 1869 of a competitive entrance examination, the introduction of which was accompanied by an increase in the time spent under training and a reduction in the number of cadets entering the ship. Since the increase in the intake of 1864 there had been a steady decline in the entry, the number having fallen to 121 by the end of the decade. The age of entry at this time was between twelve and thirteen years of age.

Britannia was now showing her age and there were signs of decay, but in spite of a smaller number on board more modern approaches to education demanded modern accommodation, and additional study areas were required. These factors led to *Britannia* being condemned as too small for what was then required of her and to her subsequent replacement. Her figurehead was removed and given pride of place on the bows of the new *Britannia*, where she remained until the old ship was broken up in 1916. The figurehead then found a home in Sandquay Woods, close to the racquet courts, before being moved to a prominent position in front of the main mast of the college, from here she was moved to the parade ground sometime in the 1920s or 1930s. Here she remains to this day, but not in her original state, for by the early 1990s she was suffering from the effects of 170 years of being exposed to the elements and the original timber had rotted beyond repair or restoration. The figurehead was transported to Nottingham where a full size resin replica was made and then returned to Dartmouth to take pride of place once more on the parade ground. Other relics of the first (1820) *Britannia* survive; these being two of the four transom figures that held up the stern gallery of the old ship. All four had been removed and brought ashore, two were located in the gymnasium at Sandquay and the other two guarded the path up to the playing fields, where they still stand to this day.

Above: The first of the Britannias *to serve as the Royal Naval College, moored in the River Dart in the condition in which she arrived circa 1863.*

Above right: HMS Britannia *and* Hindostan *moored off Sandquay.*

Right: 'Dress ship' for the King's birthday on HMS Britannia.

Britannia at Dartmouth 1869 – 1905

A much larger vessel that had been specifically adapted for the task replaced the old *Britannia* in 1869. She arrived in the Dart with only a foremast, so that her handsome hull unfortunately showed her off as a hulk from the very outset. She had been laid down as a sailing three-decker warship in 1848 but altered and lengthened during building into a screw ship that was launched as the 131 gun *Prince of Wales* in 1860. Since her launch she had been laid up at Portsmouth, a not uncommon practice in the mid nineteenth century, when ships took a long time to build, but a relatively short time to mast, rig and fit out, hence they were often built in peace time and laid

up until needed. Since her launch she had been superseded by the new ironclads that had rendered ships of her type obsolete. Surplus to operational requirements, therefore, she had her engines and boilers removed until receiving a new lease of life when fitted out for her new task, renamed HMS *Britannia* and despatched to Dartmouth.

In April 1875 the first civilian instructor was appointed to *Britannia*. The Rev. J C P Aldous, a Dartmouth resident with a family and house ashore, was appointed as the Chief Naval Instructor, causing some concern both with naval instructors on board *Britannia* and further afield. The Admiralty had decided to go outside the service for the appointment of this young man, who was to have much older and more experienced naval instructors under his authority. The Rice Committee enquiry that was conducted the previous year had looked at the health and general training of cadets and it may have been one of their recommendations to seek new blood outside the service. Although the health of the cadets was initially of concern, the committee visited the Royal Naval School at New Cross, the Greenwich Hospital School and Eton College and after comparing the physique of the cadets with similar aged boys from these institutions, came to the conclusion that they were larger and fitter, the opinion being reached that life aboard *Britannia* was good for them. The committee did however suggest a number of recommendations regarding the training and in particular the length of time spent on certain subjects. The building of a college ashore was considered at this stage but not acted upon.

It may be appropriate at this point to consider the health provision on *Britannia* and *Hindostan*. Both the Rice Committee (1875) and the Wellesley Committee (1876) reported upon the conditions prevailing on the two ships and the health of the cadets. The Admiralty Papers, housed in the Public Record Office for the period, show that there were a number of cases of illness on board, particularly in the winter, many of which were the sort of childhood infectious disease associated with schools. The sickbay on board in 1875 appears to have been very busy with cases of dysentery in January, croup and whooping cough in March and April, measles in June and chicken

Watercolour by John Mogford showing Britannia *in the Dart circa 1868.*

pox, scarlet fever and scarlatina in December. The last two, which began in the town, led to the cadets breaking up early and being sent home, as the ship could not cope with the problem. The following year there were cases recorded of diphtheria in January, followed by measles, which kept recurring between March and July, and scarlet fever was to return to Dartmouth again in 1877. Measures were taken to prevent contagion, presumably successfully since there is no subsequent record of cadets contacting the disease.

Contagion was the major concern with all the cadets living in close proximity to each other. Sick cadets were quickly moved off the ship to the cadet hospital ashore, or sent home if they were fit to travel. Measles and whooping cough cases were often sent home, particularly in March near to the end of term. There was one recorded case of dysentery when the cadet was kept on board for four days and the case for this had to be made very forcefully. In August 1877 the sick quarters ashore were inspected by the Medical Director General to ensure that no epidemic or infectious diseases had occurred, he concluded that none had.

The original cadet hospital was 'Ford House', a large former residence set in its own grounds at Townstal. However the cadet hospital referred to above was in Ridgehill from 1871 to 1891,

Crew and staff members of Britannia *during the 1860s, Captain Powell and the Reverend Inskip are prominent in the front row. (Dartmouth Museum).*

The Britannia Museum

As the site of officer training for the Royal Navy for the past century Britannia Royal Naval College in many aspects resembles a living museum, not unlike a stately home, in which modern day-to-day life exists in parallel with a rich history and tradition. This connection was recognized by lecturer and former museum curator Dr Richard Porter. In 1999 Commodore Roy Clare, who went on to become Director of the National Maritime Museum at Greenwich, agreed and enthusiastically supported the establishment of the Britannia Museum. HRH The Duke of Edinburgh KCB opened the Museum on 27th July on the occasion of his diamond jubilee reunion, held at the College.

The museum tells the story of officer training at Dartmouth from the time of the arrival of Britannia in the Dart in 1863 until the present day. The displays include artifacts associated with the history of the College and a number of prestigious works of art. At the centre of the display of life on board the old Britannia is a fully restored cadet's sea chest which would have been supplied in 1911 by Gieves, Matthews and Seagrove of Portsmouth, now Gieves and Hawkes, to a cadet when he joined the Royal Naval College at Osborne. Originally costing £5 10s, beautifully appointed with brass fittings and clips for dirk, telescope and parallel rule. The lift out trays include a 'private till' and a section containing a tooth glass

and soap tray. Mr Robert Gieve presented the sea chest to the College in 1978. The museum also has an example of the later two-tier chest with a drop down front, that was introduced, in the interests of economy, in 1912 and 1913. These remained in use at the college until 1955-6 with the introduction of the eighteen year old entry, when the 'chest flats' were divided into smaller cabins.

The museum also boasts a collection of artefacts made from timber recovered from the old Britannia and these include a fine armchair and two picture frames that hold photographs of the Royal Princes Edward and George, taken in 1877, when they joined the old ship. The dirks that belonged to the two royal cadets, both inscribed with their names,

Bone model of HMS Britannia made by Napoleonic French prisoners of war, presented to the College by Lieutenant Commander H. Morton Lee RNVR in 1947.

A standard Naval issue plate made by the Bovey Tracey Pottery Company around 1880, one of the many pieces recovered from the bed of the River Dart. The number shows which mess it belonged to, thus ensuring each mess kept its own crockery.

are also among the prestigious items on display, together with their punishment records from on board HMS Britannia.

The museum also boasts a fine collection of bone ship models made by French prisoners of war that were captured and interned in England during the Napoleonic wars. These craftsmen used the bone from their daily mutton ration, human hair for the rigging and any other material that they could find or trade to produce these intricate models. The bulk of this collection is on loan from Mrs R. A. Wootten and is a part of the late A. J. Cadbury collection. Two of the models are of the late Britannia, the large and particularly fine example being given to the college in 1947 by the Earl of Cork and Orrery. There is also an 'Admiralty Board' model of HMS Royal George. These models were made by the designer to be presented, as a proposal for a new ship, to the 'Admiralty Board' for their approval; if accepted they would then become a working model for the shipwright. Typically they are not planked below the waterline to show the method of construction, but this example is, with just one plank omitted to show the rib structure.

The collection policy of the Museum is directed at items related to the history of the College and all those who have passed through it. One area of active collection being artefacts recovered from the bed of the River Dart where the two hulks were moored. Diving on this site has revealed a large collection of pottery, bottles and other items that give a valuable insight into life on board. Many of these items are on display, some of which are in a remarkably well preserved condition.

The Heritage collection of the College is not only to be found in the museum, but many other items can be seen elsewhere, including the two Victoria Crosses, the Royal Verge and many fine paintings and ship models. Nor does it only include pictures and artefacts; the College Archive (maintained by Dr J. Harrold) is the repository for the 'Defaulters Books' from the old Britannia[1], and many 'Midshipman's Journals'. The Heritage collection also includes the fine historical collection of books of the College library that is much used by researchers of naval history.

Inside the Britannia Museum. Displays include a cadet's sea chest circa 1911, a writing desk and chair from the Royal Yacht Victoria and Albert and a chair made from timber from the old Britannia.

HRH The Prince of Wales studies a display of photographs from the College Archive during his visit to launch the Britannia Association.

HRH The Duke of Edinburgh with Dr Richard Porter, the Curator, opens the Britannia Museum during his reunion visit in July 1999.

1 The Defaulters Books list the cadets that entered the old hulks on the river and their misdemeanours and the punishments given. These leather-bound texts with their delightful copperplate script have provided many a researcher with hours of pleasure and record the amusing antics of the cadets.

Artist's impression by Michael Hill (2004) of HRH The Prince of Wales, later King Edward VII, bringing his two sons, Prince Albert Victor and Prince George aboard HMS Britannia *in 1877.*

though a photograph of the cadets outside the hospital was probably taken outside 'Coombecot' another house that was used, also in Ridgehill. However Collinson (2001) states that the hospital closed and moved to Fairview (now demolished) in February 1896. The discrepancy over the closure date and the reference to two different buildings almost certainly is because two houses ashore were in use, one as the isolation hospital and the other as a convalescent home.

The training ship attracted a great deal of attention in Parliament in 1876/7 regarding bullying and the Admiralty appointed Admiral Willes to investigate the matters raised on board the ship. He concluded that there was not a problem but no doubt it did occur, as it did in all other public schools at the time. As has been stated earlier, a competitive examination was introduced in 1869 for all new prospective entrants, this was abandoned in 1874, on the recommendation of yet another Admiralty committee, only to be re-introduced in a much more rigorous form in 1881. The following year the examination was under the control of the Civil Service Commissioners, and was described in 1887 as being 'an examination of absolutely ferocious severity' by Statham (1904). This examination attracted a great deal of interest from certain

sectors of the public as witnessed by numerous letters and several articles in *The Times* newspaper.

In January 1877 the Prince of Wales' two sons, Prince Edward, known at the time as Prince Albert Victor, and Prince George joined *Britannia*. Except for having their own private accommodation they were treated in the same way as all the other cadets on board. Their time in the ship is described elsewhere in the chapter on the Royal connection with the College.

In January 1878 Lieutenant Guy Mainwaring joined the ship as First Lieutenant. He was responsible for the introduction of two aspects of life at Dartmouth that continue into the College's centenary year. He was first of all responsible for the founding of the Britannia Beagle Pack in 1878[2], and secondly he introduced the custom of taking photographs of each term of cadets as they left the ship. Two photographs were taken of each term, one of the cadet captains and one of the rest of the term, they were framed and kept on board as a record. In the first photograph taken Lt Mainwaring himself is seen seated on the gunwale of one of the gigs with the Cadet Captains. Although all of the terms are represented in the college they are not all passing out photographs, some being term groups and others may have been taken on joining. This tradition continues today with all 'passers out' having their photograph taken as a group which is then hung on the walls of the College. The main corridor was the traditional 'rogues gallery' showing generations of naval officers, and many old cadets delighted in finding their youthful photographs and showing them to their families when they returned to their *alma mater* in later years. It was often said that this gallery of photographs linked the Chapel and Senior Gunroom with 'God at one end and Nelson at the other and generations of naval officers in between'. In the 1990s space along this corridor was running out, so the old Cadet Captains were the first to go, but this was only a temporary measure, then the side corridors were utilized, until in 1999, they were taken down and re-located to the rear of the great hall (quarterdeck). It was all part of a scheme to modernise the main corridor, but the removal of the photographs was seen by many to be a break with one of the many traditions that the old boys held so dearly. There are some gaps along the corridors but a near complete set of photographs from 1878 is held in a series of albums that are still maintained within the College and added to every term.

From September 1883 to August 1886 the captain of *Britannia* was Captain Nathaniel Bowden-Smith, he had also been Commander on board from 1870 to 1872 and in 1914 he printed a book for private circulation, prompted by an impertinent question from a cadet who asked what the Captain did, to which the answer came, 'nothing' and when further asked what the Commander did, replied, 'he helps the Captain.' Entitled *Naval Recollections – by a Retired Flag Officer,* Captain Bowden-Smith describes his time at Dartmouth, offering a unique insight into the training during those times. From his recollections of his time as the Commander he opens with a description of the

2 See section on the Beagles.

Lieutenant Guy Mainwaring in the first group photograph with the cadet captains in 1878.

A class of cadets with the seamanship instruction model.

Commander's responsibilities for discipline, upkeep of the two vessels and the supervision of seamanship instruction. He highlights that the French master had an uphill struggle in teaching his subject to unwilling cadets and the rest of his recollections mirror what has already been written elsewhere in this chapter. 'As regards minor matters, (he recalls), the cadets had been allowed to learn the piano and other instruments out of school hours, and at a slight extra charge to cover the fees of the instructor, but this was stopped by Captain Foley, who thought it effeminate for a boy to play the piano'. His recollections as Captain quoted below give us more detail on life aboard at that time.

> 'I entered upon my new duties with interest but I found
> the instruction given to the cadets little changed since I
> was Commander in 1870-1872. In the so called seamanship
> instruction too much time was still taken up with masts, square
> yards and rigging, which were fast becoming obsolete, whereas
> there were no machine shops for the cadets' instruction nor
> any vessel with engines of modern construction.[3] On the
> other hand there was a sailing yacht and plenty of boats for the
> boys to handle under oars or sail, which was excellent, and the
> instructors were all zealous in performing their duties. Every
> cadet, whatever his tastes might be, was compelled to attend the
> drawing classes, which I thought a mistake; unless a boy had
> artistic talent, he would drop this later and his time would have

3 This problem would not be addressed properly until Fisher as Second Sea Lord launched his radical new scheme for a modern navy in 1903. It can be argued that although the Royal Navy had advanced technologically, it was still manned at this time by officers and men who were of the age of sail and the instruction of the day reflected this situation.

been wasted, whereas, though all should be compelled to attend the mechanical and chart drawing, I should make the freehand drawing and colouring optional.

The only foreign language taught was French. There are of course difficulties in multiplying the number of language masters, and I entirely concur in thinking French the most useful and interesting: but although I did my best to encourage the boys to learn, or to improve themselves, in this one language, I signally failed and later reported to the Admiralty that the ordinary British boy thought his own language good enough and declined to learn any other.

I of course took great interest in the boys' cricket and other games, but I did not find my berth altogether a bed of roses. In the first place we suffered from the many epidemics to which youths of that age are liable – so much so that on one occasion we had to break up for a few weeks before the end of term. I do not mean to imply that the ships or Dartmouth were unhealthy, but these two old hulks had been there for many years and being moored 'head and stern' in the river, they were subject to great draughts in the winter months, particularly between Christmas and Easter, at which time coughs and colds were very prevalent. Other causes of irritation were complaints from the Admiralty that the boys were not properly fed, which of course were complaints by certain parents passed on to me, and at one time a well known physician in London, who had apparently attended one or two cadets, made such a report to the Admiralty that the First Lord wrote me almost a letter of censure, without any investigation of the matter, whereas not only did I frequently attend in the mess room during the boys' meals, but the officer of the day (one of the Lieutenants) was always present as a duty.'

Much activity on HMS Britannia's *starboard side.*

The meals must have improved because the following description of messing in 1899, by another writer shows that it was then of a very high standard and certainly no cause for complaint.

'The cadets' mess was aft on the lower deck and a very comfortable mess it was, and jolly well we were fed. Breakfast – porridge, huge omelettes and buttered eggs, followed by great plates of ham of tongue – tea, cocoa or coffee, all without limit or stint. Dinner was on the same lavish scale – second helpings, puddings, cheese and fruit, while servants kept passing along with big bathroom jugs filled with drink – cider, beer or ginger beer was on offer, with no limit or restriction. Tea consisted of cold meats in abundance, jams of all sorts and, three times a week Devonshire cream in huge bowls and without limit. To ensure that those who had no cash to spend at the canteen on shore were not allowed to faint from hunger during the afternoon there was a free issue of a ship's bun. On turning out in the early morning before drill there was a good issue of cocoa and a ship's biscuit at 7 o'clock.

Coming from a school where feeding was poor and insufficient and the cooking bad, I found the *Britannia* was a paradise of plenty. At that time I often wished that it was possible to have a lady housekeeper with a staff of women cooks to feed the cadets, but in later years I have quite changed my mind, when I know of a certainty that at a well known women's college at one of our universities the students are shamefully fed.

The prizes were usually distributed by the Commander-in-Chief at Plymouth or by some other officer or man of distinction and on one occasion the Duke of Edinburgh[4] honoured the establishment by performing this duty.

During these years there was some talk of moving the training establishment from Dartmouth "in consequence of its relaxing climate" but I believed it to be ideal for our naval training school. Shortly before leaving I called at the Admiralty on the Naval Lord who was responsible for all training establishments and asked permission to submit a memorandum on the *Britannia* system, proposing certain alterations to the curriculum, and also for bringing the seamanship instruction up to date, but the Admiral appeared to think that change in the existing system was so unnecessary that no further action was taken.'

At least Bowden-Smith had recognised the shortcomings of the

4 This was Queen Victoria's second son and true to tradition he entered the Royal Navy and made it his career. A large portrait of him hangs in the Britannia Museum.

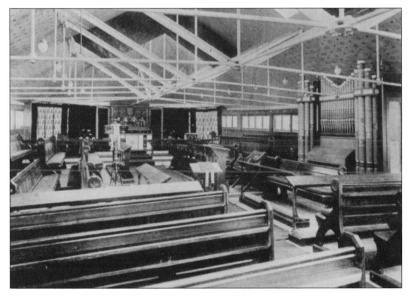

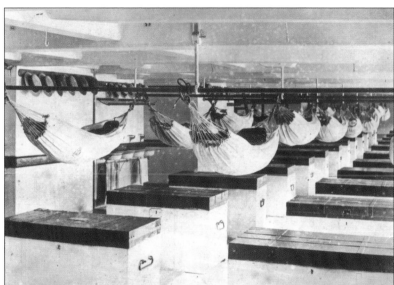

Group of photographs of the interior of HMS Britannia*; i. Cadet mess room; ii. Chapel on board* Hindostan*; iii.Morning prayers on the poopdeck;*
iv. Hammocks and cadets' chests on the sleeping deck.

seamanship training in a technologically advancing navy, but it was to be another sixteen years before Admiral Fisher was to address the problem.

In February 1884 the *Britannia Magazine* was published for the first time, the school magazine being a common feature of most other public schools. Its aims were set out in the lead article which states that every body has its organ and that 'we have opinions far too good to be limited to sanctuary chairs, far too noble to be confined to the narrow limits of the mess room, why should we not bring them out to the world.' The first editor was the Commander but he was later replaced by one of the Lieutenants. Very few of the issues from the old *Britannia* survive but the College does have an unbroken run from 1905. Some of the literary contributions are of the highest standard, as one would expect from one of the country's top public schools and later the Royal Navy's premier training and even a verse from the poet laureate John Masefield can be found amongst its pages, to commemorate the fiftieth anniversary of the College in 1955. They are the source of much valuable material for the researcher and there

are some very talented pieces of artwork within its pages, but most importantly it gives an often humorous, sometimes sad, but unique insight into College life over the past one hundred years.

Towards the end of the 1880s electric lighting was installed on the two hulks; a generator was at first located on the *Hindostan*, in a tall well ventilated structure that housed the boiler and generator on the fo'c'sle deck, but being wooden she only served to amplify the inevitable sound and vibrations that were to result, this was soon moved to an old mortar vessel that was moored just ahead of the two ships.

In 1885 yet another committee was appointed to look again at the 'vexed question of naval education' (Statham 1904). If there is one continuing thread that runs throughout this work it is surely the Navy's unease with naval education. Statham (1904) referring to the subject states that 'There has always existed, as we have seen, a sort of chronic dissatisfaction with the existing condition of affairs'. Indeed this situation was to recur time and time again over the next 120 years of the College's history. The committee was to consider and

The Britannia Beagles

Jim, first of the pack, his grave in Sandquay Woods.

HM The Queen names a beagle puppy at Lord High Admiral's Divisions in July 1972, in the presence of Rear-Admiral Tait and the kennel man.

*T*he Britannia Beagle pack owes its formation to Lt Guy Mainwaring, a First Lieutenant of the Britannia, who was appointed to the ship in 1878. Mainwaring was a man of boundless energy who possessed a keen sporting instinct. He knew that many officers and men in the Royal Navy were keen beagle pack followers and that the Gosport and Fareham pack had attracted a great deal of interest amongst the naval personnel locally. It is perhaps because the sport appealed to all ranks that he decided to start a pack in Dartmouth. He negotiated for the start of a pack, and was successful in acquiring two and a half couples of fourteen-inch hounds from kennels in Staffordshire. The ship's terrier 'Jim' supplemented these and they began hunting in the winter of 1878-9. 'Jim' had

a puppy who also hunted with the pack and was appropriately named 'Jimson'

The beagles are always referred to as hounds, never dogs, and they 'speak' not bark, they are counted or numbered as couples (thirty hounds being fifteen 'couples'), non-beagle dogs are referred to as cur-dogs and those that follow the hounds are called the 'field.' Shortly after starting the initial pack, Admiral Stokes presented another couple of hounds from a pack in South Wales and another was acquired from Battersea Dogs Home, to be named by the cadets 'Homeless.' Within three years, with further additions and breeding in the pack they numbered twelve and a half couples; they were firmly established, and the Admiralty then agreed to fund them.

Commander Raikes, Master of the Britannia Beagles, 1911.

Britannia Beagles meet outside the new College.

The initial hunts would be for hare or badgers, to be found locally on the neighbouring farms. Thus the pack became popular with local farmers who were keen to keep pests under control, indeed this close association with the local farming community is still fostered. Occasionally the local hunts would be substituted with 'drag' hunts, constituting a rabbit skin soaked with herring oil and dragged along for the hounds to chase.

The kennels were first located by the racquet court (now the badminton courts), however this site, being located in woods lacked sunshine and the necessary sanitary requirements, therefore a permanent kennel area was built near the corner of the cricket ground, where they remain to this day. 'Jim' the pioneer of the pack died in 1886 and was buried in a grave close to the site of the original kennels. An annual 'hunt breakfast' was soon established, superceded in the twentieth century by the Beagle Ball, which became the highlight of the social calendar. The beagles were originally under the care of

the Commander, who for many years hunted with the hounds on horseback. It was often quoted that the most important qualification for the post of Commander of the College was the ability to ride and to hunt with a pack of hounds. The cadets were always involved, as was Mainwaring's intention, and an entry in an early Britannia Magazine quotes; 'The chief joy in the beagle's life is hunting the hare over the hills and dales of sunny Devon, accompanied by several embryo Admirals, all letting out blood-curdling yells and valiantly trying to

Above: 'Hound speak,' one of the lingering memories of BRNC.

Left: Beagle puppy show.

crack whips almost as large as themselves.' The beagles have survived both World Wars and continue the important link that exists between the College and the local rural community.

While the formation of the pack will always be associated with Lt Mainwaring, there is one other name that for almost fifty years has been synonymous with the hounds at Dartmouth. Admiral Sir James Eberle has been very closely associated with the beagles since he was a Staff Officer at the College in 1957. Thus as the College celebrates its centenary, Admiral Eberle approaches his half centenary with the pack.

The Britannia Beagles are one of the premier packs in the country and they hunt and are exhibited all over Britain, in addition to acting as hosts for many visiting packs.

They have always been regarded as the Navy's Hounds, the reason that the Hunt Staff wear a blue uniform as opposed to the traditional green. The Admiralty no longer fund the pack, their upkeep coming from private sources. There is an active social life associated with the Beagles, such as the annual 'Puppy Show' held in May, Hunt Breakfasts, farmhouse teas after a meet, the Annual Dinner and the Beagle Ball are all part of the joys of hunting with the Britannia Beagles.

Cadets enjoying the hunt in 1932.

offer opinions or suggestions for the improvement of the education of naval executive officers, investigating the limits of age and subjects of examination for the entry of cadets and the course of study and instructional arrangements on board the *Britannia*.

In its report the committee identified a number of defects to be extant under the present system. Firstly, regarding recruitment there was a perceived 'failure to get the best material in the country, the material is good but is not the best that could be had; and we feel convinced that the special preparation of boys before coming to the *Britannia* does not tend to improve that material'. Secondly, the curriculum attempted 'to teach in the *Britannia* what cannot be properly learnt at the age of the cadets on board; the result being that the knowledge is mechanical, and that the principles are unintelligently acquired and soon forgotten;' a criticism that remains valid when applied to today's compressed system.

Among the recommendations were that the *Wave*, a small barque-rigged steamship, should be replaced by a ship-rigged corvette that be moored abreast of the two hulks, with a connecting bridge so that she could be used as a playground for the cadets, when it was not desirable to go ashore. The committee criticised the seamanship instruction and considered the *Wave* of very little use in this important area, due to her not being well adapted for drills and limited to going to sea for only a day at a time. The other major recommendation was the abolition of the nomination scheme as it was thought to place unnecessary obstacles as a route into the Navy. The committee's suggestion was that candidates sat the lower certificate of the Oxford and Cambridge local boards at the age of fifteen and a later examination at sixteen by the Civil Service Commissioners, followed by a year of practical training in a ship or shore establishment. They also considered the Solent a more suitable location. Almost a decade earlier the Solent was under consideration, along with a number of other locations, but Dartmouth was to remain as the chosen site, as none of the recommendations were implemented. Commander E. P. Statham clearly viewed committee reports of this nature with some dismay as he states; 'On the whole, one gets somewhat weary of committees; and very weary work indeed is the reading of the thousands of questions and answers so scrupulously recorded in the Blue Book'.

Despite the constant committees and critiques of the *Britannia* system, day-to-day life for the cadets continued unchanged on board. Vice Admiral W. D. Paton CB DSO MVO, arrived as a cadet on the ship in 1888, and later recorded his recollections:

'We had to go in uniform and the new term always arrived the day before to settle in. I arrived in the morning having travelled overnight from Scotland, and no other cadets came until the afternoon, so there was no lunch for me. However, I got some, I think from the Wardroom, and explored the ship and found my chest. Everything we possessed (including boots) went into a vast chest, which had a washbasin etc., and a private till in which we locked our treasures.

We slept in hammocks, which was great fun, although they were difficult to get into at first, but they were most comfortable, except in hot

Cadets swimming off Sandquay at the end of the nineteenth century.

weather when they were too warm for comfort. One of the favourite tricks was to let go the foot of the hammock when a boy was sleeping in it, and down he came with a bump. Another was to put a slippery hitch in his foot lashing, and down he came when he got in.

We all had servants, one to every three or four boys, and these had to lash up and stow away the hammocks in the mornings and get them out at night, as well as looking after our clothes, laundry, cleaning boots etc. There were sailing and pulling boats for recreation and tennis courts, football and cricket grounds, racket courts and a gymnasium on shore on the Dartmouth side of the river. In fact it was a paradise for boys.

There were four terms of cadets. The oldest were the *Niners*, then the *Sixers*, then *Threes* and lastly *News*. The *Niners* could fag the *Threes* and *News*, the *Sixers* the *News* only. There were all sorts of things which only *Niners* and *Sixers* could do, known as *Checks*, and various places where the *News* and *Threes* were not allowed known as *Sanctuaries*. Every cadet wore a white lanyard round his neck with his keys on the end of it, which were stowed in his breast pocket. These were the instruments of torture – and torture it was if one was beaten over the hands with the keys at the end of a lanyard.

Gymnastics were not popular and one did not go to the gym except on a wet day as a rule. I won my term competition every time, the prize always being a large and heavy clasp knife, full of gadgets.

The work we did consisted of navigation, seamanship (including boats, charts, construction and reading of charts), steam or naval engineering, chemistry (otherwise Stinks) and French. In our last two terms we used to go out to sea in the *Wave*, a small barque-rigged steamship, and make sail, learn to reef, tack, wear etc. for the day. The *Wave* was somewhat lively and many cadets were seasick.

I was two terms in the *Britannia* and finally passed-out 39th in the term so I had gone up a bit. I think I had passed-in fifty third out of fifty-seven.'

The beginning of the 1890s saw the question of bullying on the *Britannia* raise its head again with numerous accusations in the columns of *The Times* and the *Western Morning News*. These attacks may have had ulterior motives, other than just highlighting a problem, as many came from notable 'Wykehamists' of the time. The accusations were that cadets were being 'fagged' and particularly the younger ones were being particularly subjected to cruel treatment from older boys trying to extort money from them. It fell upon the Commanding officer at that time Captain N. S. F. Digby to investigate and put a stop to it and he afterwards made the following statement. 'It had, no doubt, been going on for a long time, and, owing to the reticence of youth, it took me a year to get to the bottom of it; but I finally succeeded in getting rid of the principal culprits'.

An insight to life on board *Britannia* and *Hindostan* towards the end of the nineteenth century is described by Fraser and Leyland (1898). This graphic description, represents the first impressions of a young cadet on joining the ship, capturing both the atmosphere of life on board at that time and providing an accurate picture of the layout of the two vessels, as seen through his eyes.

'He receives the impression, afterwards confirmed, that the *Britannia* in this land locked harbour, with wooded hills rising on every hand, lies in a very pleasant place, against which nothing, indeed, can be alleged, save the dampness that inevitably clings to the valley in winter. The old three-decker is moored by chain cables in the middle of the lake-like expanse, and just ahead of her is the *Hindostan*. He sees that a light covered bridge has been thrown from ship to ship, beneath which is a floating swimming bath, heated by steam and used for teaching swimming in winter. Both the ships are housed in over their upper decks, the roofs covering, as he afterwards finds, a fine large space for prize giving functions, concerts and recreation on the poop on the *Britannia*, and a new church on the *Hindostan*. But the larger ship still retains her foremast, bowsprit and whiskers, useful relics of her former state. Somewhat astern of her is seen at anchor, the *Racer*, a screw sloop of 970 tons, used for seamanship and navigation instruction and constant spar and sail drill with the ship under way. The *Racer's* predecessor in this service, the *Wave*, a smaller sloop of 380 tons, now lies abreast of the *Hindostan*. She has had her screw removed, and is devoted to instruction in steam and some sail drill. Just ahead of the larger ship floats a pontoon, carrying the dynamos and accumulators from which electricity is supplied to the whole establishment. The river is seen to be dotted, with skiff, dinghies, yachts and sailing cutters for the use of the cadets.

It is now time to go on board *Britannia*. The entry-port brings the newcomer to the middle deck of the ship, which is clear on the starboard side from the wardroom bulkheads aft, to the bows, and is the place where the cadets muster, and in leisure moments indulge in skylarking or dancing, though often they may be seen snugly ensconced in the gun-ports, engrossed in volumes from

HMS Racer *(tender to* Britannia*) at sea with cadets.*

their library. The cadets spend four terms on board, the two junior terms, described as the '*News*' and the '*Threes*' being berthed in the *Hindostan*, and forbidden by an unwritten law, to wear their caps on the backs of their heads, or to swing their lanyards to which their keys are attached; the two senior terms, known as '*Nines*' and '*Passers-out*' have their hammocks slung in the *Britannia*.

The newcomer, therefore, makes his way across the bridge onto the main deck of the *Hindostan*, where he also finds the starboard side is clear. Let us first descend into the sleeping deck, where the cadet's chests are ranged, and, at an appointed hour in the evening their hammocks are slung. The space is restricted, but each cadet has a 'good clear swinging billet,' and every arrangement is made for his comfort, though there is no pampering on board. At the fore-end of the sleeping deck are two very large baths, which can be heated by steam; and each cadet has his own washing place. This deck and some of the others is painted in a hard white enamel paint, so that it is easily kept dry and clean, the gangways are laid with matting and there are also strips in front of the chests. Cleanliness is the mark of the whole place. In both ships it is absolutely perfect, and even in the hold below the orlop deck, where the ballast, tanks, and store rooms are, everything is perfectly dry, and wholly fresh and sweet. Ascending to the main deck at which we entered, we will go still higher to the upper deck, where are six good sized rooms devoted to the purpose of study, under the poop of the old ship, which was raised and lengthened for the purpose. A few years ago it was the custom to take down the divisions of these studies every Saturday, so that the place might be used for service on the following day, but through the liberality of the Admiralty, and of

End of an era: Britannia *is towed out of the Dart in June 1916.*

many officers and parents of cadets, an airy chapel has been built above the studies, very tastefully decorated, and fitted with an excellent organ. The forecastle of the ship, which is roofed over, is devoted to a workshop, and each deck has been fitted with great care for the accommodation of the first and second term cadets.

Returning now to the *Britannia* where the third and fourth terms are berthed, we may visit the cadet's mess-room, which occupies a large part of the lower deck, and affords accommodation for 300 cadets, who can sit down together without overcrowding. The furniture is plain, but sufficient, and the room is in close communication with the pantries, galleys etc., which are just ahead of it, and separated by a bulkhead from the mess-room and cabins of the ship's company, which are in the forward part of the vessel. Descending a ladder to the orlop deck we reach the 'seamanship room', which is immediately under the mess-room, and is fitted with excellent models of ships, anchor gear, torpedo net booms and everything that is necessary in the training of cadets in these matters. We return now to the middle deck, where are the cadet's library, sick bay and sundry cabins, and ascend to the sleeping deck of the two senior terms, which is arranged exactly as in the *Hindostan*, with one large bathing tank at the forward end. This tank holds about twenty tons of water, which is pumped up fresh every day from the river at high water. After a good splash in the salt water there are fresh-water shower baths to stand under. Here, too are the studies, in the fitting and arrangement of which great care has been expended. Ascending next to the upper deck, we reach the poop and the large covered recreation space which has been alluded to, and in which entertainments are often contrived,

the boys looking forward to them with keen pleasure. From this place there is access to the forecastle, which is the only uncovered part of the deck, where the mast is, about which the boys clamber a good deal at certain times.'

Fraser and Leyland also describe life on board *Britannia* and *Hindostan* in the latter half of the nineteenth century. This too is included here, it may paint a rather 'rosy' picture of life at that time, but it is a contemporary account and other sources from the same period do suggest that it is an accurate portrayal. It makes an interesting comparison with life in the College today.

'As soon as a boy joins *Britannia* he is made to realise that, with his uniform, he has one foot in the Service, and is no longer a mere schoolboy[5]. Then he is quickly inducted into the meaning of the word discipline, and is imbued with a knowledge of what is implied as being 'on' and 'off' duty. The distinction between the two is sharp and rigid. 'On' duty the boy sticks closely to his work, and rare cases of shirking are sternly repressed; 'off' duty, he is encouraged to display his boyish energy and spirit in every healthy form. He learns to look on his superiors as his friends interested in his welfare.'

Before we continue with Fraser and Leyland's description of a cadet's day a short description of the organisation on board may help set the scene.

---

5 The cadets thought that they were in the navy, regarding their pocket money as naval pay, when in reality it was paid by their parents in the school fees, they were still pupils at a naval public school.

A watercolour from 1884 by L. Neville of HMS Britannia *and* Hindostan. *Note the canvas sheets on the upper deck that were later replaced by a corrugated iron-clad structure.*

'The four terms are divided into two watches, port and starboard, these alternate their duties week by week and are known as 'in study' and 'out of study'. Each term is under the charge of a lieutenant, assisted by chief petty officers (usually chief gunners' mates, under a gunner) under a gunner, who are responsible for discipline to the commander, who in turn is responsible to the captain. Each of these officers will take a term right through the ship.

On board the *Britannia* the bugle 'Cadets turn out' sounds through the ships, winter and summer, except on Sundays, at half past six in the morning. They spring from their hammocks and tumble into the baths. At seven o'clock the bugle sounds the 'fall in' and the cadets are mustered on deck for inspection. They are then sent to their morning presentation or drills, every moment is done 'at the double' and cheerfulness is the order of the day. The boys 'in study' work for an hour at mathematics, but those 'out of study' are engaged in either scripture, history or French preparation, or aloft in the tender or 'pulling boats'. Every morning of the week, weather permitting, and parties go ashore for fencing exercises, physical drill and gymnastics work.

The instructors are from the school at Aldershot to implement the new physical training system, those boys that had been in the ship eighteen months in August 1897, had increased 4.4 inches in height and 3.7 inches in chest measurements, these being considerably higher averages than previously.

'At eight o'clock the 'disperse' is sounded and the boys are dismissed from their studies and recalled from drill for breakfast in the mess-room.[6] The 'assembly' is sounded at ten minutes to nine when the cadets muster and proceed to the covered space on the upper deck, where they fall in and are inspected, as is also the ship's company, then the chaplain reads prayers. The boys then gather their books and are marched by their cadet captains to their appointed studies. The chief Naval Instructor has assistants for special subjects and it may be said that all four terms are engaged in the same work but in stages more or less

6 Breakfast consists of tea, coffee or cocoa, always rolls & butter, porridge twice a week, sometimes, hash or curry, cold meat, bacon or fish, and either bacon and fried eggs or boiled eggs and cold ham on alternate days, and sausages on Thursday.

Britannia *on her final journey, somewhere off the east coast of England.*

advanced. Fourteen hours each week are given up by the first term to algebra and plain trigonometry, theoretical and practical. In the second term time devoted to these is reduced, and practical spherical trigonometry and navigation are added. In the third and fourth terms algebra is dropped, but nautical astronomy assumes an important place. These are the subjects taken by the naval instructors; but there are extra subjects that absorb fourteen hours each week such as French, charts and instruments, drawing, seamanship, steam and Euclid. In the final two terms Euclid is displaced by theoretical spherical trigonometry. There is barely sufficient time for these subjects to be taught properly and it is only the closely–jointed system that makes it possible. Seamanship only receives three hours per week, a situation much regretted. The *Racer*, which usually lies astern of the *Britannia*, is used for practical instruction. She takes cadets out of the harbour to learn manoeuvring under sail and to grapple with the problems of seasickness. After a break of ten minutes at eleven o'clock, the dinner bugle sounds at one o'clock. On four days a week there is soup, always roast beef and mutton, sometimes stewed and corned beef, occasionally lamb or pork, veal and bacon, or meat pies or puddings, with two vegetables, and often two sweets. On Wednesdays and Saturdays, which are half-holidays, buns are served to boys in the field. All the feeding arrangements are under a mess committee, consisting of the commander, paymaster, and chief instructor and the officer of the day attends in the mess room to see that everything is good and palatable. The warning bugle at two o'clock sees the cadets once more hurrying to their studies until half past three

when they are dismissed. They then change into their flannels before tumbling into the boats where they row themselves ashore. The immediate purpose of coming ashore is bathing, where there is good deep water and an excellent place to dive from. The bugle 'sounds in' and all the boys jump in and are reluctant to get out of the water when the 'retire' is sounded. Once dressed they have a number of activities that they can avail themselves of. There are numerous boats, racquet and fives courts, gymnasium and a photographic darkroom, for the boys are encouraged through prizes to become proficient photographers. The boys climb the steep steps to the level grounds above where the playing fields are situated. In the summer cricket is played and football in the winter under both Association and Rugby rules. Sport is taken seriously, as it is in all public schools and two cricket professionals are associated with the cricket ground. There is also lacrosse, hockey, racquets and other games and sports such as beagling, the commander and officers share all the enjoyments of the boys, warmly supported by the captain, who is keenly interested in their occupations. It is in this way that the spirit of good fellowship and friendly rivalry are encouraged, and it is impossible to over estimate the advantage that results. A fine pavilion, with every convenience, is on the field, to which is attached a canteen organised by the ship, where cadets can buy their 'stodge' at moderate prices.

The 'recall' is hoisted at a quarter past six, earlier in winter, and is hauled down half an hour later, when the cadets are on board, in their change of uniform to muster for their tea of bread and butter, cold meat and watercress, and on special

'The End of the Hindostan' *by J. W. Pilcher, 1921.*

occasions jam and clotted cream.[7] Evening preparation for one hour follows where the boys attend lectures or are engaged with their cadet captain in further study. The boys take this 'on duty' time seriously and cases of skylarking are very rare. At half past eight or an hour earlier in winter the cadets gather on the middle deck, where a good band, formed of their servants, discourse music. The cadets enjoy these sessions but it is said that the waltz is not popular with them. After God Save the Queen is played there is a warning bugle, cadets assemble, prayers are said and they retire and turn in at a quarter past nine in the summer and nine o'clock in the winter.'

Such was the life of a cadet, interspersed with examinations and prize giving ceremonies until the day he left *Britannia* to join his first ship, when he proudly displayed the white flashes on his collar that denoted that he was now a Midshipman and well on his way to becoming a fully commissioned officer in the Royal Navy.

In the spring of 1901 a severe epidemic of influenza swept

through the ship, this resulted in several deaths, mostly arising from complications such as pneumonia. The result was again that the ship in general and the Captain in particular came in for some criticism in the letters pages of *The Times,* as one parent highlighted, 'that the sewage from the ship was discharged straight into the River'; one wonders where he expected it to go. On the other hand the father of another cadet, Mr N. C. Dobson, *emeritus* Professor of Surgery, said that after several visits to the ship he was quite convinced that the condition of the ship had nothing to do with the recent outbreak. The Admiralty was sufficiently concerned over the adverse publicity to commission an official report from a hygiene expert by the name of Professor Corfield. He was satisfied with the sanitary conditions on board and praised the cleanliness of the vessel, concluding that the disease got on board in

7 Jam and clotted cream was such a part of life that some years later a benevolent lady left a sum of money to the college for the purposes of providing clotted cream teas for the cadets.

The last commanding officer of the ship, Captain Charles H. Cross RN, in the captain's cabin at the stern of Britannia.

some manner which it is impossible to detect. Another letter to *The Times* attempted to blame the food and the condition of the town of Dartmouth. This prompted the following reply from the town clerk.

'Nothing, in the eyes of some people, can be commended in the poor old Brit, or the place where she is moored. The captains are all incapable, the officers and masters are worse, the position is insanitary, and nothing is right, in short, except the excellent officers, which this dreadful institution turns out! It would not be precisely fulsome if some credit were accorded to the captains and officers for this result, and a small share to the Admiralty for selecting as a rule, the right men for the post'.[8]

The conditions on board and the health of the cadets were again to the fore in the minds of their Lordships of the Admiralty. This may have been a factor in choosing at this time to finally build a college ashore. The fact that the hospital was the first part of the new college to open in September 1902, three years ahead of the main building, does give credence to this view.

Once the new college opened in September 1905, the *Hindostan* was towed away and scrapped some years later in 1920/21 after being in use as a training hulk for engine room artificers at Portsmouth and renamed HMS *Fisgard III*.

The *Britannia* however remained at Dartmouth for another eleven years. The college used her for ship's company[9] accommodation and storage, but she too was to leave Dartmouth in 1916. The ship had been sold in February 1915 to Messers Hughes, Bolckow & Co of Blyth because the copper plating on her hull and the quantities of iron and lead that she contained were needed for the war effort for munitions manufacture. While still in the river, work had begun to dismantle her upper works. Her impending departure caused a public outcry and a fund was started, called the '*Britannia* Fund' to try and secure the option to purchase the hulk for the nation and possibly turn her into an orphanage for servicemen's children. Unfortunately the appeal was unsuccessful and she was finally towed from her mooring after forty-seven years in July 1916. Her final journey was via the English Channel and the east coast of England to her final resting place where she was broken up. It was said that she was so strongly built that explosives had to be used to break her apart. Ironically, much of the salvaged metal was not used for the war effort. However parts of the old *Britannia* do survive. The figurehead that graced her and her predecessor was removed and survived for many years on the parade ground, the figure there today being a full-size resin copy. Her breakers were an entrepreneurial company that offered many artefacts for sale from their yard made from timber from the old *Britannia*, these included, tables and chairs, tea trolleys, cases for clocks, garden benches and flower troughs among the larger items, and picture frames, ink wells and miniature writing desks were offered at more moderate prices. The college is fortunate enough to possess a number of such items in the museum collection.

Thus it was that the old hulks passed into history and their familiar sight moored on the Dart was no more. However their legacy lives on in the 'stone frigate on the hill' and since the early 1990s Sandquay has had a training vessel moored alongside the jetty, appropriately named *Hindostan*. While the ships were in the Dart more than 5,000 cadets were trained on them and it is these officers that were to serve through two world wars that are the real legacy of HMS *Britannia* and *Hindostan*.

8 The Town Clerk produced statistics to defend his town and the reputation of the old ship.
9 The term 'ship's company' here probably refers to the crew other than the officers and cadets, although the term usually refers to the whole complement of the ship.

CHAPTER 2

The Stone Frigate
on the Hill:

A Masterpiece of Edwardian Architecture

*'Sir Aston Webb's enormous college buildings stretching out along the hill of Townstal, north of Dartmouth. They are
of brick and stone in a revised and vamped-up eighteenth century tradition, not successful as an ensemble, because the
Edwardian-Palladian motifs are not of sufficient bombast to fit the scale adopted. The tower is not high and broad enough
for distant view, and the side cupolas are niggling. The towers at the far ends are too small too — the same mistakes
as made by Webb in the Victoria and Albert Museum . . . The sick quarters are friendlier and less pretentious.'*

The above description is Nikolaus Pevsner's view of the College as described in *The Buildings of England – Devon*, published in 1952. Strangely, elsewhere in his book he confesses that: 'the only building to express the grandiloquence of the Edwardian period is Aston Webb's Royal Naval College at Dartmouth of 1905-9'. Indeed there are a number of inconsistencies in Pevsner's account. Many Dartmothians would not describe the college site as being in Townstal, the building dates are clearly incorrect and he goes on to describe a marble statue of George V by Hamo Thornycroft (1910) as a bronze bust given by George when he was Prince of Wales in 1908. These inaccuracies apart this German chronicler of the English architectural scene was well respected, having been Professor of History of Art at Birkbeck College of the University of London and Slade Professor of Fine Art at Cambridge, in addition to receiving the Gold Medal of the Royal Institute of British Architects for his services to architecture. One

should not, therefore, allow Pevsner to colour one's view of the College but rather concur with the 1945 guide *How to Become a Naval Officer (Dartmouth)*:

'Dartmouth College is that rare product of modern architecture on the grand scale, in that, on first sighting the building, the visitor feels instinctively that it is neither — A lunatic asylum, A prison, The house of a profiteer.'

Indeed, to many, its magnificent facade is awe-inspiring, projecting an image of British sea power that was unsurpassed a century ago.

The Decision to Build

The decision to build a college onshore dates back to 1875 when concern over the health and general training of the cadets was the subject of a report. A committee chaired by Rear Admiral E. B.

Rice, was appointed and the report recommended that a college should be constructed onshore. In the following year, 1876, another report from a committee under the chairmanship of Admiral G. G. Wellesley examined a number of sites. The findings of this committee were reported in full in the *Dartmouth and Brixham Chronicle* of 2nd March 1877. Dartmouth was not the obvious choice; in fact the committee examined thirty-two sites, including Portsmouth, Gosport, Hayling Island, Southampton Water, the Isle of Wight, Poole, Weymouth, Devonport, Milford Haven and Westward Ho. The criteria chosen, from which a decision would be made were

as follows: general salubrity, supply of water, closeness of a harbour for both boating and bathing, access to the sea, recreation grounds, absence of 'special temptations', general suitability, access by rail and proximity of a naval port. Absence of special temptations is of particular interest, as the old *Britannia* had moved from Haslar Creek in Portsmouth for this very reason. It was not surprising, therefore, that Gosport and Portsmouth were rejected but Poole, one site on the Isle of Wight, Weymouth, Devonport and one site at Milford Haven also fell foul of this ruling. Three sites in Kingswear were also considered: Hoodown, Mouthdown and Green Park.

Above: Aston Webb's original design for the college, circa 1900, showing features never actually constructed.

Right: Letter from the Director of Works at the Admiralty to the Captain of HMS Britannia, confirming the acceptance of the builder's tender of £220,600 for the construction of the new college.

Far right: Architect's drawing of interior of chapel, circa 1900.

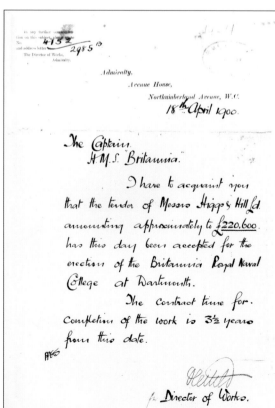

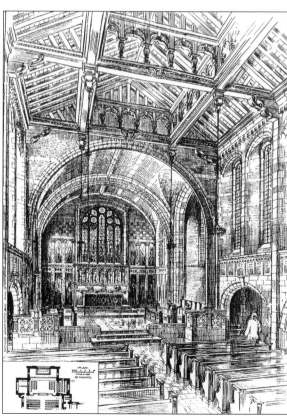

A watercolour by Frank Wood (1908) captures the well-proportioned frontage of Aston Webb's Royal Naval College.

The three Kingswear sites were rejected upon the grounds that the boating and bathing facilities were either indifferent (Hoodown) or impractical in the case of the other two. Water supply for all three was unknown and only Green Park was suitable for a recreation ground. The final analysis of the three Kingswear sites was that all three were unsuitable. Thus, after consideration of all the alternatives, only two sites were to be given serious consideration, Wootton on the Isle of Wight and Mount Boone at Dartmouth. Dartmouth was eventually chosen although Wootton is close to Osborne House, the site later chosen for the other Royal Naval College which cadets attended prior to coming to Dartmouth.

The description of the Mount Boone site in the Wellesley Report has some interesting details and is reproduced in part below.

'MOUNT BOONE SITE, DARTMOUTH.– This estate forms part of a projecting mass of old red sandstone rock and shales belonging to the Devonian series… The sides of the projection are steep and covered with grass and wood down to the waters edge… About 200ft above the water the ground slopes gently upwards to the westward, and ends in a nearly level plain about 265ft above the water level, partly enclosed by woods. Further

westwards it rises to a height of 284ft. On all sides the proposed site is sheltered by higher hills … The site is one of great natural beauty. The Commanding Royal Engineer of the district was so good as to make an examination of the site by boring in four separate places to a depth of 3ft 6ins and found it to consist of small stones overlying slate. The climate is a moist one . . . the average rainfall is 41.58 inches, which is greater than any other south-west site visited. Rain fell on 197 days in 1875. The means of drainage on all sides is ample. The best outlet for sewerage would be into the Dart.

Water from four sources in the neighbourhood of the site was submitted to analysis by the Commanding Royal Engineer, with the result that with one exception, a stream rising near Norton Dawney, which had a slight vegetable contamination, all are remarkably pure and soft, so much so that care should be taken in collecting and distributing any of these waters, to use iron pipes and tanks. The report of the Commanding Royal Engineer shows that sufficient water can be obtained. The site is completely removed from the population. There are ample means of exercise in the adjacent country. The facilities for bathing are not all that

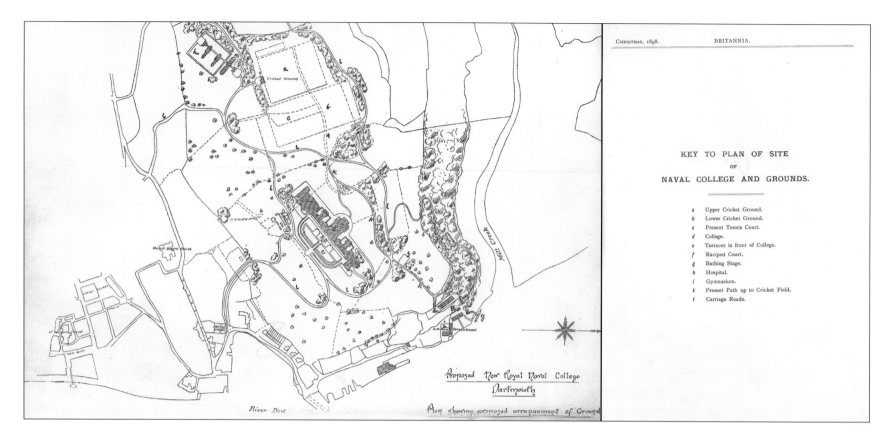

CHRISTMAS, 1898. BRITANNIA.

KEY TO PLAN OF SITE
OF
NAVAL COLLEGE AND GROUNDS.

a   Upper Cricket Ground.
b   Lower Cricket Ground.
c   Present Tennis Court.
d   College.
e   Terraces in front of College.
f   Racquet Court.
g   Bathing Stage.
h   Hospital.
i   Gymnasium.
k   Present Path up to Cricket Field.
l   Carriage Roads.

Map showing the proposed arrangement of the new college, 1905.

could be desired, but if a college were erected they might be extended and improved. The buildings could be so placed as to be sheltered from the north-east winds, and to face the mouth of the estuary, so as to receive the south-east winds. As there is no population close to the site, there are no means of ascertaining death rates, except for Dartmouth and Kingswear, where the circumstances of the population are so different from that of any that might be placed upon the proposed site that no comparison could be instituted between them. The cadets have been remarkably healthy. At the time of our visit there was not a single case in hospital, and only one of the lads on the sick list, arising from boils. Except in the moisture of the climate, the Mount Boone site must be pronounced the finest we have seen for a Cadet College, and may also be considered to be a perfectly healthy one, though not so invigorating for young lads destined to a sea life as might be desired.'

The above was used to recommend Dartmouth as the site chosen. The health of the cadets had been a major concern (as the Rice Committee of the previous year had reported) hence the importance attached to the comments above relating to water supply, rainfall, and moisture. Moreover, the Mount Boone site was considered to be free of those special temptations, a consideration

back in the 1860s, and indeed today, for countries sending their cadets to be trained at BRNC.

A site had therefore been identified in 1877, but the project did not proceed, the reasons are by no means clear, but it was probably due to financial constraints. In 1885 the Luard Committee was appointed and reported the following year on the unhealthy conditions prevailing in the old *Britannia*. The proposal of building a shore based college was once again investigated, this time recommending the removal of training to the Solent, but again no progress was made. It was not until 1895 that the Admiralty Board put forward proposals to revise the cadet training scheme at Dartmouth and to discuss the '*Britannia* Establishment, Sick Quarters etc.' It was in March the following year (1896) that the First Lord of the Admiralty, in presenting the Naval Estimates, announced that a shore based college would be built at Dartmouth, almost twenty years after the site had been initially identified as suitable. One further advantage was that the site, which belonged to the Raleigh estate, was already in use as playing fields and by the Beagle pack for their kennels. The Admiralty then entered into negotiations with the Raleigh Estate to purchase the required land. However, the negotiations soon became difficult and eventually collapsed in October 1896 and were not to be resolved until almost two years later. The funding for the new college was to come from the 1895 Naval Works Loan Act, and it was thought that under this

The foundation stone underneath the temporary pavilion, constructed for the ceremony. The hook and wire rope used for laying the stone are visible above it.

legislation the land could be purchased for £25,000. However, this ran into legal difficulties and the Defence Act of 1842 had to be invoked for compulsory purchase. Judgement was eventually given in favour of the Admiralty in November 1897 and the owner's representatives then began to co-operate to ensure the highest possible price. The final purchase was affected in June 1898 and it is understood that should the Navy ever vacate the site that the land is to be offered back to the Raleigh Estate for the original purchase price.

In the College Archive there survives a memorandum from R. H. Watson JP, a magistrate of Totnes who was appointed to determine the outcome of the dispute between the Government and the Raleigh Estate. To bring the Act of Parliament into force two Deputy Lieutenants of the County had to be appointed, one by the Lord

Their Majesties the King and Queen arrive for the laying of the foundation stone.

The College Chapel

As the College celebrates its one hundredth anniversary, so does the Chapel. This Anglican Chapel has been the focus of worship for cadets and staff of all denominations since it was dedicated by the Venerable Stuart Harris, Chaplain of the Fleet, on September 17th 1905.

The Chapel shares the architectural features of Aston Webb's building, with its interior red brick and Bath stone, enhanced by an assortment of marble features on the walls and floors.[1] All the stained glass windows were paid for by subscription, the most noticeable of which is the east window, portraying Christ enthroned in majesty surrounded by angels, bearing the Emblems of the Passion and given by the parents of cadets from HMS Britannia from 1900-1905. The side windows, depicting the Archangels Iophiel and Raphael, were donated by cadets' parents and members of the College in 1907-1909. Those in the nave depict various saints, given in memory of loved ones, while the three central ones were commissioned after the Second World War. Admiral of the Fleet Sir Dudley Pound, First Sea Lord 1939-1943, is commemorated by a depiction of St. Wilfred; St Columba represents the United States Navy; and St Boniface commemorates those who served in Combined Operations at Dartmouth.

In the south transept there is a window to the memory of Captain Robert Falcon Scott, a cadet on board Britannia, and his comrades who perished in the Antarctic on their return from the South Pole. Below this is a small chapel, the altar of which has the original First World War Memorial carved in Devon oak on the back. It portrays the Virgin Mary and St. John at the foot of the cross with St. George and St. Nicholas on either side.

The main altar boasts a number of frontals, the most notable of which is made of white brocade from the same bolt of cloth as Queen Victoria's wedding dress. The Queen originally gave it to her daughter Princess Louise, Duchess of Argyll, who subsequently gave it to her niece Mrs Meade, on her marriage in 1911. Her husband, Captain the Hon. H. Meade (later Admiral the Honourable Sir Herbert Meade-Fetherstonhaugh) was captain of the College between 1923-1926, and in 1925 Mrs Meade gifted the cloth to the Chapel. At the same time Captain Meade's father, the Earl of Clanwilliam, presented the College with an altar Cross and candlesticks of gilded brass and two brass standard lights, designed by Sir Ninian Comper. The Cross is notable for its fine work in Champleve enamel with four plaques representing St. Edward the Confessor; St. George, patron saint of England; King Alfred, the founder of the Navy; and St. Nicholas, patron saint of sailors. Both the Cross and candlesticks are inscribed; 'To the Glory of God and in memory of Admiral of the Fleet the Earl of Clanwilliam, the countess of Clanwilliam and their daughter Lady Elizabeth Dawson.'

The original organ, completed in 1924, had two manuals and a pedal board with twenty-two speaking stops. It was enlarged in 1952, when the noisy and worn action was renewed, with the console being moved to the south transept under the Scott Memorial. This three manual organ was again enlarged to give forty-two speaking stops in 1972.

The ship that hangs above the nave is a model of the first Britannia (1682) and was the gift of Rear Admiral Dunbar-Nasmith VC, who commanded the College between 1926 and 1928. The model, like the ship herself, was built in Chatham Dockyard, by apprentices.

The kneelers in the nave and choir were designed by Jane Blair, wife of the then Commander of the College in 1979. They were worked by a number of people associated with the College, based on ten designs and dedicated to the seventy-fifth anniversary of the College in 1980.

The original wooden doors to the chapel were replaced in 2000, to commemorate the new millennium, by two Dartington cut glass doors, etched with the words; 'They that go down to the sea in ships see the works of the Lord and the wonders of the deep.' While unmistakably twenty-first century in design, the new doors continue one of Aston Webb's themes, with the styling of the handles as dolphins. Moreover, the glass doors allow for a view of the complete length of the interior of the College, with God at one end and Nelson, in the Senior Gunroom, at the other.

Immediately outside the chapel are housed the war memorial shrine and opposite, in what

Early photograph of the Chapel, probably 1920s, showing the original light fittings or electroliers.

The Chapel as it is today.

was originally the chaplain's office, a small chapel dedicated to the memory of Midshipman Bret Ince, who was killed in action in HMS Prince of Wales *in 1941. Within the war memorial itself is an imposing green bronze sculpture of a west of England cog, copied from the earliest Dartmouth town seal. Such vessels were used by crusaders in the thirteenth century and are also evocative of the ships and small boats that left Dartmouth for Normandy in 1944. On the walls are carved the names of Dartmouth cadets and members of staff who gave their lives in both world wars. In addition these names and more details are recorded in the memorial books, which also include those who have perished in subsequent conflicts.*

While the Chapel remains the focus for worship on such occasions as the end of term and Remembrance Sunday, two additional chapels exist within the College. In 1956 the first chaplain of the Church of Scotland and Free Churches was appointed, although he and his successors were to make do with a lecture room (E2), which would be converted for services on a Sunday, until it was finally decided to convert the room into a permanent chapel, St. Giles, in October 1963. In 1969 a bronze Celtic Cross and wrought iron communion rails, designed and made by the men at Sandquay were added and in 1981 the Alice Fawcett Walker[2] Memorial Window was installed, completing the transformation from classroom to chapel.

The first Roman Catholic chaplain did not arrive at BRNC until 1980, when Sir Julian Oswald (later First Sea Lord), himself a Roman Catholic, was Captain. A chapel was created at the back of O block and named St. Philip Howard, after an English martyr from the period of Catholic persecution in England. The first chaplain was Father Couch RN, who was also a monk at the local Benedictine monastery at Buckfast.

It is not just the Chapel, however, that has contributed to the life and well-being of the College. The three chaplains themselves provide invaluable support to students and staff alike through their pastoral care.

i.

ii.

iii.

iv.

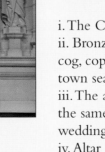

v.

1 See Chapter 2 on Architecture.

2 Whose bequest also paid for the painting of the crests on the Senior Gun Room ceiling.

i. The Chapel's millennium doors.

ii. Bronze sculpture of a west of England cog, copied from the earliest Dartmouth town seal, in the war memorial shrine.

iii. The altar frontal of white brocade from the same bolt of cloth as Queen Victoria's wedding dress.

iv. Altar Cross by Sir Ninian Comper.

v. The reredos carved in Bath stone, depicting Christ and six of the disciples.

Building commences with the garden (Parade Ground) retaining walls in place. A rare early photograph.

Lieutenant, who appointed Kelly, of Kelly & Watson Solicitors, and the other by the Chairman of the Quarter sessions last preceding the date of the action, for which position Judge Edge appointed Watson. Watson's account of the business is reproduced below.

'On receiving notice

We met at the Royal Hotel, Plymouth. The Naval and Military authorities, were present with maps and co. They gave their views etc. Having heard all they had to say we retired "now Kelly what is your opinion?" he replied "I am decidedly against making an Order. I do not approve of taking any mans land against his will".

I then said; "I am definitely for making an Order". "Taking into account the great advantages to the West of England and the County as well as the local benefits that must necessarily accrue we must make an Order to take the Land. If the Raleigh Estate show fight let the Govt fight it out," Kelly gave way and we signed an order to take possession.

1 The act of erecting an ash pole was a symbolic act of establishing and taking possession.

Next Day

A marine was sent who erected an ash pole in the centre of the Estate.[1]

An action was then brought against us on trespass in the High Court which decided in our favour.

The building of the Naval College commenced forthwith'

Architect Appointed

All that remained was to find a suitable architect to launch this prestigious project. Captain A. W. Moore was Captain of *Britannia* from 1894–97 and when the decision to build was announced he recalled:

'It having been decided to build a college onshore to replace the *Britannia* our excellent drawing master, Mr Spanton, prepared plans of the design, which in our opinion would fulfil the requirements, and I sent it up to the Director of Works at the Admiralty. He declined it and returned it remarking he had his own staff and would not require to avail himself of the services of the *Britannia* drawing master. This was followed by the arrival at Dartmouth of one of his staff, who proceeded to draw up plans which were quite

Sir Aston Webb portrait by Solomon Joseph Solomon

National Portrait Gallery

Above: The original gatehouse shortly before its demolition prior to the building of a new road in the 1960s (College Way).

Top left: The three isolation wings of the hospital, opened in 1902.

Left: General view of the front of the College and sunken garden in the summer of 1905.

impossible, so I wrote to a friend at Osborne (Osborne House, the residence of Queen Victoria and not the College that was not built until some years later) of what was going on and hoped Queen Victoria would hear. The reply was a telegram commanding me to Osborne. I dined with the Queen and told her about it. The next day the First Lord of the Admiralty was sent for and shortly afterwards Mr Aston Webb was appointed as architect to the new naval college. When Mr Aston Webb came to Dartmouth I showed him Mr Spanton's plans and he was a big enough man to accept them in the main. So the present naval college is to all intents along the lines we worked for. The Easter holidays gave me plenty of time to consider the best site. On one of my walks ashore I went up to the playing fields on the hill which overlooks the harbour. I covered a great deal of ground, but came back to the cricket field with its magnificent outlook. Standing there for a few minutes I was convinced that the site could not be improved upon. I recommended it to their Lordships, and there stands
the naval college today[2].'

2 Account taken from the reminiscences of Capt Moore's niece Miss E M Moore.
(Pack 1966 p.96)

The appointment of Aston Webb (1849-1930) was not surprising. He was one of the country's most respected architects with some impressive public buildings to his name, most notably the main block of the Victoria and Albert Museum in South Kensington (1899-1909) and the Victoria Law Courts in Birmingham (1885). The commission to design the new university in Birmingham in 1900 rewarded the reputation that he had earned in the city. The early years of the twentieth century were to prove fruitful to Aston Webb, for not only did he have the commissions for two major educational establishments (Birmingham and Dartmouth), he also became President of the Royal Institute of British Architects from 1902-4 and was knighted for his Presidency and services to architecture in 1904. His work at Dartmouth was not to be his last major naval building, for in 1911 he was commissioned to design Admiralty Arch. His reputation for educational buildings was rewarded again when he was offered the commission to design the Royal School of Mines in South Kensington, (1903-13). This latter appointment was hardly surprising as he had the contract to design the Chemistry and Physics building at Imperial College, started in 1898, this was unfortunately destroyed in a fire and now only the tower survives. His appointment by the Admiralty to build the new college at Dartmouth demonstrated the

i. Interior of the Chapel shortly before completion. Note the winged cherub faces carved on the roof cross beams.

ii. Interior of the Quarterdeck shortly after opening. Note the elaborate electroliers.

iii. Interior of the dining hall (Senior Gun Room) shortly before completion.

iv. Bath stone resplendent in the main stair well.

Navy's commitment to the College, in addition its grand appearance would dominate the town's skyline and be a testimony to the fact that, *Britannia* still ruled the waves. The Royal Navy was the most powerful in the world and still had an empire to defend. Such symbolism was important at a time when it was government policy to maintain a navy that could outnumber the next two largest naval powers, particularly, Germany, the United States of America and Japan, with Germany posing the greatest threat to British interests.

The College was being built as architectural trends were changing from the Victorian era of what was often described as an 'aggressive and assertive Gothic Revival' period to a more relaxed and eclectic scene. One aspect of the Edwardian architectural scene was the coming together of artists and architects. Architects now wished to be associated with artists, and through the Arts and Crafts movement they often included the work of artists in their buildings. One of the aims of the movement was to break down the barriers that kept art compartmentalised; architects now started to commission artists to execute carved friezes and sculptures, both features of the new college at Dartmouth. The Art Workers' Guild[3] was formed at this time and the fruits of their labours also appeared on the interior of buildings. Aston Webb was responsible for overseeing much of the ornate interior decoration and artwork at the College and when the Bromsgrove Guild[4] became a company in 1901 he had no hesitation in using the Guild for some of the fittings in the college. The Guild's handiwork can still be seen in the Senior Gunroom light fittings (electroliers) and the ornate main doorknocker, which were both specially designed for the College.

Appointment of the Builders

Tenders were invited for the building of the new college, and the well-established firm of Higgs and Hill were successful with their submission for £220,600 and an estimate of three and a half years to finish the works. The Director of Works at the Admiralty accepted the estimate in a letter dated 18th April 1900. The builders Higgs and Hill had been formed in 1874, from two smaller concerns, that of William Matthews Hill (founded in 1850) and William Higgs (founded in 1867), and by 1900 had gained a good reputation, but the college at Dartmouth was the biggest contract that they had ever won. The company's recent completion of the Tate Gallery in London in 1897 had certainly enhanced their reputation and must have impressed the Director of Works that the builders were capable of such a large undertaking as the new College.

The builders decided that all the joinery and stonework would be carried out at their own works in London. Portland and Bath stone was taken to the company's works in Vauxhall and each week a boat left the Free Trade Wharf on the Thames, with dressed stone, for Dartmouth. The company sent Mr Edmond Hill (Company Secretary and grandson of William Hill) to be resident director of works in Dartmouth, an act that demonstrated the company's commitment to the project.

Laying of The Foundation Stone

Although work on the site had started in 1898, the Foundation Stone for the main building was not laid until 1902 when on 2nd March King Edward VII accompanied by Queen Alexandra, travelled to Devon by the Royal Train for the stone laying ceremony. They boarded

Watercolour by Michael Hill showing the College from the Commodore's garden.

3 Formed along with the Arts and Crafts Exhibition Society in the 1880s to give direction to the Arts and Crafts movement.
4 The Bromsgrove Guild, which became a company in 1901, produced decorative plasterwork, wrought iron and carving.

the train at Paddington, for what would be one of the longest non-stop runs that the Great Western Railway had ever attempted. Not only was this the longest run, but the first non-stop train from Paddington to Kingswear. The King took a great personal interest in the running of the train and the railway had chosen one of their best footplate staff, Driver Burden, for the journey. With Burden in charge and the King's interest in the journey, there were no inhibitions regarding speed and the train was allowed to run somewhat ahead of time, reaching Kingswear at 14.55, more than twenty minutes ahead of schedule. The train had maintained a steady average of 60 mph on the open stretches of the line, and recorded an average of 56 mph between Paddington and Exeter, a remarkable feat for 1902. The locomotive hauling the train had been re-named *Britannia* for the day, special nameplates had been made at the GWR's Swindon works, and, as a mark of respect for the Royal Navy, the gleaming brass letters had their sides painted red, as this was the tradition with nameplates on Royal Naval ships. Although Kingswear and Dartmouth had been preparing for this visit for some months, the early arrival of the train must have caused some consternation amongst the waiting dignitaries. The royal party crossed the river in a refurbished paddle steamer called the *Dolphin*. They were met by the Mayor, the Corporation and the Commissioners of the Dart Harbour before leaving by landau for the college site.

A temporary wooden pavilion had been erected over the stone to give protection from the weather should it prove inclement. This measured one hundred and twenty feet by thirty-six feet, there was a raised dais around the stone with seating for the royal party and dignitaries and tiered seating at either end. The walls were covered with red and white drapes and flags, and behind the stone were floral displays and plans and drawings of the new college. The stone was laid in place by a chain and wire rope mechanism operated from outside the pavilion, with orders being communicated by a voice pipe. The inscription on the stone originally had a gilded background, which has unfortunately not survived.

At the stone laying ceremony a casket was laid in the foundation stone. The *Dartmouth Chronicle* described the casket as being of solid silver, richly gilded and enamelled and medallioned on each side, with images of Dartmouth Castle on one side and Kingswear Castle on the other, and containing an illuminated loyal address. The King is said to have locked the casket with a solid gold key, which he took with him. There is, however, a second description of a casket in an edition of *The Sphere* for March 15th 1902. *The Sphere's* description is as follows.

'The casket … measures about 16 inches long by 10 inches wide. It is formed of oak taken from the old *Britannia* training ship and is partly encased in a framing of copper fretted in an appropriate design to show the oak body beneath, the metalwork at the ends being beaten into fixed handles of conventional design to take the ribbons by which the casket will be lifted into the aperture of the foundation stone. The oak lid has a wide framing of copper held by rivets of the same metal and the royal initials 'E. R. VII.' with the

Top: Aston Webb's design for the electroliers in the Chapel and dining hall (Senior Gun Room).

Bottom: Electrolier in the Senior Gun Room today, with an additional two lampshades.

Mess Silver

Military silver has a long tradition in the armed services where its significance lies not merely as a piece of beautifully crafted precious metalwork, but in the story recalled by the inscription upon it, as Roger Perkins describes it (1999) 'This is silver with a human face'. The inventory of silver artefacts owned by the Royal Navy numbers some eight thousand items, many of these given to Wardrooms by 'The Leavers'[1]. In contrast the relatively small Corps of seven thousand officers and men of The Royal Marines boast four thousand such items on their inventory of silver, and this does not include items given directly to the Messes of individual units.

Statue of Britannia:
A table centrepiece given by seven officers in 1896. It was made by a London silversmith from drawings made by J. Humphrey Spanton who was the senior drawing master on *Britannia* from 1867 to 1904. This item is still in regular use as the centrepiece for the top table in both the Wardroom dining room and the Senior Gunroom.

Statue of Britannia with the Prince of Wales Feathers:
This silver centrepiece of Britannia with the Prince of Wales plume of three ostrich feathers rising from the helmet was presented to the College by the Prince of Wales to commemorate his initial Naval Training at the College from September to October 1971. The statue stands on a mahogany pedestal, reputed to be made from the boss of an aircraft propeller; the Prince of Wales trained as an aviator.

The Beagle Trophy:
Made in 1898 with a London hallmark, the BB standing for the Britannia Beagles. Although this is a handsome piece of silver it is more interesting for its provenance. It was given by Commander C. Cradock to the 'Wardroom Officers'. He later became Rear Admiral Sir Christopher Cradock KCVO CB, and commanded the British squadron at the Battle of Coronel, where on 1st November 1914, he went down with HMS *Good Hope*.

Cigarette Box:
A casket pattern cigarette box with a fine enamelled coloured image of HMS *Britannia* and *Hindostan* on the lid. Made in London in 1896 it is inscribed 'Presented to the Officers of the Wardroom HMS *Britannia* by D. Potts Chatto, July 1896.'

Plate from Nelson's Dinner Service:
In 1919, twenty-three dinner plates formerly belonging to Admiral Nelson were presented to the Royal Navy by the Navy League to honour the services of the Royal Navy in the Great War. The plates were divided amongst various ships and the College received that of HMS *Lion* in 1928. This was recalled for the new *Lion* in 1961 and the College received the one formerly belonging to HMS *Queen Elizabeth*. It bears a London hallmark of 1801; the plate is engraved with Nelson's coat of arms, together with the Viscount's coronet awarded at the Battle of Copenhagen in April 1801.

The Hamilton Cup:
This cup was commissioned by Admiral Nelson and was a favourite piece of Lady Emma Hamilton. After Nelson's death Lady Hamilton took the cup as a keepsake, but when she fell upon hard times the government of the day took it in lieu of debt. It was later presented to the College.

Alms Dish:
Silver alms dish presented to the College in 1963 by the Mayor, Aldermen and Burgesses of the Borough of Clifton Dartmouth Hardness in commemoration of one hundred years of Naval Officer Training inaugurated at Dartmouth in HMS *Britannia*, 30th September 1863. The emblems within the gilt roundels on the rim are of the four Evangelists.

Sports Trophy on Oak Base:
This trophy presented to the Wardroom Officers of HMS *Britannia* in 1888, consists of three figures depicting the sports of rugby, cricket and fencing surmounted by a naval crown held aloft by entwined dolphins.

1 The average length of appointment for a Naval Officer being two years probably accounts in part for the large number of silver items, as silver was a traditional gift to the Wardroom Mess.

Dormitory ventilation tower over A block.

Architect's original drawing of the headmaster's house, April 1905.

Tudor crown are finely carved in high relief on the surface of the oak lid. The interior of the casket, which contained the usual coins and records, was lined with royal blue velvet, and the whole was secured by a Chubb's patent lock actuated by a gold key of unusual design, introducing the acorn and oak leaves in reference to the 'wooden wall' from which the material was obtained. On the front of the casket was the following inscription:

> This casket, made from oak from HMS *Britannia*, was deposited in the foundation stone of the *Britannia* Royal Naval College by his Majesty King Edward VII, March 7, 1902.'

The descriptions of both caskets are very detailed and as such are likely to be accurate; *The Sphere* also carries a photograph of the wooden casket that matches its own description. It is therefore possible that there were two caskets interred at the ceremony, one from the Town of Dartmouth (the gilded and enamelled silver one) containing the loyal address, and the wooden one from the Navy containing the coins and papers. *The Sphere* carries an illustration with the Captain of *Britannia* handing coins and papers to the King, which would support this theory. The whole ceremony only lasted for one hour and fifteen minutes and the Royal Train departed for Plymouth at ten past four in the afternoon.

A Masterpiece of Edwardian Architecture

The College was initially designed by Aston Webb as a public school to replace the two hulks on the river. Public schools at the time reflected the architecture of the homes of the landed gentry, as the pupils, who were largely from the middle classes, aspired to be seen in a similar light (Wiener 1981 and Perkin 1990). The sons of the aristocracy almost invariably went to public schools, but the majority (and Dartmouth was no exception) were from middle class backgrounds (Kalton 1966). Dartmouth also conformed in its architecture, echoing the design of many English country houses at the time. The building's division into two wings either side of a central tower, its sweeping drives to the entrance and setting in open parkland all emulating the English country estate. The acquisition of the Raleigh estate also had its corollary in that many public schools sought to acquire surrounding lands from the gentry to protect their isolation. Indeed, Harrow School bought 220 acres for £90,000 in 1885 'to keep a distance from the rising tide of bricks and mortar'. This connection is also illustrated in the following passage from the Gieves 1935 booklet *How to become a Naval Officer, and Life at the Royal Naval College, Dartmouth*:

> 'As the officer goes from ship to ship and wardroom to wardroom he always feels at home; it is as if his quarters had been moved from another wing of the family mansion.'

Above: Crown and monogram surmount the hopper of a drainpipe. Such was Aston Webb's attention to architectural detail.

Right: Construction of D block, 1914-1917.

Below: Warship development carved in stone. These four prow models adorn the front of the building.

It is this visual analogy with aristocratic life that almost certainly determined the architect's thoughts when he designed his public school at Dartmouth. It reflected many of the great houses and public schools with the inclusion of a great hall, a central tower with dormitory and recreational wings either side. The proportions of the rooms and height of the ceilings were more than the average cadet would have been used to at home, the panelled and vaulted dining hall with its gallery was reminiscent of many Tudor or Elizabethan mansions. It is therefore not surprising that during his time as architect at Dartmouth, Aston Webb was also commissioned to design a war memorial for Harrow School (Colville 2003).

In spite of the above constraints and Aston Webb's reputation for being 'hopelessly eclectic' (Fellows 1995) the Royal Naval College is undeniably Edwardian in appearance. In his opening words Fellows (1995) describes 'the images of Edwardian architecture' as 'alluring: a lofty gable projecting high above the street, rising from a wall of warm red brick striped with creamy coloured stone; a richly craved frieze running below, a bay window framed in stone

Architectural idiosyncrasy in the balustrades outside the Wardroom.

and set about with allegorical figures; over all a copper clad dome with lantern and gilded weather vane'. Except for the reference to rising above the street and the copper cladding of the dome, this description could very well refer to Dartmouth.

The site sits 180 feet above sea level and slopes steeply down to the River Dart, both to the south and to the east. Aston Webb accommodated the slope to the east by first choosing the site where the slope is less steep, and secondly by the use of stairs from the dining hall and the chapel. The main corridor is level, but at the eastern end there is a short flight of steps down to the level of the chapel and two short flights at the western end, leading up to the dining room. The slope to the south has resulted in the architect building the College as a series of terraces that are hardly obvious from the front elevation.

The parade ground, originally conceived as a sunken garden, is below the level of the thirty-foot wide main terrace. There are then steps into the main building, more steps to the main corridor, steps to the great hall and steps beyond to the buildings at the rear of the great hall, the entire building being a series of levels rising to the north. The College was originally designed to accommodate 260 cadets with dormitories and recreation rooms in the two wings (now known as A & B blocks) and classrooms off the great hall (now known as the quarterdeck). However, after the announcement of Lord Selborne's scheme there were to be 390 cadets in six terms of sixty-five each. The College was therefore inadequate for the intended numbers, a situation that has plagued Dartmouth ever since the College was built. To accommodate this increased number, an extra accommodation block was added at the time of building at right angles to the chapel (now known as C block), with its own sanitary annexe. The sick quarters were opened in 1902, a sign that the health of the cadets was still of great concern to the Admiralty. These quarters consisted of sixty-four beds, forty for infectious and twenty-four for non-infectious cases, these were in three isolated two-storey wings. In addition there are nurses quarters at one end and a day-room and administrative block at the other. The block also boasts operating rooms and a dispensary, in addition to a large house for the doctor[5]. In the 1960s the old doctor's house became the residence of the Commander of the College.

The fresh water supply for the College was originally taken from a spring at Sandquay and pumped to a reservoir situated one hundred feet above the College; this fed a large cistern in the clock tower, which fed the entire College. The salt water supply for the swimming pool was pumped from the river and this also fed the plunge baths and the hydrants. The heating for the College was from a boiler and engine house at Sandquay, and this reached the College via a service duct, which in recent years has been the roost of

5 The first patient in the new hospital was Cadet C W Graham, who broke his leg in the first game of the 1902-3 season, 'quite a proper and appropriate baptism' the *Britannia Magazine* reported. Fatalities were not uncommon and on 11th June 1904 Cadet Boycott died at the hospital.

Architectural detail in Portland stone.

Construction of D block, 1914-1917.

a colony of Lesser Horseshoe bats. The location of the boiler house at Sandquay was so that coals and ashes need not be transported up and down the hill to the College. The College is now heated from a modern boiler located to the rear of D Block.

Externally the dressings are of Portland stone and the red bricks, so typical of many Edwardian buildings, were supplied by Thomas Lawrence & Sons of Bracknell, Berkshire.[6] The roofs are covered with Delabole slates from Cornwall, characterised by their delicate green colouration, as seen on so many West Country buildings. The walls of the terrace are of Torquay limestone and they are topped with parapets of Cornish granite, which also forms the base upon which

6 The bricks were all stamped with the initials DNC, for Dartmouth Naval College

Previous pages: The Battle of Trafalgar: 2.30pm by W. L. Wyllie ARA. Arguably the College's finest work of art, painted for the centenary of Trafalgar it is signed and dated 1905. TRANSPARENCY SUPPLIED BY MARITIME PRINTS & ORIGINALS

the college frontage stands. The internal stonework is Bath stone from the Monks Park limestone quarries, located at Corsham, Wiltshire, and still operated by Bath Stone Firms Ltd. One of the most notable internal features of the College is the use of glazed bricks along the main corridor and some of the stairways leading off this corridor. Those along the main passageway are a delicate shade of green and those on the stairs a rich deep brown colour. Unfortunately those lining the stairs have for the most part been painted over; but those on the corridor remain, some showing damage from the bombing in 1942, some of the more intricately moulded ones having been replaced by painted wooden blocks during the refurbishment. All of the glazed bricks were supplied by the Farnley Iron Company of Leeds, and were transported to Dartmouth from Leeds in a small steamer via the Aire and Calder Navigation, then down the East Coast and the English Channel to Dartmouth where they were unloaded at a specially built pier at Sandquay. Many of the building materials were brought in this way

The Commodore's house.

and transported to the College site via a narrow gauge rope hauled tramway. A small quarry was opened at Sandquay that was used to supply local stone for the boundary walling. Some sand for building purposes was removed from a small beach near Stoke Gabriel, a few miles up river.

The interior of the chapel combines Bath Stone with the red bricks that dominate the exterior. The high vaulted ceiling above the chancel show this feature to good effect, while the roof of the main aisle has a wooden beamed roof with delicately carved cherubs on the main bosses of the beam work. Originally the chapel was illuminated by electroliers similar to those in the main dining room (Senior Gunroom), but with cherubs as the main theme. It is traditional for the chapels of public schools and colleges to have the seating running longitudinally, facing each other, but here Aston Webb broke with tradition and somewhat controversially for the time, placed the seating across the main body of the chapel, as would be found in a traditional church.

The chapel displays a wide variety of decorative marble work, this was entrusted to the local company of H. T. Jenkins and Son, of Torquay. This reflected Aston Webb's desire to use local materials whenever possible. To help with the marble work, four stonemasons were brought over from Italy, all of whom settled in Dartmouth, their descendants living locally today. Their work was not only confined to the College, several shop doorways in Dartmouth still show evidence of their skills.

The twelve-foot high marble panelling in the chancel is Italian in origin and has been cut and opened out to give a very striking pattern, the colouring subtly changing to become lighter nearer to the altar, signifying the transition 'from darkness into light'. In between these panels are columns of local Devonian limestone from Jenkins' Kingsley quarry and in the panel at the top are decorations of a green marble, which is possibly from Connemara in western Ireland. The chancel floor is laid with a dark veined variety of marble and white Cararra marble from Italy, while the

The College nearing completion, with the headmaster's house still only partially built. The inclined ropeway and temporary jetty, used during construction, are clearly visible (Dartmouth Museum).

side ambones are of beautiful deep red Victoria marble from Cork. The steps to the chancel, the altar rail step, and the plinths to both the ambones and the altar are all of locally quarried dark Devonian limestone (known as Ashburton marble and from Jenkins' quarries) close examination will reveal fossil corals within.

The above is a description of the College as it opened in 1905, with the Master's Hostel and the swimming pool opening the following year. However, as in the past fluctuations in the student population, due to changes in entry regulations and the demands of the fleet for new officers, was soon to apply pressure on the available accommodation. It was therefore only two years before the first substantial extension was opened in 1907. This has always been known as E Block, and has for more than forty years contained the Chapel of the Church of Scotland and Free Churches. (The Chapel celebrated its 40th anniversary in 2003). The rest of the Block now houses the computer training rooms.

Further Expansion of the College

The first major extension was the addition of what is now known as D Block, which was completed in 1917. In the years after the College was opened there was an increasing requirement for more naval officers. This demand was to be met in part by the introduction of the 'Special Entry' for boys who had previously completed an education at public school. Nevertheless, the total expected entry to the Naval College of 110 per term was almost double that of

1905, which clearly required additional accommodation. The result was an entirely new block, to be constructed to the north of the original main buildings, and to house an extra dining room (now called the Junior Gunroom), three large gunrooms for recreational purposes and more dormitory space, in addition to more studies (classrooms) and a Common Room for the Masters. Aston Webb's practice in London was awarded the contract, although it has been suggested by Davies and Grove (1980) that he no longer controlled the work there at that time. It is also a popular myth that upon seeing the completed extension and the scar on the skyline view of the original College, that he washed his hands of Dartmouth and was never to return. There is however no evidence at all to support this view, and it is believed by some students of architecture to be pure speculation. Aston Webb was sixty-five years of age when these works were started in the summer of 1914 and he may have not have been as involved as he was in the original building. However, it was only three years earlier that he was responsible designing and overseeing the building of Admiralty Arch in London. How much the architect was involved in the design of D Block we shall probably never know, but when viewed from the south it does bear more than a passing resemblance to the façade of Buckingham Palace, a project which was his entirely. The arrangement of terraced and mezzanine floors in the original building is continued through into D Block, at least in keeping with Aston Webb's original theme. The construction is of red brick and Portland stone, just as in the original College, but it is of

The College as it approaches its centenary.

a much more utilitarian design, probably reflecting its wartime period of building. There are few Portland stone courses to relieve the vast area of brick, and the front elevation is flat, in contrast to that of the original College, which is relieved with projecting gables and bays. It has a flat roof unlike the original 1905 building with its lofty slate clad, hipped and gabled roofs. The new block does have an imposing entrance with a Portland stone gable, above it at roof height, is an elaborately carved royal coat of arms[7]. Nevertheless, while the lower floors do possess elaborate large windows with gracefully curved upper portions and ornate brickwork, mirroring that at the rear of the main building which this block faces, the two upper floors are flat and without relief. Unfortunately it is only the two upper floors that are visible from a distance, as the original building hides the more elaborate lower floors. The upper floors were completed towards the end of the first world war, and wartime shortages of both materials and labour may be the reason why the upper two floors are much more austere than the lower floors.

Although the lower floors do bear all the hallmarks of Aston Webb design it is likely that he did not design the upper two floors. New studies were completed in May 1917 that also joined the new block to the existing building, which itself was opened in September of that year.

Aston Webb's magnificent College suffered bomb damage in 1942[8], but only makeshift repairs could be carried out because of wartime shortages of labour and materials. Repairs were started after the war and were completed in time for the return of the cadets to the College in September 1946. Also in that year, the foundations were laid for a new building to accommodate areas for the teaching of the new additions to the curriculum, music and art. This brick building of utilitarian design is rectangular, and flat-roofed, but functional, reflecting the modern outlook of the time. Fortunately it is hidden behind D Block, and so does not detract from the fine proportions of the original 1905 building, nor indeed the 1917 D Block. Its large open rooms, originally intended for music and art are now used for classes in navigation, it also houses the College's modern 'Bridge Trainer' *Daring*. The building, now referred to as F Block, is the Navigation Department Block.

The major changes in training as a result of the COST Committee report[9], saw the College cease to be a naval public school and become a naval training college for naval officers. This had major implications for the building. A sub-committee was set up in June 1954 to examine the necessary works and buildings that would be required. It was decided at an early stage that COST's solution of providing extra instructional and living accommodation by putting up standard Ministry of Supply buildings was out of the question. As far as the Navy was concerned, Dartmouth was an ancient monument and so must not be spoilt. Throughout the discussions and subsequent planning, thought was given to keeping the buildings viewed from the south, the main aspect of the building, 'architecturally in accord with the existing buildings'. Fortunately the need for this was also recognised by the Treasury.

The first major change was to be in sleeping accommodation, where the existing dormitories on the first and second floors were to be altered into single cabin accommodation for the midshipmen and four berth cabins for cadets. It was felt that the cadets would more easily be acclimatised to communal life in non-single cabins, a belief that remains the case today. The house or divisional system was to continue and therefore the gunrooms only changed in how they were used. They became purely recreational spaces instead of working/recreational spaces, and hence only the furnishings were altered. The report recommended that midshipmen should enjoy a higher 'standard of elegance' in their messing, so it became necessary for the midshipmen and cadets to mess separately, leading

---

7 This carving was originally on the exterior of the northern gable of the great hall (quarterdeck), it being removed to this position when D Block was built.

8 See Chapter 5 The College at War.

9 See Chapter 6 Education, 1945-2005.

to the reactivation of the D Block mess and galley. This necessitated a great deal of work in both messes (dining halls) and galleys. These two messes became the Junior Gunroom for the cadets (juniors) and the Senior Gunroom for the seniors, these arrangements continue to this day. A separate bar and billiard room was set up in the gunroom nearest to the seniors dining hall (Senior Gunroom), and it remains to this day as a television room.

The Wardroom, which was originally built to house about twenty-five officers, became quite inadequate for the new role, as officer numbers were expected to rise to fifty or more. As an extension was necessary, it was decided to make possible the provision of a combined mess of which officers and lecturers could be full members. As stated in the Captain's report of the time 'cohesion between the Service and Civilian staff has always been desirable but under the new scheme it is even more essential and this seemed a good way of helping it on'. (Captain's Report of the COST Scheme Recommendations. – College Archive). The Wardroom extension that followed displaced a number of storerooms; hence a new victualling block was built, incorporating some victualling offices and a Catering Officers Flat (this is now known as the Wardroom Flat). The extension to the Wardroom and the alterations to the Senior Gunroom resulted in a major refurbishment of the attached galleys. This resulted in a movement of one of the large doors from the Senior Gunroom to the galley. The work was skilfully executed and the original wooden panelling was taken out and replaced with great care. The only evidence of the move is that the carved names of the battles and admirals at the top of the panelling are now out of date sequence in two of the panels.

Other building work involved the building of a new annexe to D Block, containing additional cabins, to accommodate the increased numbers with the COST scheme. The firm of Stanbury of Plymouth was to be the main contractor for all the new works. A new lecture hall was included in the original plan, but the Treasury did not sanction its building at this stage. Other moves involved the clothing store moving from D Block to C wing of the old hospital, recently vacated by the Admiralty Interview Board.

The College would have to wait almost ten years to get the new lecture hall originally suggested in the COST scheme, and this was to be the last major new building to date. The impetus for the commencement of building of the new hall was the 'Unison 63' conference to be held at Dartmouth in September 1963. This was a gathering of Commonwealth armed forces and was planned by Lord Mountbatten as Chief of Defence Staff. It was to be a multi-purpose building seating 485, intended for lectures, discussions, cinema and theatrical shows, musical recitals (previously held in the chapel or gymnasium) and examinations. It was for the latter that the removable tip-up seating was installed. It is used for a wide variety of purposes but not examinations, latterly the gymnasium was used, but now with small groups sitting classrooms are used. The sloping site suited the building well, as the architects could make use of the slope for the raked seating. The architects Messrs Playne, Lacy and Partners of Westminster, were appointed; they now incorporated the practice of Sir Aston Webb and Son, the original architect for the College, producing an unbroken line from 1905 to 1963. The building is in red brick with a broad Portland stone band at the top, so as to harmonise with the other College buildings. The building has a cinema projection room over a generously proportioned entrance foyer, with cloakrooms. It is apparent that when built it was for a predominantly all male college population, as the ladies' facilities are totally inadequate – ask any lady who has ever needed to make use of them. The hall has a generous stage made of maple some twenty feet in depth, with changing rooms beneath. The main auditorium has a suspended ceiling and its back wall is treated acoustically; the plain plaster walls have a beech veneer dado and the entrance foyer an attractive terrazzo floor. The hall was first used by Admiral of the Fleet Sir Casper John[10] to address the young officers' passing out in the summer of 1963. The hall was named *Casper John Hall* in his honour, an act that may have been thought insensitive as it was Lord Mountbatten who provided initial impetus to its building. 'Unison 63' took place in the September of that year, when there were 220 representatives from twelve nations.

It is perhaps therefore fitting that the last major building at Dartmouth should be designed by Messrs Playne and Lacy and Partners, the company that incorporated the practice of the original architect of the college, Sir Aston Webb. More than one hundred years since the doors on Aston Webb's masterpiece opened to its first term of cadets, it continues to symbolise the pride and traditions of the Royal Navy.

10 Casper John was christened in the College chapel in March 1918. His father was the artist Augustus John, who had no obvious naval connections, and why the ceremony took place at Dartmouth remains a mystery.

CHAPTER 3

A Revolution in Education:

The Selborne Scheme at Dartmouth, 1905-1945

'If the Navy is not supreme, no Army however large is of the slightest use. It's not invasion we have to fear if our Navy is beaten, it's starvation' (Admiral Sir John Arbuthnot Fisher, 1904)

Admiral of the Fleet, Lord Fisher of Kilverstore. Painting by Robert Swan after Sir Hubert von Herkomer

To describe the Selborne Scheme of naval education as a revolution is not mere hyperbole. It offered boys destined to become Naval Officers a very modern education, in particular through its inclusion of theoretical and practical engineering. With some modification, it was to form the basis of training and education at Dartmouth for over forty years – an unprecedented period of continuity in the history of the College. The success of the scheme was in large part due to the energies of Second Sea Lord, Admiral Sir John Arbuthnot Fisher, for whom the new scheme was but one component of the reforms he was to institute during his time as Second and later First Sea Lord, although it is after the First Lord of the Admiralty, Lord Selborne, that the scheme is generally known. Inevitably Fisher and Selborne's plans met with opposition when first published, on Christmas Day 1902, particularly from older and more conservative officers, active and retired, whose principal objection focused on the introduction of engineering instruction for executive as well as engineering officers and the apparent 'inter-changeability' between the two branches. Indeed, some of the original objectives of the scheme, such as the full inclusion of Royal Marine and Engineering officers into a common entry and training, failed to materialise fully.

'The Founders of the College,' at the opening of the Royal Naval College Osborne, circa 1904. The group includes Admiral Sir John Fisher, HRH The Prince of Wales (later King George V) HRH Princess Mary of Teck (later Queen Mary), Captain Rosslyn Wemyss the first captain of Osborne and other officers of the establishment.

Nevertheless, the Selborne-Fisher Scheme succeeded in establishing Dartmouth as a respectable and unique form of public school, which was to survive in amended form through the upheavals of two world wars, until finally succumbing to the demands of social equality when the thirteen-year-old entry was abolished by the post-war Labour government in 1948.

The Selborne Scheme

It would not be overstating the facts to suggest that at the turn of the twentieth century the soundness and efficiency of the Royal Navy was of grave concern. Since the Battle of Trafalgar it had enjoyed almost unchallenged command of the sea, due in large part to the weaknesses of its principal rivals. Such superiority had however bred complacency. While other newer navies had been quick to assimilate advances in technology the Royal Navy

remained psychologically attached to a world in which sails and masts, rather than steam and engines, were the life force of a navy. The system on board HMS *Britannia* reflected this illusion with its emphasis on traditional seamanship. As one contemporary critic of the *Britannia* observed:

'For the perpetuation of a system which time and the engineer has rendered obsolete, the *Britannia* must be held largely responsible. The vessel was established fifty years too late … Science was already perfecting a system of propulsion which was destined not merely to give the lie to the statement on which the *Britannia* system was based, that "ships cannot be navigated on long voyages without masts and sails" but to supersede old-time methods of propulsion' (Commander Hon. Henry N. Shore, in Kemp 1964 p.210).

While such criticism might seem overly harsh, it nevertheless underlines one of the key driving forces behind what was to become

Sir Cyril Ashford, first Headmaster at Osborne and Dartmouth.

a revolutionary new scheme of education. The introduction of steam propulsion in the latter half of the nineteenth century had led to the rise of a new breed of naval officer; the engineer. However, coming generally from a lower social class, and engaged in a technical and often dirty occupation the engineer was denied the same status and opportunities as the executive officer, who had received his education on board *Britannia*. As a result a sharp class divide was distinguishable through the officer corps, while for the vast majority of executive or deck officers, the workings of the engine room remained a mystery. To resolve these problems a new system of entry and education would be necessary in which all officers would receive instruction in engineering, allowing those from all social backgrounds to become specialist engineers. Similarly, Royal Marine officers were found to be largely idle when embarked on ships, lacking any knowledge of the workings of the ship itself, which was a waste of valuable human resources. In addition and perhaps more importantly, a system had to be devised which would provide a wider pool of young officers for the growing number of RN ships, particularly the smaller more modern vessels such as torpedo boats and submarines.

The institution of such a scheme would inevitably require an individual of tremendous energy and vision; this man was to be Admiral Sir John Fisher, who would be responsible during his career in the Admiralty for a series of major reforms, including the introduction of the all-big-gun battleship and the regrouping of fleets on a modern strategic basis. Before his appointment as Second Sea Lord, Fisher had been Commander-in-Chief in the Mediterranean. It was in this post that he was to observe many of the deficiencies of the service, which he was to attempt to remedy later in his career. In 1901, Fisher had written that engineers should 'enter as Midshipmen in the Naval College at Dartmouth' (Marder 1953, p.212). Also in that year he was visited by First Lord Selborne, who was most concerned about growing agitation among the broader engineering community, backed by the trades unions. As he wrote to the First Sea Lord, Admiral Kerr; 'I think it is a very bad thing for the Navy that so large a body of its officers should be growing up in a different atmosphere of tradition and aspiration to the executive officers.' (Boyce 1990, p.119). Consequently, Selborne concluded:

> 'The whole root of the matter is the difference in social origin, difference of entry, and difference of training of the two branches of officers. It is my profound conviction that this matter can only be finally dealt with without detriment to the service by going to its root, and that is why I point to the entry through the *Britannia* for both Executive and Engineer officers as the one and only final cure.' (Ibid. p.140)

Subsequently Selborne invited Fisher to take up the position of Second Sea Lord, the member of the Admiralty Board with responsibility for personnel. Usually this post would have been held by a rear admiral, whereas Fisher was a full admiral, but in order to deal with his concerns for the naval training and education Fisher accepted the challenge. On February 25th 1902, before leaving his post in the Mediterranean, Fisher outlined his ideas in a paper:

> 'All must now admit we have been slow to appreciate the alteration in the status of the Engineer, consequent on the abolition of sails.
>
> The deck officers have no longer what really was an all absorbing task in becoming proficient in handling a ship under sail. Men's lives aloft were absolutely dependent on the skill of the Officer of the Watch…
>
> These qualities no longer required on the deck are acquired now and required now (but both in lesser degree) amongst the engines and boilers.
>
> … The general good and efficiency of the Navy renders it imperative that the entry of Engineer Students as at present[1] arranged should be gradually stopped and the entry of

---

1 Engineers had been trained at the Royal Naval Engineering College Keyham, Devonport, since it opened in 1880.

Naval Cadets gradually increased in like proportion, and that instruction from the moment of entry into the College at Dartmouth should in large measure, *at least half the time,* be devoted to engineering. That like Gunnery, Torpedo and Navigating as at present, there should be Engineer Officers, Sub-Lieutenants, Lieutenants and Commanders, and going on perhaps to the Captain's List and the Flag List, but the pay in view of greater responsibilities (the extra pay, that is) should be such as would perhaps induce officers to prefer remaining in the Engineer Class.' (Mackay 1973, p.267)

Fisher's ideas were by no means original. The defence writer and former Royal Marine Sir John Colomb, for example, had been advocating the idea of a common entry for twenty years, and some aspects of the proposed instruction at Dartmouth had been elaborated in an article in *National Review,* in June 1900, by Rear Admiral C. C. Penrose Fitzgerald. Fisher also sought inspiration and advice from such authorities as Sir Julian Corbett and Captain Christopher Cradock. Consequently Fisher is occasionally criticised for stealing other people's ideas, while amassing the credit for himself. However, as Hughes observes Fisher 'was big enough not to be ignorant of his ignorance.' (Hughes 1950, p.25) This was particularly evident in the brilliant appointment of J. A. Ewing, Professor of Mechanical Engineering at Cambridge University, to the newly established post of Director of Naval Education.

The new scheme was to be based upon four fundamental principles, outlined by Fisher in 1905:

Common entry for Executive, Engineer and Royal Marine officers
Amalgamation of the three branches
Emphasis on engineering
Completion of general education and training before going to sea. (Fisher 1919, p.156).

The Admiralty scheme for the entry and training of officer cadets, warrant officers, petty officers and men, was published on December 25th 1902 (Brassey 1903). It commenced with the recognition that the 'Navy has reached a critical period in its development – a development which, steady and comparatively slow for the greater part of the last century, has now for fifteen years proceeded with startling rapidity.' During this period steam had replaced sail, wood had been superseded by iron then steel, and cannon replaced by quick-firing guns. The number of officers and men in the Royal Navy and Royal Marines had more than doubled from 60,000 to over 120,000, while a number of foreign navies were now more powerful than the British Navy had been fifteen years ago, although the Royal Navy remained supreme[2]. Nevertheless:

2 Under the 'two power standard' the Royal Navy was to be maintained at a strength greater than the next two naval powers combined.

'Throughout this period the [Admiralty] Board never lost sight of the most important question of all those which confronted them, the education and training of the officers and men of the Navy, and the adaptation of that education and training to the new conditions under which the Navy has to work.' (Ibid. p.465)

In particular it was necessary to recognise, with the demise of masts and yards, the growing importance of engineering. 'In the old days it sufficed if a naval officer were a seaman. Now he must be a seaman, a gunner, a soldier, an engineer, and a man of science.' However, this could not be at the expense of 'preserving to the naval officer his unmistakable naval character.' (Ibid. p.465-6) Therefore now, as ever, 'the highest type of naval officer is that wherein great professional knowledge is added to force of character.' A combination of character building, practical training and professional knowledge, acquired through education, were required for the modern naval officer:

'The danger within the Navy itself is lest insufficient importance should be attached to the importance of study, and lest the value of what is called the practical character should be placed higher than it deserves … no seaman, however practical, will be fit to rise beyond a certain rank unless he has thought out the problems of his calling as a student.' (Ibid. p.466)

Engineering, practical and theoretical, was to be of greater importance to all naval officers. Moreover executive, engineer and Royal Marine officers would all receive the same training and education until they reached the rank of sub-lieutenant, at the age of about twenty, when they could select their preferred branch, based upon their original preferences as stated on entry. All officer cadets would therefore join under the same conditions. The younger age of entry, which had been raised to between fourteen and a half and fifteen and a half when Goschen was First Lord in 1896, was reverted to in an attempt to increase the number of sub-lieutenants available for the fleet. The reasons for returning to the younger entry were spelt out as being two-fold:

'The age of 12 to 13 not only corresponds to that at which the history of the Navy shows that boys have been most successfully moulded to sea character, but also corresponds to the age at which boys would leave private schools, and, therefore, to a natural period in the system of education which obtains in this country.' (Ibid. p.468)

Entry under the new scheme was to be by nomination following a suitability interview, a qualifying examination and a medical. It was intended to end the competitive nature of the *Britannia* exam, which had encouraged cramming and subsequently mental exhaustion among cadets. It would be of 'an elementary kind, and confined to those subjects in which a carefully-educated boy has been instructed

The College Library

The College Library can trace its origins to the shelves of leather spined books lining the deckheads of the hulks moored in the Dart. Indeed many of those books still line the shelves of the present library, providing a tangible link with the past.

Upon opening, the College did not have a central library, one having not been called for during design. Instead, there were scattered collections, such as the Common Room reference library, the cadets' reference library and the cadets' lending library, together with others, reflecting specific interests, such as those for the Field, Art and Music Clubs. These were finally consolidated into one location in 1933, when accommodation was made available in what is now the Lower Library, toward the rear of O Block. This was enlarged to encompass three former classrooms on the Upper level upon the College's return to Dartmouth in 1946.

Prior to 1955, the library was in essence a school library, designed to meet the needs of a public school, albeit with a slightly unusual curriculum. During this period, the task of Librarian was performed part-time by a member of the History and English Department, most notable of which in the post war period being Cyril Barnes-Lawrence, who held the post from 1928 to 1958. He was followed by Captain Pack, author of the former standard College history, *Britannia at Dartmouth*. However, as the College continued its transformation into a tertiary educational training establishment, demand

A student at work in the lower library.

grew for the post to be upgraded to full time. The first professional librarian was Graham White, appointed in 1964. He was followed in 1974 by Michael Chapman and from 1977 to 2009 by Richard Kennell. Staffing now consists of a Librarian and an Assistant.

Today, the library fulfills several functions, whilst providing a quiet study space amidst the bustle of college life. It boasts a substantial book-stock of some 61,000 volumes, subscriptions to almost 200 journals, around 1,500 videos and DVDs as well as CD ROMs. Access to the Internet is also provided. Primarily, the library exists to support the core educational and training function. However, its breadth of coverage also supports many recreational and historical pursuits, including research by students from local universities, authors and historians, who utilise the particular blend of historical resources, built up over the years. These have been augmented by material gleaned from many closed establishments, beginning with RNC Osborne and most recently RNC Greenwich.

As the College Library enters the twenty-first century, its primary role in support of student learning and development is being challenged by changes in the syllabus and the availability of electronic sources. However, it would be difficult to completely replace the vast collection of knowledge contained on the shelves. Similarly, it would be hard to replace the sense of shared history experienced when consulting a book which may have been thumbed by George VI, Mountbatten, Leach or Lewin and what is more, within the environment in which they did it.

A group of students enjoying the resources of the upper library.

up to the age of thirteen.' (Ibid. p.468) The interview board, consisting of naval officers, including a captain, and a headmaster, was designed to assess the general suitability of the boy, aided by a report from the boy's headmaster. The examination which followed the approval of the First Sea Lord as to the boy's suitability, aimed to ensure a level of academic ability. The exam, which 'seems to have been of an enlightened nature for those days.' (Pack 1966, p.148) was divided into two parts. The first consisted of tests in English, history, geography, French or German, arithmetic, algebra, and geometry; in the second part there was a choice between Latin, another modern language, or an essay question in science. The objective was to allow open competition, enabling the best possible candidates to come forward. The reality was, however, that most boys 'were simply not able to take advantage of the new system. Their parents lacked the financial resources to put them through the private education system.' (Davies 2003, p.25) For Dartmouth was a public school, run by the Navy; its pupils were not yet in the Navy, but the sole purpose of the school was to provide the Navy with specially educated boys who would become the officers of the future. Fisher himself had reservations about charging fees for a naval education (a sum of £75 per annum plus cost of uniform and other kit and equipment), restricting the pool of 'future Nelsons,' but the system was in fact designed to catch a particular type of boy from a particular middle to upper class background. The aim to abolish the class distinction between the executive and engineering branches, as claimed by an Admiralty memorandum from 1905 (Kemp 1964, p.159) should be more accurately interpreted as attempting to draw both from the same class, rather than extending entry to the lower classes.

Having successfully passed the selection procedure cadets would spend four years at the Royal Naval College. During this time, as Professor Ewing explained in 1906, they would 'receive a general education on modern lines which should include an exceptionally large element of practical science and engineering.' (Kemp 1964, p.174) The curriculum which, according to Ewing, would resemble that of 'a good public school,' covered instruction in 'mathematics, heat, electricity; in the science and practice of engineering; in French [plus German for the more able], English composition and literature; in history, both general and naval; in geography, navigation and the elements of seamanship; and in religious knowledge.' A good deal of time would also be spent in workshops, including instruction in 'carpentering and pattern making, in turning, moulding and casting, in blacksmithing and coppersmithing, and in mechanical drawing.' (Ibid. p.179) The result was to provide 'an education for the boy who is to become a man of action, not a philosopher.' (Ibid. p.180)

Inevitably, given the extent of the reforms being proposed, Fisher and Selborne were met with criticism and opposition for their scheme. As Fisher wrote in 1904, 'in our recent naval revolution in regard to entry and education of officers, all the senior officers of the Navy were against it to a man! *Never were such bitter things said!*' (Marder 1953, p.301) Selborne too admitted to 'some bad "quarters of an hour" in reconciling conflicting views and interests...' at the Admiralty (Boyce 1990, p.152). Fisher was driven to exclaim, 'I am not sure the "training of our Admirals" is not equally pressing with the 'training of our Midshipmen'!'. (Marder 1953, p.255) Objections centred round the common training of executive and engineer officers. Much of

Hobbies: model aircraft club.

Attentive cadets at study in a classroom in the 1920s.

Engineering instruction in the powerhouse at Sandquay.

the detractor's opposition seems to have been based on sheer snobbery, not wishing to 'taint the glory of the executive officer with the oil, grime, and heat of the engine-room.' (Mackay 1973, p.277)[3] Indeed *The Times* journalist James Thursfield[4], wrote to Fisher telling him of a conversation with Lord Spencer who had been approached by 'a distinguished person' to lead an attack on the scheme. When Lord Spencer refused to do so, the anonymous 'great man' replied; *'Are you prepared to defend our officers going down in the coal hole?'* (Marder 1953, p.268) But underlying this there was a genuine concern about 'interchangeability' between the branches reducing the degree of specialist knowledge on board ship. The intention, however, was merely to give deck officers sufficient engineering and scientific knowledge to understand the workings of their ships and weapons systems, while providing engineers (and Marines) with an appreciation of the art of seamanship, thus creating the 'lifelong community of sentiment' Fisher wished to establish. (Penn 2000, p.88) In so doing, however, there was the danger that the specialist engineer would

lack the technical knowledge of his predecessors. For Fisher, though, this was to miss the point as 'all are going to be educated as Engineer Officers from their first entry…we only want a Faraday and a George Stephenson about every two or three years.' (Marder 1953, p.269)

Not all contemporary opinion was against the Fisher-Selborne scheme. The Prince of Wales, a former *Britannia* cadet, wrote to Fisher:

'I call it a grand scheme and wish it every success. No doubt it will be severely criticised by the old ones, who are too conservative for our modern days … I am certain the Navy will greatly benefit by having your Engineer and Marine officers drawn from the same class as your Executive officers …' (Ibid. p.266-7)

3 It was often said of engineers that it had taken an act of Parliament to make them officers, but it would take an act of God to make them gentlemen.

4 Fisher was adept at using the media to promote his ideas and rewarded those who supported him with privileged information. *The Times* journalist James Thursfield was the most privileged amongst this group.

Still Life.

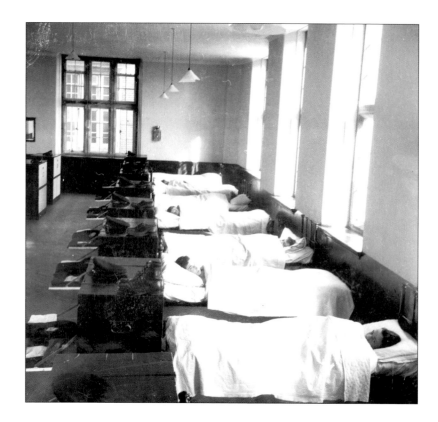

And so to bed.

Even Admiral Lord Charles Beresford, with whom Fisher was later to fall out over his war plans, described the scheme as 'a brilliant and statesmanlike effort to grapple with *a problem upon the sound settlement of which depends the future efficiency of the British Navy*.' (Fisher 1919, p.167) Indeed by the time the scheme was published, Fisher was to claim that it had been *'the unanimous decision of the whole Board of the Admiralty ...'* (Ibid. p.267) He went on in 1904 to write:

'Now they all see an immense success looming in the distance, magnifying the efficiency of the Navy beyond any present conception, and all hands are beginning to "Hosanna," when a year ago they wanted to "crucify"!' (Ibid. p.302)

The real proof, of course, would come when the first naval cadets entered under the new system.

Two New Naval Colleges

The reduction in the age of entry and subsequent lengthening of the course meant that it would take longer for a new cadet to be added to the active list than under the old *Britannia* system. The new College being built at Dartmouth had been designed for the existing, shorter (two year rather than four year) course and was therefore of insufficient size to take all new scheme cadets. Moreover, the building was not going to be ready for completion until 1905. It was therefore decided to look for an additional college, which

could be made ready to receive its first cadets by September 1903. The solution was found through the bequest from King Edward VII of his parents' home on the Isle of Wight, Osborne House. The main house was to be used as a convalescence home for service men but the stable block was converted to provide gunrooms and classrooms for a new naval college. The stables, together with a number of additional huts, were therefore hurriedly constructed within seven months to become the Royal Naval College, Osborne. Cadets would subsequently spend two years at Osborne, before progressing to the extended senior college at Dartmouth[5]. The first cadets to make the transition arrived at Britannia Royal Naval College on September 14th 1905. Meanwhile, the old *Britannia* system, with the older entry was to run concurrently with the new system for two and a half years, in order to maintain the flow of officers into the service. The architects of the new scheme were determined to ensure that there would be as little influence as possible from the old scheme. Captain Cross, the last Captain of *Britannia*, was thus most disappointed to be denied command of what he had originally regarded as his College. When both groups of cadets entered the new College in September 1905, it was ensured that the new schemers would outnumber the old, an additional two of the *Britannia* terms having been sent off to complete their training at sea.

5 See Chapter 2 Architecture.

Initial impressions of the new scheme from those involved were positive. Captain Rosslyn Wemyss, the first captain of Osborne felt sure that '… these young gentlemen will turn out more capable all-round officers than the present generation of young officers at sea.' (Kemp 1964, p.165) While Captain Goodenough, the first captain of Dartmouth was satisfied that instruction in engineering and science at an early age had '… in no way taken from the cadets their independence of character or boyish enthusiasm. It has in reality much increased those qualities and the somewhat more strenuous life they lead in comparison with other schools has in every way brought out the best points of the boys character.' (Ibid. p.167) The only serious reservation held by both was that boys were being discouraged from opting to take engineering as their specialisation.

One of the initial problems encountered at the new naval colleges was to combine naval and academic organisation with a captain and a headmaster. However, as Ewing observed; 'thanks to the good sense and good feeling of the persons concerned and to the constant desire, which all share, to make the College effective for their purpose, these difficulties are surmountable.' (Kemp 1964, p.180) Indeed, such was to remain the case, save but a few exceptions, until the academic community at Dartmouth was integrated with the naval staff, under a Commander Naval Education and Training, in 2004.

In another of his perceptive appointments, Fisher had bestowed the position of Headmaster of Osborne to Cyril Ashford, senior science master at Harrow School. On the completion by the first new scheme entry of their two years at Osborne, Ashford was to join them as Headmaster of Dartmouth. His comments were once again essentially positive, dismissing a number of the concerns previously raised, and emphasising the public school mould in which Osborne and Dartmouth were formed:

'I have no hesitation in saying that the broader education now given will immensely increase the officer's control over his men and his power of getting the best work out of the subordinate engine-room artificers.

'… the fact that the future engineer officer will have studied the subjects considered the province of the executive officer who specialises in torpedo work, will set him on a plane above his men; it is proverbial in civil life that a public schoolboy, although in most cases grossly ignorant of all scientific matters, makes a better works-manager than the more highly trained product of the technical schools, if the education and social environment of the latter man has been bounded by that limited horizon. I believe I am right in saying that the personal qualities which are developed by a non-specialised education in an atmosphere such as that of Osborne or the more strenuous of the old public schools, are more valuable in claiming respect in the engine-room of a battleship than in a factory. The well-educated English boy of the upper classes possesses sanctions of conduct that lie outside the mental equipment of a man who has devoted his time to the perfection of his manual, or even his exclusively scientific powers … In part, no doubt, these qualities which shine out in emergencies are the results of

Pen and ink sketch by Frank Wood of the Officers' quarters and mast at the RNC Osborne, 1908.

heredity and home influence … but the public school system of England is sadly at fault if they are not in part due to education in the humanities and to the companionship, during the formative years of youth, of other boys who are being trained to command their fellow men by all agencies, even games, that have been found effective. This education and these agencies are an integral factor of the new scheme, and I venture to assure that in these respects Osborne is inferior to no public school both in the appreciation of their importance which is possessed by those in control, and in the enthusiasm with which the cadets take advantage of the opportunities.' (Ibid. p.173)

It is apparent from Ashford's comments that he regarded a good general education along the lines of the best public schools as more than adequate compensation for greater scientific or technical instruction. This was not necessarily the case in Fisher's mind, having originally intended for half rather than a third of cadets' time to have been spent on engineering. As he wrote in his memoirs in 1919;

'… we wanted "Machinery Education," both with officers and men; and also that education should be the education of common sense. My full idea of Osborne was alas! emasculated by the schoolmasters of the nation.' (Fisher 1919, p.123)

Again the suggestion is that the equality aimed at was to take all officers from the same class thus ending class distinction between branches, rather than opening up opportunities for boys of all classes to become naval officers.

The aim to provide more officers for the service, however, remained only partially fulfilled. Consequently in 1913 First Lord of the Admiralty Winston Churchill introduced the Special Entry scheme. Under this system boys aged between seventeen and a half and eighteen and a half that had completed their education at a public school, could join the Navy as cadets for a six-month course on board a training ship, initially HMS *Highflyer*. By admitting more mature boys who had received a non-naval based general education the Special Entry scheme ran counter to some of the core principles

Meal time in the Senior Gun Room.

Receiving pocket money on the Quarterdeck.

Seamanship instruction in rope work. This room is currently the E-learning centre.

of the Selborne Scheme. Nevertheless, the two systems were to run concurrently until the thirteen-year-old entry was abolished after the Second World War. During that time both systems were to produce their share of competent officers, with Special Entry at times providing more officers than Dartmouth.[6]

From War to Peace to War Again

Nine years after the first cadets arrived at Dartmouth from Osborne the long anticipated conflict with Germany finally broke out. The response at Dartmouth was swift and decisive. The entire College was mobilized for war on August 1st 1914, sending cadets, most of whom had yet to complete their training, into the

fleet. Although students did arrive from Osborne in September 1914 numbers at the College were to fluctuate throughout the war, depending on the need for officers at sea.[7]

The end of the war was to be the cause of even greater disruption. By 1920 the combination of peace and economic stringency had led to the 'Geddes axe', cutting throughout the Navy. In addition to reducing the entry into the Naval Colleges there was also to be a forty per cent reduction among the existing terms at Osborne and Dartmouth. On the whole these reductions seem to have been voluntary and less drastic than originally feared (Davis & Grove 1980, p. 15). However, with the reduction in the number of cadets there was now enough room to accommodate them in one rather than two colleges. With its still largely temporary buildings and poor health record, Osborne was the natural casualty. In May 1920 two terms from Osborne started to move to Dartmouth. One year later the remaining

6 According to John Beattie, in the period 1913-55 about half the officers in the Royal Navy (including Paymasters, Mates and Upper Yardmen) were not entered to the College as 13 and 16 year old entries. Of the Flag Officers in the 1970s 50% were Special Entries, 25% Darts, 25% from other routes.

7 For a full account of the impact of both World Wars on BRNC see Chapter 5, The College at War.

College Sport

'With the re-opening of the College on September 11th all our thoughts were at once concentrated – on the River in preparation for the coming Regatta.' This quotation from the Britannia Magazine of Christmas 1915 underlines how highly sport at BRNC was regarded, one might have thought that 'our thoughts' should have been with those former cadets who were on active service, but alas no, sport was uppermost in the editor's thoughts. After all the College was a public school and sport has always been a major part of public school life. In previous histories of HMS Britannia and the College such as Statham (1904), Hughes (1950) and Pack (1966) the progress of the cricket and rugby football teams have featured, given almost as high a priority as the major historical events chronicled by the authors. One of the criteria in choosing a location for the old Britannia was the availability of level land for use as playing fields in the locality. The College has always offered a wide range of sporting activities as the sports trophy cabinet can testify, the sports of sailing and rowing remaining as popular today as they were in the days of the old Britannia.

Cricket has always been one of the main sports enjoyed at the College, and the importance

Swimming regatta.

The *Britannia* team that played against W. G. Grace and the MCC in 1889.

attached to it is shown by the fact that in the days of the old Britannia two cricket professionals were employed. One was a professional groundsman to look after the 'square' on the playing fields, but the other was the professional coach; in 1889 this was a Mr Underwood, who coached the boys until the summer of 1893. In July 1889 a two-day match was organized between HMS Britannia and the MCC. W. G. Grace[1] captained the MCC team and Lt Abdy of HMS Britannia, who had played with W. G. at Lord's, arranged the match. W. G. only played for the second day as he had agreed to play at Bristol for Gloucestershire against the Gentlemen of Philadelphia. On the first day Britannia had to follow on, scoring only sixty-one against the MCC's 156 and they won by seven wickets. W. G. did not arrive until the evening of the first day so another game was played on the second day. In the second match the MCC went in first and declared at 118 for two wickets. W. G. made forty-eight before being bowled out. In reply Britannia's boys made eighty-two for nine wickets, W G taking seven of them. The local paper reported that the 'cadets fielded very well', when in fact they had a very good match indeed against one of England's top sides, used to making high scores and taking their fair share of

'Assault at Arms' summer of 1906.

wickets in top class cricket. By 1902 the cadets had a cricket professional again, by the name of Lord, and the playing fields were maintained to a very high standard. It was Wellington who said that 'the Battle of Waterloo was won on the playing fields of Eton'. The Admiralty funded the upkeep of the playing fields so that the Navy had no excuse for not winning their victories on the cricket fields of Dartmouth.

Rugby football was the main winter sport and matches were reported with the same enthusiasm as was shown for cricket matches, especially in the Britannia Magazine. One former cadet who joined HMS Britannia in 1902 is immortalized at the home of English Rugby at Twickenham where his name is proudly displayed on the honours board. That was Arthur Leyland Harrison who gained two international caps while playing for the United Services team against Ireland and France in the 1913-14 season. He is better known at Dartmouth as the recipient of the Victoria Cross that is on display in the College.[2]

In 1897 the sport of hockey was introduced and matches of Cadet Captains v Ship; Officers v Ship and Britannia v Hindostan, were to become features of the sporting field. Beagling was introduced

Tug of war at New Entry sports on the Parade Ground.

in the winter of 1878/9, as reported elsewhere in this book, as a sport for those cadets who were less competitive in the more traditional sports. Indeed, the sporting programme remained varied. Clay pigeon shooting was introduced by Captain Cross, the last Captain of the Britannia *and remains a popular sport today. Another sporting tradition at Dartmouth*

For the high jump!

is the cross-country race, this is a regular event in which all cadets take part; the pain of running up 'Britannia Steps' still etched on many a former cadet or young officer's mind. This event dates back to the days of the old Britannia *and was run across the surrounding farmland, but today it merely takes in a circuit of the College grounds.*

The river has always played a major part in the activities at Dartmouth and sailing and rowing have always been popular pastimes, for both recreational and sporting pursuits. The College maintains a large quantity of craft, which includes boats for practical seamanship instruction and as well for pleasure and sport. Many former members of the College will remember 'away all boats', when all the College would walk down to Sandquay and take part in a scratch race, that in effect was an exercise in seamanship against the clock. The College has also had a close association with the Port of Dartmouth and always taken part in the annual Port of Dartmouth Royal Regatta.

The College also boasts a nine-hole golf course for the use of the young officers and staff. The College grounds occupy approximately 117 acres of which about thirty eight can be regarded as parkland.[3] This parkland was at one time leased to a local farmer as grazing. This provided a pleasant pastoral scene but did necessitate the use of an ugly wire fence around the establishment. In 1965 it was decided to turn this parkland into a golf course. The work was started at the beginning of the summer term, with cadets providing the labour, the youngest of whom, P. St. A. Sweet was given the privilege of cutting the first sod. A start was made on the third green as this was considered to be one of the two most difficult, and the insistence of the farmer that machinery must not be taken over his precious pasture, made it particularly hard work. It soon became apparent that the voluntary system of labour would not be sufficient for the task in hand, so each division was given a green

and asked to finish it by the end of term, so that the greens could be sown in the autumn. The value of golf as an officer's sport was recognized prior to the Second World War when a golf professional used to attend once a week and give tuition on Norton Fields. In 1965 the College paid for a block subscription to Thurlestone Golf Club, but as first year cadets were not allowed cars at the College the sport of golf was denied to them. As the ground available for the course was limited, future players ought to be masters of the 'short game,' however it was possible to include two long holes. Initially the greens had to be fenced, because of the farmer and his grazing, but today one can enjoy a round without the obstacle of the fences and appreciate the magnificent views of Dartmouth.

Sport at Dartmouth remains very much a part of College life and Wednesday and Saturday afternoons are traditionally set aside for the young officers to participate in their chosen sporting activity. The College also has strong sporting links with both the Army and Royal Air Force initial training establishments and games weekends against both the Royal Military Academy Sandhurst and RAF Cranwell are still regular features of the College sporting calendar.

Running the cross-country.

1. W. G. Grace had family connections in South Devon and in January 1890, his son H. E. Grace joined HMS *Britannia*, as a cadet.

2. Arthur Leyland Harrison was born in Torquay and was awarded the VC for his part in commanding the Naval storming parties at Zeebrugge on 22nd-23rd April 1918, losing his life in that action. His brother Percy Harrison was a master at the Royal Naval College Osborne, but he came out of retirement to teach at Dartmouth during the Second World War as there was a shortage of teaching staff, many being on active service.

3 The College for many years kept a horse named Daisy whose primary task was to keep the parkland mown. She was a feature of the College for many years and in the winter, when she would otherwise be under-utilized she was loaned to a local farmer.

four terms moved to Dartmouth, along with the first new entries to join Dartmouth directly since the end of the old *Britannia* system. Captain Marten had been appointed captain of Osborne during the College's last term and transferred to Dartmouth with the last of the Osborne cadets to become Captain of Dartmouth.

The 1920s at Dartmouth have been described by Davies and Grove as a 'Golden Age', by Pack as 'Halcyon Days', while Hughes remembered the period between the wars as 'in many ways the happiest.' (1950, p.89) Indeed, having successfully integrated the junior and senior colleges into eleven Dartmouth terms, staff and students settled into a regular and comfortable regime. The curriculum had already changed in 1921 when the amount of engineering instruction was cut by two-thirds, 'to be treated less from the vocational and more from the educational standpoint.' (Ibid. p.96) Henceforth, sufficient engineer officers could be obtained voluntarily from the Special Entry, enabling all Dartmouth cadets to become executive officers, unless they chose otherwise.

With the arrival of the Osborne cadets Ashford introduced a number of special courses to broaden cadets' interest. For one period a week they could follow courses covering a variety of subjects from astronomy and Greek art to archaeology and architecture. Cadets at Dartmouth had always been encouraged to develop hobbies and pastimes to occupy their leisure time. Numerous clubs and societies existed as a browse though the *Britannia Magazine* from the early part of the twentieth century shows, with reports of the clubs' activities often appearing with both photographic and artistic contributions submitted by the cadets.

Music often played a large part in the life of the boys with both a band and choir performing regularly. The band in summer term of 1917 had fifty-five members, of whom forty-two were cadets, the rest being from the college staff (masters and naval officers and one Chief Petty Officer). The instruments played were varied in both number and variety, for example eighteen banjo players, five clarinets, six mandolins, six violins and a variety of other instruments including bassoon, trombone, timpani, euphonium and glockenspiel, under the supervision of the conductors Mr Piggott[8] and Mr Ovenden. The band would perform concerts for the cadets and play for the regular Saturday evening dances. There was also an active choir with thirty cadets regularly attending choir practice in the summer of 1917, all again under the direction of Mr Piggott, with Mr Ovenden playing the organ. The cadets made up the trebles and alto sections with the staff forming the tenors and the majority of the bass voices. In July of that year sixty cadets, seven masters, the Padre and the Medical Officer, enjoyed the Choir and Band outing to Paignton.

Drawing classes were part of the curriculum and the cadets were encouraged to develop their creative talents, as the frequent artistic contributions to illustrate the *Britannia Magazine* testify.

8 Mr H. E. Piggott became Head of Mathematics and the Second Master.

Belly muster.

Photography was also popular, with a darkroom having been available to cadets since the latter days of the old *Britannia*. Their contributions were frequently used to illustrate the *Britannia Magazine*. The study of Natural History had a strong following, supported by the College Field Club, here cadets would take rambles in the countryside and observe the local fauna and flora, birds and in particular their nests. There is no doubt that collecting bird's eggs was a popular hobby at this time, as photographs of nests with eggs frequently appear in the *Britannia Magazine* (one cadet had lost his life in the quest to collect eggs, falling from a cliff, when the *Britannia* was moored at Portland in 1862).

Drama productions have also been a part of College life from the days of the hulks on the river up to the present day and cadets were encouraged to take part in all aspects of the production. Model making too was a hobby enjoyed by young boys. Naturally boats were a particularly popular theme for modelling, with the Britannia Model Boat Club meeting at Sandquay, where they sailed their

Seamanship instruction utilising the fo'c'sle of HMS Rodney. *This bow model was built by the engineering company of Basset-Lowke Ltd. of Northampton and is fondly remembered by generations of naval officers. It was dismantled in 1997 but the two anchors survive to serve as doorstops.*

'The Old Canteen,' a watercolour appearing in the Britannia Magazine, *by Cadet W. St. J. Ainslie, before it was replaced in 1930.*

craft. In 1917 there had been 150 members of the Britannia Model Boat Club, a not inconsiderable proportion of the College population. One of the more unusual clubs met in the classroom of Mr J. S. Sampson, the History and English Master. He had an interest in medieval weaponry and built models of the types of weapons used to storm and defend great castles. The top edge of the blackboard in his classroom was decorated with castellated battlements resembling a medieval castle. The club would meet in the afternoon, after lessons, and he would demonstrate how these weapons worked by firing projectiles at the battlements. As a special treat at the end of term the cadets would be allowed to operate the miniature weapons themselves.

Sport played a highly significant part in the daily life of the College, recognised as providing not just recreational activity but a means of instilling the qualities of team spirit and leadership, vital for a Naval Officer. [9] The prominence of sport was spelt out very clearly in the guide *How to Become a Naval Officer (Dartmouth)* (1945):

'From the point of view of sport, Dartmouth challenges comparison with any school in the world.

9 See box on College Sport.

There are eighteen acres of playing grounds, devoted to rugger, soccer, cricket and hockey. The College maintains a pack of beagles, started over fifty years ago, and famous throughout the district.

Half-way down to the river are the racquet courts, and on the river itself are the boat houses containing skiffs and gigs. Above the College are a large gymnasium and a swimming-bath, the latter the scene of strenuous water-polo matches. The keenest competition rages between the various Houses as to which can accumulate the greatest number of trophies in their gun-rooms, as every branch of sport, from rugger to cross-country running, including rifle shooting, has a challenge cup for competition ... Last, but not least, we must not forget the canteen, which stands so conveniently among the playing grounds, and beneath whose hospitable roofs vast quantities of delicious food are consumed by a seething mass of cadets straight from the battlefields of sport.

Without the slightest fear of contradiction one may assert that to 99 per cent of the cadets who pass through Dartmouth, the period spent there remains for all times the happiest of memories.'

Officers and Masters in the Common Room in 1941. Among those assembled are the Headmaster Mr. Kempson (standing third from right) and keen photographer Mr John Barlee (second from right).

Within this idyll there could have been the temptation to become complacent. In 1926 HM Inspectorate of Schools observed that 'the staff was tending to become a smooth-running, efficient machine rather than a body of pioneers developing new ideas and a new system.' (Davies & Grove 1980, p.15) This otherwise complimentary report also remarked that while great care was taken of weaker students there was little opportunity for the intellectual development of the most able. It was against this background in 1927 that second Headmaster Mr E. W. Kempson took over from Cyril Ashford, who was awarded a knighthood for his services. An engineer, Kempson had taught at Dartmouth before the war as both a Naval Instructor and civilian master, before becoming head of the science department at Rugby School. During the war he had served with the Royal Engineers and won the Military Cross. After the war he had returned to the field of education as an Inspector of

Schools.[10] One of Kempson's first acts, in 1928, was the introduction of 'Alpha classes'. Under this system the ablest students in the eighth term would be chosen to take one subject (not mathematics, but science, modern languages or history and English) at a subsidiary level, allowing more time to be spent on the remaining three. Much of this additional work would involve private study thus affording cadets the opportunity to manage their own time under a slightly more relaxed routine.

By the early 1930s the College was once again coming under outside scrutiny. Against the backdrop of economic depression and continuing disarmament Dartmouth appeared an extravagance with 412 staff to 408 students in 1932. Part of the problem was that a naval career was simply not felt to be an attractive proposition at the time, thus reducing the number of suitable applicants. Those for whom a career in the Navy might appeal were increasingly drawn towards the more flexible arrangements of the Special Entry. There was also mounting concern over the quality of the Dartmouth cadet, particularly when compared to the public school boys of the Special

10 His eldest daughter, Rachel became an actress and married the actor Sir Michael Redgrave. The celebrity couple were married in the College Chapel in 1935.

Entry. As a mark of this concern the captains of ships taking cadets into the fleet were asked to report back to Dartmouth on their progress (BRNC Archive). The results were mixed. One captain observed:

'The main difference between the Dartmouth and the Special Entry officer is the narrowness of outlook of the former; this is shown in their conversation and lack of knowledge on matters outside the Service. The main topics of conversation on Officers' messes are 'shop' and 'games.'… The Public School man is wider read and more knowledgeable about the least detraction to his job.

The Dartmouth system tends to create officers of the deserving, unimaginative type who take matters as they find them. The Late Entry on the other hand produces officers who lead their men and are more inclined to strike out on a line of their own.'

The captain of HMS *Valiant* was more sympathetic:

'I think there is very little wrong with the modern Naval Cadet as he leaves Dartmouth. He is bound to suffer in comparison with the Public School boy when each joins his first ship because the Dartmouth boy is one to one and a half years younger.

The world rarely makes allowances; people are judged at their face value, and the Public School boy, with his greater age and more self-assurance, gets away with it every time.'

Part of the problem was perceived to be the independence and responsibility that was afforded to the public school boy in his sixth form, for which there was no equivalent at Dartmouth. Consequently when Admiral Dunbar-Nasmith VC, Captain of the College 1926-29, became Second Sea Lord in 1936 he determined to introduce a house system at Dartmouth. Following a whistle-stop tour of seven public schools undertaken by Captain Dalrymple-Hamilton and having taken advice from various headmasters, the House system was introduced in 1937. Under this new organisation there were to be five houses, – Blake, Exmouth, Grenville, Hawke and St. Vincent, plus a separate 'Drake' house for cadets in their first two terms. By replacing the term system with that of houses, cadets were able to mix with boys of different ages and develop a sense of loyalty and attachment to a house that would not change at the end of every term. The system also allowed for increased responsibility to be devolved to senior cadets as both cadet and house captains.

The problem of staff turnover remained, with house officers having to move on after two or three years but it now became possible to affiliate masters to a specific house to act as tutors and assist with the organisation of games. Indeed inter-house sports became more competitive as in term competitions the advantage had usually rested with the more senior term. Despite some initial concerns about laxity of discipline the house system was to prove most successful and continued until the end of the thirteen-year-old entry after the Second World War.

Meanwhile, in the outside world, international relations continued to deteriorate. In September 1938, as the leaders of Britain, France, Germany and Italy met at Munich, sandbags were filled by cadets and placed around the College. In May 1939 Special Entry cadets arrived at Dartmouth for the first time. Their training cruiser HMS *Frobisher* was being refitted for active service, so instead of going to sea the eighteen-year-olds were accommodated in the ship's company barracks block (now Beatty). Finally war was declared on 3rd September 1939. The initial impact of the war upon the College was minimal, until 18th September 1942 when the College was bombed and rendered unfit to continue as a place of education. Despite the subsequent evacuation to Eaton Hall in Cheshire the routine of the College was to remain unchanged throughout the rest of the conflict.[11]

That the scheme fought for by Fisher and Selborne lasted for almost half a century is a mark of the forethought that had contributed to a unique system of naval education. Arguably many of its original objectives failed to transpire; engineers were to remain at a disadvantage and after 1921 were not generally to receive a Dartmouth education, while an increasing number of officers of all branches were to enter the service via the Special Entry at the age of eighteen, too old to be properly moulded for life at sea. Nevertheless Dartmouth had been successfully established as a public school for naval officers, in which it was possible to combine the staff and curriculum for what was recognised as a good general education with the unique professional training the Navy required. However, as the College returned to Dartmouth in September 1946 few could have anticipated the changes that were about to be wrought. The world and Britain's place in it had changed and so would Dartmouth.

11 See Chapter 5 The College at War.

CHAPTER 4

The Royal College

The Verge carried by the usher (left of photograph) ahead of Her Majesty Queen Elizabeth as she inspects the Guard at Lord High Admiral's Divisions in 1972.

The Royal connection with the British Navy is centuries old. The Royal Family's association with Dartmouth, as frequent visitors, cadets and indeed the parents, grandparents, and brothers and sisters of cadets dates back to the College's earliest years.

To prescribe a date to the origins of the modern Royal Navy would be to invoke controversy, although the Restoration Navy of 1660 is often accepted as such. The Senior Gunroom panelling of the College, however, chooses a much earlier date at which to start the connection of King and Navy. Elaborately carved in the upper parts of the panelling are commemorated famous naval engagements and the personalities associated with them. Prominently over the entrance door the carved letters covered with gold-leaf, proclaim 'ALFRED: THE DANES: 897'. This was only a minor encounter but demonstrated the use of ships by a King for the defence of our shores and makes Alfred the first English monarch to recognise the importance of sea power to an island nation. Thus Alfred is often regarded as the 'Father of the Navy'. However, his victory over the Danes as commemorated in the Senior Gun Room was not his first seagoing engagement, an action in 875 has that distinction (Rodger 1997, p.10). Moreover, the *Anglo-Saxon Chronicles* record the date of the engagement as 896 (ibid. p.16). The controversy over the precise date of the engagement might in fact be due to the English civil calendar dating the start of the New Year from Lady Day (25 March) (see Rodger page xix). Nevertheless, the choice of this action and this date probably has as much to do with the Diamond Jubilee of Queen Victoria in 1897 as it does with historical accuracy and thus emphasises the thousand-year association of the Monarch and the Navy. Hence the royal connection can be said to be well in excess of a thousand years.

The Princes Albert Victor and George in their cadet uniforms. These official photographs were taken, as they were about to join HMS Britannia *in 1877.*

Edward III became known as 'The King of the Seas' after his bowmen gained victory at the battle of Sluys in 1340, another battle commemorated in the carved panelling of the Senior Gunroom.

It was under Henry VIII that a true navy was born, and he is often referred to as 'The Father of the English Navy' but it was his daughter Elizabeth I, who recognised the potential of a maritime fleet. Francis Drake was appointed as Rear Admiral and he played a major role in the defence of our shores by repelling the Spanish Armada. It was men such as Frobisher, Grenville, Hawkins, Howard and Raleigh, who gained notoriety at this time, the first two giving their names to 'Terms' at the College.

It was during the English Civil War that a number of generals established some command of the sea and such men as Robert Blake and George Monck were recognised as both seamen and leaders. The name of Blake for many years was one of the College Divisions and Monck is another name celebrated in the Senior Gunroom panelling. Admiral Blake had gained a reputation in the war against the Dutch and this in turn led to a fleet being raised and sent to Holland under Monck to bring back Charles II to the throne of England. It was with the restoration of Charles II that the Navy was truly established, indeed it was Charles who granted the Royal prefix in 1660. The Royal Navy was now truly born.

The Naval Discipline Act of 1661 founded the Royal Navy by permanent Statute. The act bore the following in its preamble: 'His Majesty's Navies, ships of War, and forces by Sea, wherein under the good Providence and Protection of God, the Wealth, Safety and Strength of his Kingdom is so much concerned.' This view was first expressed by the Commons in 1415 as '*La dit Naveye est la griendre substance du bein, profit et prosperitee du vostre dit Rioalme*' and is misquoted rather elegantly, carved in Portland stone, on the front of the College as:

IT. IS: ON. THE: NAVY UNDER: THE: GOOD:
PROVIDENCE OF: GOD: THAT. OUR WEALTH:
PROSPERITY: AND PEACE: DEPEND

Even though the Act received minor amendments in 1749 and 1816 to '...wealth, safety and strength of the Kingdom chiefly depend' the carving on the College front is still not as originally quoted and was probably shortened and altered to fit the space available.

The Lord High Admiral

When the High Court of Admiralty was formed early in the fifteenth century, The Earl of Dorset was placed at its head with the title Admiral of England, Ireland and Aquitaine in 1408 (Rodger 1997, p.149). Subsequent heads of the Court were referred to as Great Admiral or Lord Admiral, and in 1547 Baron Seymour of Sudeley was appointed Lord High Admiral. In the reign of Henry VIII they took command of the fleet at sea, and through the Navy Board, also took charge of naval administration. The judicial functions finally passed to

A College cutter at the service of the Prince and Princess of Wales when they visited HMS Britannia on 23rd and 24th July 1878. Prince George is the second bow oar, nearest to the camera. Prince Edward (Albert Victor) is the coxswain.

the High Court of Justice in 1875. During the years from 1628 to 1964 the office was vested in committees, commissions or boards.

The post of Lord High Admiral has been held by James, Duke of York (later King James II) from 1660 to 1673; King Charles II (1685); King James II (1685); Prince George of Denmark (Consort of Queen Anne) from 1702 – 1708; and from 1827 – 1828 William, Duke of Clarence (later King William IV).

In 1964 when the Admiralty, along with the War Office and Air Ministry combined to form the Ministry of Defence, the Admiralty became the Admiralty Board of the Defence Council and Her Majesty Queen Elizabeth II graciously consented to assume the title of Lord High Admiral. On 10th June 2011 Her Majesty appointed HRH The Prince Philip as Lord High Admiral, on the occasion of his 90th birthday.

In 1970 Her Majesty approved Admiral of the Fleet Earl Mountbatten of Burma's proposal that each year one of the passing out parades at the Britannia Royal Naval College should be called the Lord High Admiral's Divisions. In addition the salute at these Divisions should be taken by the Lord High Admiral or by her/his personal representative, nearly always a member of the Royal Family.

The Royal Verge or Wand

The Verge or Wand was made in 1662 for James, Duke of York, as a symbol of the authority and jurisdiction of the Lord High Admiral. It is carried by the usher ahead of the Lord High Admiral or his representative at Lord High Admiral's Divisions. The head is of solid silver and was kept on board the Royal Yacht *Britannia*. When the Royal Yacht was decommissioned it was given to the College and can still be seen in a case near the front entrance.

The Royal Princes Edward (Albert Victor) and George on board HMS Britannia. *The photograph is dated 3rd March 1878 and signed by both Princes. It is framed with wood taken from the old* Britannia *when she was broken up in 1916. The photograph is inscribed on the back 'Sprat' and 'Herring'. Sprat referring to Prince George and Herring, Prince Edward.*

Royal Cadets

The Princes Albert Victor and George

It had long been a tradition for the second son of the monarch or heir apparent to join the Royal Navy. This had been so in the case of Queen Victoria's second son, Alfred Duke of Edinburgh, who had been a cadet on board HMS *Illustrious* and *Britannia*, at Portsmouth. It was therefore natural that Prince George, the second son of Prince Edward the Prince of Wales (later Edward VII) should follow a career in the Navy. By the time Prince George was twelve years old (one of the youngest cadets to ever join the ship) the route of entry for a naval cadet began on board the training ship HMS *Britannia*, moored in the River Dart.

However, a problem existed in sending Prince George away to Dartmouth. His elder brother, Albert Victor (also known as Prince Edward or 'Eddy') the Duke of Clarence, was a rather backward child who relied heavily upon his younger brother for support. The boys' tutor, Canon Dalton, therefore suggested that both Princes should join *Britannia*, thus affording Albert Victor the opportunity to develop 'those habits of promptitude and method, of manliness and self-reliance, in which he is somewhat deficient.' (Rose 1983, p.6.) The Prince of Wales agreed that the education and discipline they would receive in the Navy would prove invaluable and approved of the suggestion. The Queen, however, while agreeing that George should make the Navy his career, had reservations about the suitability of the lifestyle for a future monarch: 'The very rough sort of life to which boys are exposed on board ship is the very thing not calculated to make a refined and amiable prince.' (Hampshire 1971, p.116.) Moreover, she expressed her concern that a 'nautical education' might 'engender and encourage national prejudices and make them think that their own Country is superior to any other.' (Rose 1983, p.7.) The First Lord of the Admiralty and the Prime Minister, Mr Disraeli, who advised the Queen against the idea, shared her concerns.

Finally the Queen acquiesced on the condition that Canon Dalton accompany the Princes on board the ship. Subsequently, the boys sat the entrance exam for the Royal Naval College, which included arithmetic, algebra, geometry, diction, reading English 'intelligently', French translation, the Scriptures, geography and English history, in April 1877, achieving satisfactory results. In October of that year the Prince of Wales, wearing the full dress uniform of a captain in the Royal Naval Reserve, accompanied his sons and their tutor on board *Britannia*. They were to be treated as any other cadet on the ship, their only privilege being to sling their hammocks in a private cabin on the poop deck, above the captain's. In common with many of the cadets they were given their own nicknames, 'Sprat' and 'Herring', as befitting the sons of the Prince of W(h)ales. They messed with all their classmates and were subject to the same restrictions, including the ban on food on board and the limit of one shilling a week pocket money, as George V was later to recount to his librarian, Sir Owen Morshead:

'It never did me any good to be a Prince, I can tell you, and many was the time I wished I hadn't been. It was a pretty tough place and, so far from making any allowances for our disadvantages, the other boys made a point of taking it out on us on the grounds that they'd never be able to do it later on . . . Then we had a sort of tuck-shop on land, up the steep hill; only we weren't allowed to bring any eatables into the ship, and they used to search you as you came aboard. Well the big boys used to fag me to bring them back a whole lot of stuff – and I was always found out and got into trouble in addition to having the stuff confiscated . . . we were only given a shilling a week pocket money, so it meant a lot to me I can tell you.' (Rose 1983, p.7.)

George seemed to suffer particularly from financial hardships, his pleas to his Grandmother to send him a sovereign to tide him over meeting with a kindly but firm refusal on the basis that it would be inappropriate to break the restrictions placed upon all the cadets. Fortunately not all cadets' families were so inflexible, and on recounting his story to a wealthy friend, George was offered three pounds for the Queen's letter, which he accepted.

Being directly in line for the throne it was recognised that Albert Victor would not be making the Navy his career, a point not missed

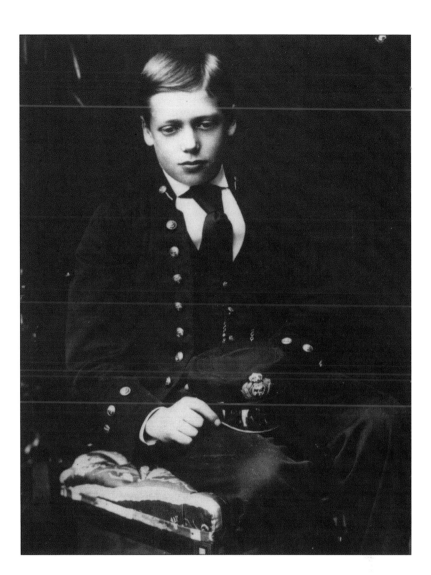

Official photograph of Prince George while he was a cadet on Britannia.

A drawing by Prince Edward, Duke of Clarence, recently discovered in the College archive. Drawing and art classes were held on board Britannia, *after all this was a school and the normal school subjects were taught in addition to seamanship etc. The drawing shows some grasp of both perspective and light and shade and such skills would be useful to a naval officer later in his career when as a Midshipman he would need to be able to illustrate his 'Journal'.*

by his younger brother who allegedly advised his instructors to focus their attention upon him. Indeed while the Duke of Clarence remained distant and lethargic, George fitted into the naval lifestyle with ease. He took his training seriously, dutifully performing the most lowly of tasks, such as scrubbing the deck, thoroughly and with care. He was skilful in seamanship and handling boats and was also good at mathematics. His sense of humour also suited life aboard *Britannia*, entering into the spirit of all the pranks, while his brother chose to take no notice. Finally, in 1879, the two princes passed out of *Britannia* to join their first sea-going ship, HMS *Bacchante*. Prince George was to see service for a total of almost twenty-two years, serving in a number of battleships before taking command of a torpedo boat in 1889. He subsequently commanded the gunboat HMS *Thrush* and (as a Captain) the cruisers *Melampus* and *Crescent*. However, in January 1892 Victor Albert, who had suffered from ill health throughout his life, died leaving George as his father's successor to the throne.

The Princes Albert Victor and George on board Britannia, *c.1878.*

The Princes Edward and Albert

As Prince of Wales, George recognised that his naval education had not perhaps been the most appropriate preparation for a future monarch, and that an understanding of politics, international affairs, history and languages would have been more valuable than the practicalities of seamanship and navigation. Nevertheless, when it was suggested by their tutor, Henry Hansell, that his sons Edward and Albert might benefit from attending prep school his reply was emphatic: 'My brother and I never went to prep school, the Navy will teach them all they need to know.' (Hampshire 1971, p.146.) So it was that the next generation of royal princes entered the Royal Navy.

By 1907, when Prince Edward was twelve years old, the *Britannia* on which his father and uncle had received their education had been replaced by the shore based College. However, before he could enter Dartmouth, the naval cadet of the twentieth century had first to spend two years at the Royal Naval College Osborne, built around the stables of the late Queen Victoria's residence. Edward arrived at Osborne in May 1907, with his father on board the Admiralty yacht, *Enchantress*, to join the Exmouth Term. In common with all the other new cadets, Edward had undergone both oral and written examinations before joining. He did well in the oral exam, in which one of the questions was whether he was afraid of the dark, but did rather less well in the written part, failing to achieve the minimum mark required by five points. He was not, however, the only boy to have done so and still make it on to the College. Indeed, the Prince of Wales was insistent that his son should be treated the same as any other cadet, a decree that naval outfitter Mr Gieve found difficult to accept, replacing Prince Edward's standard issue rough blue rug for one of fine quality cashmere. His fellow cadets, however, had rather less difficulty in treating him as one of their own, subjecting him to the same initiation ordeals and mild bullying that everyone incurred. On one occasion classmates used a classroom window to re-enact the beheading of Charles I and on another poured red ink over his head. The latter incident caused Edward to miss evening quarters rather than give away his persecutors, a move that earned him three days' extra drill. He was also christened with the obligatory nickname, in this case 'Sardines', a not exactly original reference to his father's royal title.

Both Edward and his younger brother joined Osborne at a distinct disadvantage, not merely because of their royal status. Until the age of twelve or thirteen neither had experienced being taught in a classroom of more than three pupils, by a tutor whose teaching failed to prepare them fully for the Naval College's curriculum. They had not spent much time in the company of children their own age, slept in a dormitory or been away from home. In contrast, their peers at Osborne and Dartmouth would have had up to seven years at prep school to get used to such conditions. Nevertheless, by the end of his final term at Osborne Edward had become a popular if not brilliant student. The next step was Dartmouth.

Name *Prince George*	Date of Entry *Oct 1..*		Page
Date.	Offence.	Punishment.	
Nov 15 1878	Improper behaviour in lecture room	1 day 3	
July 3ᵈ 1878	Improper behaviour at Tea table	1 " 5	
1879 March 3	*March 1879* Throwing bread at dinner	1 days 5	
May 3ʳᵈ	~~Very troublesome~~		
May 3ʳᵈ 22ᵈ	Very disorderly marching to Study	1 " 3.	

The punishment record of Prince George. The misdemeanours include 'improper behaviour' in both the lecture room and baths, 'very disorderly marching to Study and throwing bread at dinner'. The punishments are 1 days no. 3 or no. 5. These numbers refer to various chores or cleaning duties that the cadets carry out as a punishment. Similar punishments exist at the College today.

Edward found Dartmouth a distinct improvement, as he wrote to his mother: 'This is a very nice place, much nicer than Osborne . . . There is a very nice chapel here and I think I am going to join the choir.' Although life was still conducted at the double: 'There is an awful rush here and everything has to be done so quickly. We are only allowed 3 minutes to undress in the evening.' This final remark greatly concerned the Princess, who was anxious that her son should have ample time to take proper care of his teeth. A further letter home, however, assured her that the three minutes did not include time for cleaning teeth and that he was taking due care with regard to his oral hygiene. (Ziegler 1990, p.23.)

Academically Edward performed very well in English, German, French and history but was dragged down by his inability to grasp any branch of mathematics. He participated in amateur dramatics and was a good runner and rower. He enjoyed team sports, although he did not excel in them, and was often to be seen coming down

Page 148

Name *Prince Edward* Date of Entry *Oct 1877*

Date.	Offence.	Punishment.	By whom Punished.
Nov 7	Misbehaviour in drawing study	1 day 3	Com?

February 1878

Feb 14th	Inattention at Extra drill	1 days 3	Lieut. Corpe
" 22nd	Having a Catapult in his possession	1 " 3	" Pigott

1878 *September 1878*

Sept 22nd	Skylarking after Silence Gong Struck	1 days 5	Lieut. Pigott
Oct 10th	Skylarking at Seamanship Instruction	1 " 4	" "
12th	Not obeying Orders	1 " 5	" Treadon
21st	Skylarking after Silence Gong was Struck	1 " 5	" Pigott

Prince Edward's (Albert Victor) punishment record. His misdemeanours were more varied, and indeed more numerous than those of his younger brother. They include; 'inattention at Extra drill, having a catapult in his possession, skylarking at Seamanship instruction and skylarking after silence gong struck' (twice). Prince Edward appears to have become more bold as his time in Britannia progressed, there being one record for November 1877, the month after he joined, two in February 1878 and no fewer than four offences for the following September – October. These records are however very few in number compared to some cadets whose transgressions when recorded may fill much more than one page.

from the playing field loaded with boots so that boys could claim in later life that the King had once carried their boots. Edward was not, however, to be able properly to finish his time at Dartmouth.

On 7th May 1910 Princes Edward and Albert were both at their parents' London residence, Marlborough House, in their cadet uniforms, packing to return to Dartmouth and Osborne respectively, when Edward noticed the Royal Standard on Buckingham Palace flying (incorrectly)[1] at half-mast. Edward VII had died the previous night and the boys' father was now King. Prince Edward was now heir to the throne, automatically gaining the title Duke of Cornwall;

1 As discovered in the wake of the death of Diana, Princess of Wales, the Royal Standard should never fly at half-mast, as George V himself remarked when being given the news by his eldest son: 'That's all wrong. The King is dead, long live the King!' (Bradford 1989, p. 60.)

A signed photograph of Prince Edward (Edward VIII), as he was about to leave and pass out from the College.

Prince Edward (Edward VIII) in his cadet's uniform, with his mother and father, the future King George V and Queen Mary, at the entrance to the Captain's House on 7th May 1909. The framed original of this photograph now hangs in the entrance porch to the House, just to left of where Prince Edward is standing.

it was decided that he would not be created Prince of Wales until after his sixteenth birthday, a year later. On his return to Dartmouth after the King's funeral, a few subtle changes were noticeable. Fellow cadets started calling him Prince Edward instead of 'Sardines', a course of Civics was introduced and he began to follow the daily papers, *The Times* and *Westminster Gazette*, recognising that 'in years to come when I am obliged to follow politics, I shall know something about it.' (Ziegler 1990, p.25.)

However, with his father's accession and his own elevation Edward's last few terms at Dartmouth became increasingly disrupted. In February 1911 there was an outbreak of measles and mumps, which was to claim the lives of two cadets. Edward and his brother, who had joined the senior college the previous month,

were immediately put into quarantine in the Captain's House, but to no avail. Both Princes fell victim to the epidemic, their condition severe enough for bulletins to be published in the press. Despite the assurances of *The Lancet* that the boys were at the least susceptible age to any complications, they were in fact at the most vulnerable. One such complication of mumps is orchitis, which can lead to varying degrees of infertility in its victims. Edward was to go on not to have any children, despite a sexually active life. The possible knowledge that he was unable to father children may even have had some influence on his willingness to abdicate the throne.

Before leaving Dartmouth, however, Edward was able to perform his first official duty – returning to the town a silver oar, belonging to the Duchy of Cornwall, a symbol of the rights of the Duke over

The Queen's Visits

*S*ince the times of HMS Britannia *Royal visits have been a frequent occurrence at Dartmouth, whether visiting royal cadets or simply inspecting day-to-day College life. HM Queen Elizabeth II first visited the Royal Naval College, Dartmouth as a thirteen year old princess, together with her parents HM King George VI and HM Queen Elizabeth and her younger sister HRH The Princess Margaret. The occasion, during which the Princesses were hosted by Cadet Prince Philip of Greece and Denmark, would prove to be a defining moment in the life of the future Queen and one which would also shape the modern monarchy. A decade later the recently married Princess Elizabeth and Prince Philip returned to Dartmouth to take a parade.*

Since ascending to the throne in 1952 Her Majesty has visited the College on a number of occasions, whether to take the salute at a Lord High Admiral's Divisions or visiting her sons Princes Charles and Andrew as cadets.

1. HM Queen and HRH The Duke of Edinburgh depart from Sandquay on completion of Her Majesty's first visit to the College as Queen in 1962.

2. In 1972 Her Majesty was accompanied by HRH The Duke of Edinburgh, HRH The Princess Anne and a young HRH The Prince Andrew (pictured).

3. HM Queen and HRH The Duke of Edinburgh with Captain N J S Hunt and Commander P N Blair. HM is about to present the 'Queen's Telescope' to a cadet who has performed particularly well. This passing out parade in 1972 was of particular significance to the Royal couple as HRH The Prince Andrew was among those passing out. It was also the year in which the College celebrated its 75th anniversary.

1.

2.

3.

4.

Totnes Image Bank/South Hams Newspapers

5.

Totnes Image Bank/South Hams Newspapers

6.

7.

4. HM The Queen chats to Britannia Beagles kennelman David Trinnick after naming one of the beagle puppies in 1988.

5. HM The Queen inspects the Officer cadets at Lord High Admiral's Divisions, April 1988.

6. HM The Queen inspects the Colour Party with Commodore Philip Masterton-Smith at Lord High Admiral's Divisions, April 1997.

7. In 2008 Her Majesty inspected Lord High Admiral's Divisions with Commodore Martin Alabaster.

the water of Dartmouth. His next step as a cadet should have been a six-month training cruise in one of the cruisers attached to the College, HMS *Cumberland* or *Cornwall*. Unfortunately, with the coronation due to take place on 22nd June 1911, he was unable to join his classmates, being instead promoted to the rank of midshipman by his father on the eve of the coronation and later joining the battleship *Hindustan*. Nevertheless Dartmouth seemed to have made a good impression on the Royal Family, the King noting, 'I certainly think the College is the best school in England.' A sentiment which was apparently shared by Prince Edward, who following a visit to Winchester School, wrote to his father; 'It is amusing to see the difference between an ordinary school and Dartmouth . . . Their life is not half as strenuous as it is at Dartmouth and we were more contented. There can be no better education than a naval one.' (Ziegler, 1990, p.28.)

For Prince Albert, though, his naval education still had a long way to go. Albert had joined Osborne as a member of the Grenville Term in January 1909. It was Edward's final term there and he was tasked by his father to look after his younger brother, to 'put him up to the ropes' and make sure that he worked hard. (Ziegler 1990, p.22.) This task was not easy as boys from different Terms were not supposed to mix with each other, causing the royal brothers to meet clandestinely at the top of the playing fields. Albert inevitably suffered from comparison with his brother, suffering as he did from the extra disadvantages of being shy and nervous. Mr Watt, Albert's Osborne tutor, wrote: 'One could wish that he had more of Prince Edward's keenness and application.' While a contemporary of the two princes at Osborne and Dartmouth commented that it was: 'like comparing an ugly duckling with a cock pheasant.' (Bradford 1989, p.63.) His stammer contributed to the bullying of other cadets while his determination to hide it baffled and irritated his masters who thought him either stupid or very shy. As he was later to confide to a friend, he chose to remain silent in maths classes to avoid pronouncing the letter 'f' in 'fraction'. Fortunately his father seemed to appreciate his problem, writing to the brothers' old tutor, Hansell: 'Watt thinks Bertie shy in class. I expect it is his dislike of showing his hesitating speech that prevents him from answering.' (Bradford 1989, p.56.) One senior staff officer, who knew them both, remarked that he considered 'the younger will outstrip the elder.' (Hampshire 1971, p.159.)

Albert was not good at rugby or cricket but had an aptitude for athletics, winning him the appreciation and respect of his peers. Academically, however, he struggled, regularly occupying the lower few places in end of term results. Indeed there was real concern that Albert would not make the grade to move up to Dartmouth, prompting the Prince of Wales to write sternly to his son:

'I am sorry to say that the last reports from Mr Watt with regard to your work are not at all satisfactory, he says you don't seem to take your work seriously, nor do you appear to be very keen about it. My dear boy this will not do, if you go on like this you will be at the bottom of your Term, you are now 71st and you won't pass your examination and very probably will be warned this term if you don't take care . . . everything rests with you and you are quite intelligent and can do very well if you like. I trust that you will take to heart what I have written and that the next report will be a good one and the others to come until the end of term.' (Wheeler-Bennett, 1958, p.45 – 46.)

Prince Albert seemed to take his father's warning to heart, with noted improvement in his powers of concentration and willingness to use them, causing Mr Watt to report that 'His Royal Highness has done better and more consistent work than he has done in any previous term.' (Ibid. p.46 – 47.) However, as the final examinations approached so did the Christmas holidays and in the excitement Albert, in Mr Watt's words, seemed to go 'a mucker', finishing sixty-eighth out of sixty-eight.

Nevertheless, in January 1911 Albert joined his elder brother at Dartmouth, only to find himself one month later laid up by the latest epidemic of measles and mumps. This was followed by a period of sick-leave and recuperation in Newquay, Cornwall. He returned to Dartmouth two days before the end of term, having spent no more than a total of four weeks of his first term at the College. Albert's second term was also disrupted, this time by his father's coronation on 22nd June, an occasion for which he wore his Naval Cadet's uniform.

The regime at Dartmouth expected more maturity from its cadets than Osborne, allowing greater responsibilities and freedoms. Albert's new term officer, Lieutenant Henry Spencer Cooper, encouraged the young prince to pursue cross-country running, riding and to follow the Britannia Beagles. He also became good at tennis and sailing, seizing the opportunity to take the College boats up the River Dart to Totnes and Dittisham to enjoy tea with the locals. Sports were not the only extra-curricular activity in which Albert participated. On one occasion he was caught along with sixteen other cadets letting off illicit fireworks on Guy Fawkes' Night. As punishment for this misdemeanour he received 'six of the best', although he always maintained an injustice had occurred as the cane had broken after four strokes. Such escapades or 'skylarking' were not unusual but one such episode was to have more impact than the average prank. In February 1912, the King and Queen returned home from the great Coronation Durbar in India, planning to visit the Naval College in March. But the Britain to which they had returned was in the grip of industrial unrest and anti-establishment protest. A rumour started to circulate around Dartmouth that some of the senior cadets planned to mark the forthcoming royal visit by painting the newly installed statue of the King with red paint. The Captain of the College took the rumour seriously, ordering a twenty-four hour watch to be posted on the statue. Some of the civilian staff required to form the guard threatened to strike and were subsequently sacked. In a letter to his parents Prince

R. T. Bower, P. F. P. Wood, V. G. Snow, H. B. Deedes, H. T. Dawson, W. B. Price, C. V. Powel, Prince Edward, M. J. Bethell.

ut. Beasley, Mr. McKean, Mr Arkwright, J. M. Mansfield, Eng.-Lieut. Foster, H. R. K. Bamber, Mr. Bryant, G. H. Warner, Y. H. F. G. Wells, J. M. P. Rowlandson, Mr. Anstie, Mr. Piggott, G. R. Cousins

H. S. Barker, W. S. R. King-Hall, Lieut. Nicholson, Mr. Hope, C. Jenkin, Dr. Pick, D. Wainwright, Mr. Megson, J. L. Davies, Mr. Mercer, Lieut. Ford.

H.M.S. PINAFORE, CHRISTMAS 1909.

The College production of 'HMS Pinafore', staged at Christmas 1909. Prince Edward played the First Lord's sister and can be seen standing at the back, second from the right. The photograph is taken at the rear of O block, or what is now the lower library.

WAR SERVICES.

(Giving full particulars of campaigns, engagements, wounds, mentions in despatches, medals, awards, decorations, etc.)

I served in the Grand Fleet in August 1914 in the "Collingwood". Again from February 1915 to August 1915. Again from May 1916 to August 1916 and from May 1917 to August 1917 in the "Malaya". In February 1918 I was attached to the R.N.A.S. at Cranwell Lines, and remained on there in the R.A.F. till August when I was appointed to the R.A.F. Cadet Brigade Hastings and subsequently transferred to Shorncliffe when the Brigade moved in September.

I was present at the Battle of Jutland on May 31st 1916.

I was mentioned in despatches

Knight of the Garter
Queen Victoria's Diamond Jubilee Medal
King Edward's Coronation Medal
King George's Coronation Medal
Order of the White Eagle (I Class) Serbian.
Order of St Vladimir (IV class) Russian.

I hereby certify that I am satisfied of the general correctness of all the above particulars as to qualifications, services, etc., set out on pages 2, 3 and 4.

_____ Commanding Officer.

Station _____ Regiment.

Army Form B. 199.

RECORD OF SERVICES.

of Captain H.R.H. Prince Albert
(Rank, Christian Names and Surname in full, printed).

Regiment Royal Navy (attached Royal Air Force)
Lieutenant

PERSONAL PARTICULARS.

1. Date and Place of Birth ... ...
(If promoted from the ranks, age as given on attestation and date of attestation should be stated in lieu of date of birth.)
York Cottage Sandringham Norfolk December 14th 1895.

2. Religious persuasion ... ...
Church of England

3. Where educated, specifying Schools or University ... ...
Royal Naval College Osborne " " Dartmouth.

4. Date of first Commission ... ...
May 15th 1916.

5. Height ... ...
5 ft. 9 inches

6. Married or Single ... ...
Single

7. If married, date of marriage ... ...
—

8. Name and Address of next of kin (stating relationship), guardian or agent for reference in case of emergency ... ...
His Majesty The King Buckingham Palace London S.W.

also

A second name (as an alternative) ... ...
Her Majesty The Queen

I do hereby certify that to the best of my knowledge and belief this statement of personal particulars is in all respects correct and true.

Albert _____ Signature of Officer.

Place Dibgate Camp Shorncliffe Captain Rank.

Date October 3rd 1918 Royal Air Force Regiment.

(A9113) Wt. W930/P120 60.000 10/17 D. D. & L. Sch. 28. Gen No. 1357

The Record of War Service of Prince Albert, later King George VI dated 3rd October 1918, is on Army Form B99 and is in the King's own handwriting.

Albert innocently informed them of the episode:

'Papa's statue has been placed at the end of the Quarterdeck today with Grandpapa's picture on the right of it. It looks very well indeed. Have you seen the small paragraph in today's Daily Graphic on page nine. It is headed "The Statue and the Strike". It is supposed that some cadets were going to paint it, so the cadets' servants were told to watch it at night, to prevent anyone from doing so.' (Wheeler-Bennett 1958, p.55.)

In the end the visit had to be cancelled due to a five-week long coal strike. Albert failed to persuade his father to grant an extra week's leave as compensation.

In his last term at Dartmouth Albert was given the opportunity to accompany his father on board the Royal Yacht, *Victoria and Albert*, to witness the review of the Fleet off Weymouth, in May 1912. It was during this excursion that the future king met his future prime minister, Winston Churchill, who was then First Lord of the Admiralty.

Overall, Dartmouth seemed to have a positive impact upon Prince Albert. He was never to excel academically but to finish sixty-first out of sixty-seven could be seen as a relative improvement, leading Captain Evan-Thomas to conclude, 'I think he will do'. (Wheeler-Bennett 1958, p.58.) In terms of personal development Albert had clearly matured and achieved general popularity among fellow cadets, masters, staff officers and civilian workers. He was respected for his persistence, generosity, loyalty and sense of humour, but most of all because he never talked 'up' or 'down' to anyone. All this stood him in great stead for the next part of his training on board HMS *Cumberland*, which would lead to his promotion to the rank of midshipman and a career in the Royal Navy. He would next visit Dartmouth on the eve of the Second World War, accompanied by his wife and two daughters.

The last of King George's children to be educated by the Navy, was Prince George, the Duke of Kent. By the time he joined Osborne in September 1916 the First World War was already well underway. The Royal Navy was contemplating the outcome of the Battle of Jutland that had taken place earlier that year and at which Prince Albert had been present, serving on board HMS *Collingwood*. For George the war meant a foreshortening of his education, spending just three, instead of the usual six terms at Osborne before joining Dartmouth in September 1917. By way of compensation he was to spend, along with his classmates, seven terms at Dartmouth but the overall experience was to prove an unhappy one. Temperamentally unsuited to naval life George hated his time at Dartmouth and indeed was to spend most of his career pleading to be allowed to leave the Navy. This was reflected in his performance at the College, where he passed out eighty-fifth out of eighty-six. Prince George finally left the Royal Navy in 1934 but he was to find himself back in uniform at the outbreak of World War Two. Tragically on the 25th August 1942 the plane in which he was flying

Prince Albert, the future King George VI, at the front door of the College in 1911.

HOBSON	E.A.	KEENE	A.N.R.	LUKE	J.C.
HOFFMAN	A.A.	KELLETT	W.B.	LOVATT	R.S.
HOLBROOK	G.N.	KELSEY	V.H.		
HOLLAND	K.T.	KEMP	N.McI.	McCLINTOCK	J.L.E.
HOLLOWAY	D.R.	KENNAWAY	C.S.H.	McCULLOCH	A.C.
HOOPER	B.R.	KENNEDY	M.H.McL.	MACDERMOTT	A.
HOPE	C.W.	KENNEDY	R.	MACDONNELL	L.W.A.
HORNELL	D.A.H.	H.R.H.DUKE OF KENT	G.E.A.E.	MACHIN	J.L.
HOSKIN	M.C.	KERR	R.	MACHIN	M.N.
HOTHAM	C.E.	KETTLE	L.H.	MACK	P.J.
HOUSTON	D.A.	KINDER	R.	MACKENDRICK	D.W.
HOWARD	H.G.P.	KINDERSLEY	A.T.J.	MACKINNON	A.H.I.
HOWDEN	I.C.	KING	H.V.	MACKINNON	D.S.
HUDDART	G.P.	KING-CHURCH	J.B.	MACLEISH	A.A.F.
HUDDART	J.S.	KIPLING	R.F.	MACPHERSON	M.H.
HULBERT	W.B.	KNOWLES	A.	MAINPRICE	W.J.
HUMPHREYS	P.N.	KNOWLES	H.G.	MANDEVILLE	G.F.
HUNT	H.G.	KNOWLING	R.G.K.	MANSELL	J.F.
HUNT	J.P.	KNOX	W.N.R.	MANSELL	J.O.
HUNT	M.H.			MANWARING	A.H.

*HRH Prince George outside the main entrance of the College in 1920.
In common with all former cadets who lost their life during the Second
World, the Duke of Kent's name is recorded on the College war memorial.*

crashed, killing all on board. Having lost his life in the service of his country, the Duke of Kent's name was added to the College war memorial alongside those of fellow former cadets.

Prince Louis of Battenberg

Prince Louis joined the Royal Naval College Osborne as a member of the Exmouth Term in May 1913. He had done well in his entrance exam, passing fifteenth out of eighty-three, doing best in English and German and worst in arithmetic. He entered the College at potentially a double disadvantage, being not only royal, but the son of the First Sea Lord, the Marquis of Milford Haven. His royal status was reflected in the particularly small writing on the brass plaque on his sea chest, so as to accommodate the title 'Serene Highness'. In common with all the other royal cadets 'Dickie' was subjected to the same bullying as the other boys. On joining his 'ordeal' was to climb the flagstaff and sing 'A Life on the Ocean Wave'. On the whole, however, Prince Louis was able to stand his own against the bullies, even challenging an older boy to a fight and winning. Usually this would have been considered a cardinal sin but his opponent was unpopular with the rest of the College, henceforth Louis was something of a hero amongst his classmates. Nor was the son of the most senior Naval Officer in the country exempt from punishment, on one occasion he was rapped so hard over the knuckles with a steel ruler for giggling in bed that he still bore the mark a week later.

In August 1914 war broke out between Britain and Germany. Louis's father, having been born a German, soon found himself victim of the anti-German sentiment that not unnaturally swept the country, finally being forced to resign in October. Back at Osborne Louis found himself ostracised for a short time but this never really amounted to persecution.

Prince Louis arrived at Dartmouth in January 1915, he wrote to his mother giving his first impressions of the Senior College:

'This is an enormous place, almost like a palace. We are all quite lost in it, and as we are apparently not going to be shown round, we will have to find out things for ourselves . . .
The Captain gave us a speech on the quarterdeck after prayers, and then we had to turn in. I was about half-way down my rank, and when we got outside it was literally a race, in which I gained to be about 6th. I then just had time to run off the rusty water in the tap, fill my mug, give one scrub with my brush, and fly back through the passages, nearly lost . . . I went to sleep shortly after 10. In the morning I woke up with the first notes of the old reveille in my ears. I was out of bed with my pyjamas off and my towel on just as the bugle ceased. I then simply flew for the bathroom and was second to get into the plunge. The plunge is not sunk into the ground like the Osborne ones are, but stands up and has only about 2'6" of water in, so I kind of slid in with my mouth open. Alas, I swallowed a mouthful

before I realised it was salt water. Then I hurried off to wash, once more raced up to the dormitory, where I dressed as fast as I could and yet I was only just out within 3 seconds of the time the Cadet Captain gave us. We then had cocoa at about 5 minutes past 7, and then dashed off in the vain hope of finding the right classroom.' (Ziegler 1985, p.37.)

Good academically, Prince Louis was less accomplished when it came to sport, not helped on one occasion when his shorts fell down during a hundred yard race! Some of his letters home hinted of homosexuality being practised among a proportion of the cadets, as he wrote to his mother: 'Some people in the other dormitory have even begun to do filthy things, I have heard.' But Louis himself was far more interested in Admiral Palmer's daughter, Rosamond.

The war was never very far away. In August 1914, the College had received a telegram from the Admiralty, ordering mobilisation, leading to all the cadets being sent to sea ahead of completing their training. There were constant fears that the College would come under attack. During Louis's first term instructions to evacuate were given when it was thought German armed trawlers were nearby and might fire on the College. The incident proved to be a false alarm but from then on Mountbatten kept his greatcoat at the ready and a bag of warm clothes under his bed should it be necessary to leave in a hurry. Then in September 1915, after being at Dartmouth for less than a year, Louis wrote excitedly to his mother: '. . . we are going to sea in January. This has far surpassed my faintest hopes.' (Ziegler 1985, p.39.) However, he was later to be disappointed when the Exmouth Term's departure was postponed until April. Worse was to come though when it was announced that Louis was one of the seventy-two cadets to be sent to the Royal Naval Engineering College at Keyham, Devonport; as Lord Louis was to reflect in the *Britannia Magazine* (July 1965, p.7), 'to our intense indignation we missed the Battle of Jutland by six weeks.' He passed out of Dartmouth eighteenth in his class and subsequently went on to pass out top of his class at Keyham, to commence a naval career which would lead to his appointment as First Sea Lord, making him and his father the only father and son to both hold the post.

Right: The full dress naval uniform of King George VI. It was presented to the College in 1953 by HM Queen Elizabeth and Queen Elizabeth the Queen Mother: "in memory of His late Majesty and of his career in and his devotion for the Royal Navy" (letter dated 5th February 1953 from the Private Secretary to the Queen). The uniform consists of the full dress coat in rank of Admiral of the Fleet, full dress trousers, cocked hat, epaulettes, full dress belt and shoes. In July 1959, Field Marshal Viscount Montgomery of Alamein, KG, visited the College to take the salute at the Passing Out Parade; he forgot to bring his Garter star and so borrowed the one from the King's uniform.

The Royal Marine Band

While the origins of the Royal Marine Band Service can be traced back just over a century, (they celebrated their centenary in 2003), Dartmouth has only hosted its own for just under fifty years. Prior to that the Voluntary College Band, formed when the College opened, provided all the music. This band consisted of cadets, civilian staff and officers and it served the College well for fifty years, playing for parades, ballroom dancing lessons and other functions.

It was in July 1903 that the Royal Naval Band marched into the newly formed Royal Naval School of Music at Eastney. The Royal Naval Bandsmen became Royal Marines and they took responsibility for the provision of music for the Royal Navy. However, their arrival at Dartmouth was not until the beginning of 1956 when the Band of HMS Triumph, the ship that had been used for many years as an RN Officer Cadet training ship, marched into the College to assume their new title of the Band of HM Royal Marines Britannia Royal Naval College.

The latter half of the twentieth century has seen huge reductions in the number of ships and of shore establishments and a consequent reduction in the number of bands. The last two ships to retain a band were HMS Ark Royal, which decommissioned in 1978 and HMY Britannia, decommissioned in 1998. By 2005 there were five Royal Marine Bands one of which was based in Dartmouth. In addition to their musical duties the bandsmen were trained as medical orderlies and to assist the local community, such as fire fighting duties, as they were required to do in Operation Fresco during the firefighters strikes in 2002/3. However, following the deployment of a number of bandsmen to support 3 Commando Brigade Royal Marines in Afghanistan in March 2008 the BRNC band was suspended and finally disbanded in May 2009. In its place the Volunteer Band was reformed, consisting of College staff and former members of the RM band.

The Voluntary College Band made up of cadets and civilians, many of them stewards, in 1955 just prior to its demise a year later when the Royal Marine Band arrived.

The Royal Marine Band concert in the Caspar John Hall.

HM Royal Marine Band of Britannia Royal Naval College receives the freedom of the town of Dartmouth, 28th April 2004. The Band parades the illuminated charter, the work of Mr. Melvyn Stone, granting their freedom. Picture courtesy of South Hams Newspapers.

A posed photograph on the parade ground in full dress uniform.

The Royal Marine Band Fanfare Team.

The Corps Drum Major poses for an official photograph in front of the College.

The Corps of Drums.

The Last Post.

Edward, Prince of Wales with Mr Jasper Bartlett, Chairman of the Dartmouth Harbour Commission aboard the pinnace landing at Dartmouth for the official ceremonial opening of the town's War Memorial in 1921. Reproduced by kind permission of Mrs Sally Pidsley.

Prince Philip of Greece and the Royal Visit of 1939

The son of Prince and Princess Andrew of Greece, Prince Philip was exiled from his homeland a year after his birth, following the abdication of his uncle, King Constantine of Greece. Eventually Philip found himself in Britain, under the guardianship of Lord Milford Haven, and upon his death in 1938 Milford Haven's younger brother Lord Louis Mountbatten. During this time Philip was sent to school in Salem, Germany until the school's founder, Kurt Hahn, was forced out of the country by the Nazis. Subsequently Dr Hahn re-established his new school at Gordonstoun in Scotland, to which Philip followed. On leaving Gordonstoun, encouraged by the Mountbattens, Philip decided to join the Royal Navy. After spending some time in Cheltenham with a Mr and Mrs Mercer, to cram for the forthcoming examinations, Philip took the entrance exam to the Royal Naval College at Dartmouth, passing sixteenth out of thirty-four. Having already received a public school education Philip, aged seventeen, joined the

On Saturday 22nd July 1939 King George VI and Queen Elizabeth visited the College accompanied by their daughters the Princesses Elizabeth and Margaret. Here the Royal Yacht Victoria & Albert III *is entering the Dart and passing Dartmouth Castle. A few locals braved the wet and blustery conditions hoping to catch a sight of the Royal Family. This small group belies the fact that the visit was immensely popular with the local population as in excess of 20,000 loyal subjects turned out to greet the visitors over the two-day visit.*

'Special Entry' cadets, created by Winston Churchill in 1913 to boost numbers by recruiting young men who had already received their secondary education. These cadets were known as the 'Frobishers', after the training ship HMS *Frobisher*, on which they would normally receive their three terms' training. However, when Philip joined in May 1939, *Frobisher* was being rearmed in preparation for war so the Special Entry Cadets were housed in the Naval College to complete a foreshortened course of eight months, instead of the usual twelve.

The royal party arrives at the Town Quay in the Royal Barge. July 1939.

The royal party is introduced to the Captain of the College, and the Headmaster Mr E. W. E. Kempson, who is nearest the camera. July 1939.

Nevertheless there was still time to enjoy the pleasures of the River Dart, as the Prince fondly remembers:

'My most vivid recollection is of the boatwork in cutters and whalers. I was fortunate in having learnt to sail in a boat at my school on the Moray Firth. There was only one other cadet in my term who knew how to sail a boat. With only two term officers, we were delegated to take charge of other cadets in our term under instruction in pulling and sailing naval cutters and whalers.

I remember one occasion when four cutters were beating up the Dart on the way home, two with officers in charge and two with us in charge. At one point one of the cutters commanded by an officer made to cross my bows while he was on port tack and I was on the starboard tack. I expected him to give way, but he ploughed on, and although I did my best to go under his stern, I hit him smartly not far from where he was sitting. Fortunately no harm was done and there was no further mention of the subject!!

On another occasion I was steering a whaler in a race just outside the mouth of the river. I had discovered that the art of going-about quickly in a whaler was for the helmsman to push the yard of the mizzen to windward while holding the tiller hard down with his knees. The crew, meanwhile, were busy dipping the lug of the mainsail and shifting jib sheets. On this occasion we hit a slightly bigger wave as we went about and I was pitched overboard to leeward. Fortunately I was holding on to the mizzen sheet and managed to scramble back before anyone noticed. However they were all a bit puzzled to see me sitting in the stern sheets soaking wet.'[2]

2 Personal correspondence of HRH Prince Philip

Although brief, Philip's time at Dartmouth ended in success, culminating in the presentation of the 'King's Dirk' for best overall cadet.

However, Dartmouth was to become more than merely the gateway to a great naval career for the young prince, when in July 1939 King George VI visited the College, accompanied by Queen Elizabeth and the Princesses Elizabeth and Margaret. The true significance of the visit has become shrouded in myth, romanticism and controversy. The legend has it that this was the first time Prince Philip and Princess Elizabeth met each other and that, particularly from the latter's point of view, it was love at first sight. Certainly this is the impression given by the account of the Princesses' governess, Miss Crawford, quoting, for example, Princess Elizabeth as exclaiming 'How good he is,' as he showed off, by jumping over a tennis net. The reality however, may be more mundane.

The Royal Family had arrived at Dartmouth, in the rain, on board HMY *Victoria & Albert* on Saturday 22nd July. Among the royal party was Prince Philip's uncle, the King's *aide de camp*, Louis Mountbatten. Not unusually the College was in the middle of an epidemic of chicken-pox and mumps. It was, therefore necessary to keep the Princesses away from the risk of infection. At this point it is believed that Mountbatten intervened, suggesting that his nephew might be dragged away from his regular routine to join the Princesses. This suggestion has been interpreted as a deliberate manoeuvre on the part of Mountbatten, to throw his nephew and the future Queen together. To what extent this may be true is difficult to decipher, as a royal prince Philip was a natural choice to act as host. Mountbatten himself gave little away, noting in his diary on the first day of the visit merely that 'Philip accompanied us and dined on board' the Royal Yacht, with a number of other cadets. Next day he noted: 'Philip came back aboard *Victoria & Albert* for tea and was a great success with the children.' (Ziegler 1985, p.102.)

HM Queen Elizabeth plants a tree just to the west of the College in the grounds. The King and the two Princesses also planted trees. All of these trees still survive in what has become known as the Royal Plot. This started a tradition of royal tree planting that continues to this day.

The gallery of the gymnasium where the royal party are seen watching a demonstration by the cadets. The Princesses and the King and Queen are all seated. Behind the King, standing without a cap, is Captain Mountbatten, aide de camp to the King, and to the right of him, in a cap, is Prince Philip of Greece.

The Dartmouth visit was certainly not the first time that Philip and Elizabeth had seen each other. They had both been at George VI's coronation and at the wedding of Philip's cousin Marina in 1934. However, it is probably fair to say that at the age of thirteen this was the first time Princess Elizabeth had 'noticed' Prince Philip, even if it took some time for him fully to reciprocate the feelings of someone whom to an eighteen-year-old officer-cadet must still have appeared a child. As Mountbatten was to write many years later when advising Prince Charles on the subject of marriage: 'After all Mummy never seriously thought of anyone else after the Dartmouth encounter when she was 13.' (Ziegler 1985, p.687.)

The Captain of the College at the time, Sir Fredrick D. G. Dalrymple-Hamilton, kept a detailed diary throughout his distinguished naval career. His entries provide a fascinating insight into the visit, although they throw little light upon any emerging royal romance.

'July, 1939. Saturday 22 R.N.C.D.
V. Wet am. Showers pm.

The Royal Yacht escorted by *Keppel* (de Winton) and *Versatile* (Hussey) arrived at about 10 o'clock and secured to Nos 1 and 2 buoys. Almost as soon as she had done so the rain commenced to descend in torrents and continued doing so until about 4pm. I went aboard at 1030 and was most kindly received by the King and Queen and stayed about half an hour discussing plans and was given a glass of Port! I then returned to R.N.C. and gave orders for wet weather programme to be put into effect . . . At 3 o'clock C in C and Justina Commander and I & N Kisty and Graeme repaired to the gym. All the cadets were assembled

lining the road outside. Headmaster joined us with Revd. and Mrs Gordon (Headmaster of Blundells) and Joan (Peek). The two latter being with their respective cricket teams who had been scheduled to play here today but of course could not on account of the weather. The King and Queen and Princesses arrived at 1515 and we received them there . . . We went straight up to the gym gallery where I presented Formby and then the 9th term gave their "passing out" display and did it extremely well. Thence to the swimming bath . . . They walked down to Q.D. [quarterdeck] via D Block and officers and masters wives were presented on Q.D. after which we walked up to the Canteen stopping on the way to plant trees on the bit of grass just to the westward of west end steps. The King, Queen and Princesses each planted one and it was a rather amusing interlude. Parsloe produced shovels etc all burnished up. Then to the Canteen for tea. Headmaster next to the Queen. Others present at tea included Prince Philip of Greece, Joan, Gortons, and Seldon Cricket master at Blundells who gatecrashed and I never spotted him until after the Queen had asked who he was! Tea went off V. well with traditional Raspberries and Cream mixed with Strawberry ice – Banana and Cream and so on . . . After tea we looked at the Beagles and puppies and then made our way to Sandquay . . . All cadets were assembled there and as soon as T.M. [Their Majesties] were seated Walter Starkie started a dinghy race 21 dinghies competing . . . Then the barge came along-side and T.M. and Princesses embarked and returned to the yacht. This concluded the first day's programme at R.N.C. but in the evening T.M. gave a dinner party on the yacht . . . A wonderful party for us

all. I had the honour of sitting next to the Queen . . .
I introduced the cadets to T.M. We returned to R.N.C. about
1115 (Cadets earlier).

'July, 1939. Sunday 23
Mostly fine

The King visited escorting destroyers and arrived at our main
entrance at 1015. Cadets at Divisions. I receive H.M and H.M
the Queen and Princesses. The King walked out onto the
Bridge and was received with a Royal Salute and the Standard
was broken on the College Tower flag staff. Divisions went
off very well. Black cloud rolling up but only 1 short shower
thank God! The King presented Cups . . . Cadets marched
past. The Officers and Masters were presented on the Parade
Ground. Next off swords in the Visitors Room and Church. The
Princesses left off church owing to Mumps infection possibilities
and had a good rag in our house with North, Kisty, Graeme and
Prince Philip assisting . . . After a short interval for elevenses in
our house during which the Queen presented cakes to winning
sailing crews we went out to Parade Ground the King and
Queen went down to inspect the College employees (300 or so
mustered). They did this very thoroughly and talked to many of

*A rare private photograph of Prince Philip showing the young Princesses
the essentials of croquet on the lawn of the Captain's House. Princess
Margaret nearest to the camera and Princess Elizabeth partially hidden
behind the lady dressed in black. This was supposedly the first meeting
of Princess Elizabeth and Prince Philip.*

*The Captain, Fredrick Dalrymple-Hamilton escorts the King to the Parade
Ground for the Inspection of Divisions. The Commander of the College,
Cdr. Charles Addis is to the left behind the hand of the Captain and
Captain Mountbatten can be seen between the Captain and the King.*

them . . . Then to the Wardroom where a happy half hour
and H.M. much amused by the defaulters book etc . . . On
leaving I asked the King and Queen to look inside the Dining
Hall where cadets were all at dinner. The moment they got
inside the door the whole 500 Cadets leaped to their feet and
cheered themselves to a standstill for about 3 minutes. A quite
unrehearsed item and shook me to the core! Along the corridor
past his photograph and so to luncheon at our house . . . I
sat next to the Queen, on her left, and Prince Philip on her
right. Lady K Seymour on the King's left. Miss Crawford the
Princesses governess' on my left then Princess Margaret, Graeme,
Tommy Lascelles, Madge, H.M. the King and Lady K.S., Dickie
Mountbatten, Harold Campbell, Kisty North, Princess Elizabeth,
Prince Philip – H.M. Queen and self. After luncheon the
Princesses and young played croquet game outside. We visited
Grenville House, Seamanship Room, Library, then sick quarters,
walked through one garden then out into garden . . .
Goodbyes were said H.M. presented G and I with signed
photographs of himself and the Queen and we all walked down
to Sandquay and they re-embarked for V & A. Nothing could
have been easier than they have made this visit – We all enjoyed
every minute of it and the whole thing went with a swing despite
the weather at the beginning . . . T.M. were most kind in their
appreciation of all they had seen. The event of the evening was
the send off to the Yacht. Cadets [including Prince Philip] manned
every boat we had in the place and the whole party proceeded to
lie off the starboard side of the Yacht . . . Whilst we were waiting a
blue dinghy was called alongside and a message lowered into it. This
contained a signal from H.M. the King giving 4 extra days leave at

The March – Past after the Inspection of Divisions and the King is taking the Salute. This area is known as the Bridge, and on it can be seen the headmaster, Mr Kempson, his staff in their gowns and mortarboards are to the left of the Bridge, with the officers to the right. The practice of wearing academic dress at Divisions is still continued to this day. In the distance in the garden of the Captain's House can be seen one of the Princesses.

The King inspecting Divisions on a very wet and blustery 23rd July 1939. The Royal Yacht can be seen anchored in the Bight in the distance.

the end of the summer holidays and a request to me to impart the news there and then which I did to all the boats round and produced a splendid storm of cheering. Later on when V & A was aweigh we gave more cheers for King and Queen . . . We then slipped all boats as V & A gathered way they all rowed their hardest and the whole party accompanied her to sea . . . We followed until she stopped to drop the pilot and then as she got under way again one final cheer and turned towards her and so back. It was a wonderful sight and I shall never forget it seeing the old yacht steaming along slowly with all the boats accompanying her and the King and Queen and Princesses on the bridge waving and everyone cheering and so ended our much looked forward to Royal Visit and we returned to our harbour and college tired and pleased with ourselves and everybody else but particularly so with our Visitors who couldn't have made a greater success of the whole visit.'

Thus the summer term of 1939 came successfully to a conclusion. However, by the time the College returned for the autumn term Britain was once again at war. The Second World War would see even greater losses for the Royal Navy than the first. Amongst those involved were former royal cadets Lord Mountbatten, the Duke of Kent, Prince Philip and of course HM King George VI, who won the respect and admiration of his people as he led them through the nation's darkest hours until victory in 1945. After the war the tradition of royal princes at Dartmouth was to continue when Prince Charles joined Dartmouth on 16th September 1971, as a member of Blake Division. Prince Andrew followed his elder brother to Dartmouth as a member of Hawke Division in September 1979. A hundred and two years since Princes Edward and George had first stepped on board *Britannia* in 1877 the Naval College could once again claim to be truly Royal.

Lord Louis Mountbatten shares a moment with Prince Philip outside the newly opened Casper John Hall on 11th September 1963 built for the 'Unison 63' gathering of senior representatives of the Commonwealth Armed Forces.

Following pages: 'Memories' – watercolour by Michael Hill based upon the reminiscences of former cadets of the College. Published as a limited edition print by Barbican Gallery, Plymouth.

His Royal Highness the Prince of Wales

*P*rince Charles joined Dartmouth on 16th September 1971, as a member of Blake Division, having completed a period of service with the RAF. As a graduate entrant, he spent just six weeks at the College, learning about leadership, navigation and the ways of the Royal Navy. In common with many graduate students at the time Prince Charles found the constraints of Dartmouth irksome: 'It was exactly like being locked up at school again and we weren't allowed out, except on rare weekends. It really was quite a business . . . endless rushing about, drill . . . quite a shock to the system.' (Dimbleby, 1994, p. 196.) He was, though, popular among his classmates who identified with his self-deprecating manner and his willingness to join in. At the time, he may have been relieved that he was only to suffer the pressures of Dartmouth for a short spell, but he later agreed with changes to the training pattern, which resulted in extended courses for all young officers, admitting that as a Naval Officer he would have benefited from a longer stay: 'There is no substitute for professional training'. (Winton, 1981 p. 90). Although he did not consider himself to be a natural seaman, Prince Charles was a proficient handler of the College picket boats on the river, experience that was to underpin his effectiveness and professional flair in command of the minehunter HMS Bronington in 1976, his final appointment in the Senior Service.

Above: Prince Charles at a Passing Out Parade in 1971.

Right: HRH Prince Charles arrives at the College to commence his training. The term had started the previous day but Charles arrived in his Aston Martin and drew up on the Bridge to be greeted by the Captain of the College, Captain Gordon Tait. 16th September 1971.

Above: Prince Charles aboard the College yacht *Bluebottle*, formerly his father's yacht..

His Royal Highness the Duke of York

The Duke of York followed his elder brother to Dartmouth for two terms in September 1979, joining as a short service Seaman Officer, specialising as a pilot. He was in Hawke Division, which at the time was housed in the old sick quarters. Like his elder brother before him, Prince Andrew applied himself to his studies and performed well, even finding time and energy to complete successfully commando training at the Royal Marine Commando Training Centre, Lympstone. Prince Andrew proudly received the coveted Green Beret one week before passing out from Dartmouth, in front of Her Majesty The Queen, at Lord High Admiral's Divisions. Unlike his elder brother with prior responsibilities as heir to the throne, Prince Andrew was in a position to make the Navy a longer career. In 1982, as a member of 820 Naval Air squadron he embarked in the aircraft carrier HMS Invincible, he followed in his father's and grandfather's footsteps, going to war in the South Atlantic to retake the Falkland Islands. Subsequently, he served in various appointments, including frigates and commanding a mine countermeasures vessel, before earning promotion to Commander and seeing service in the Ministry of Defence. Prince Andrew finally stepped outside the Service to other State duties in 2002.

HRH The Prince Andrew at the front door to the College while he was under training from September 1979 to April 1980.

Above: Passing Out Platoon marching with Prince Andrew on the back row nearest the camera. April 1980.

Right: On the ceiling of the Wardroom at the College, there are three signatures, Prince Charles, Prince Andrew and Prince Edward (at BRNC for a short introductory course while with the Royal Marines). 'Signing the ceiling', or deckhead as it is known at College is one of the after mess-dinner pastimes of Naval Officers. Indeed legend has it that the deckhead was covered with signatures before it was painted over and just three left. The method of signing is to support the signatory with the aid of a human pyramid. In this rare private photograph, Prince Andrew can be seen 'in action'. More than one officer has suffered broken bones in the past from this and other precarious stunts.

His Royal Highness the Duke of Cambridge

*P*rince William followed in the footsteps of his forbears when he joined Britannia Royal Naval College in June 2008. Having completed his Army Officer Training at the Royal Military Academy Sandhurst in December 2006, Sub-Lieutenant William Wales joined BRNC as part of a two month detachment with the Royal Navy, having completed a similar period with the Royal Air Force. During his time with the Royal Navy the latest Royal student at Dartmouth spent time with the Royal Marines, the Fleet Air Arm and finally saw active service in HMS Iron Duke, engaged in anti-narcotics operations in the West Indies.

In his four days at BRNC Prince William undertook an intensive course covering core skills such as navigation, seamanship and practical boat handling. He was also introduced to the fundamentals of ship behaviour, naval history and enjoyed a historical tour of the College, when he learnt of the experiences of his father, uncle, grandfather and great grandfather; lingering for a while to admire the full dress uniform of King George VI. He concluded his time at the College by continuing a family tradition, signing the ceiling of the Wardroom atop a human pyramid, before completing the even more impressive challenge of circumnavigating the Wardroom without touching the ground.

In August 2006 HM The Queen appointed Prince William Commodore-in-Chief of both Scotland and Submarines.

Right: Sub-Lieutenant W Wales, as he was referred to during his attachment with the Royal Navy, at Sandquay with his classmates.

Above top: William Wales at the helm of a Picket Boat.

Above bottom: Picket Boats on the River Dart during Prince William's visit. These vessels mimic in many respects the handling of a frigate or destroyer thus providing the ideal opportunity for the Prince to practice his boat-handling skills.

CHAPTER 5

The College at War

As the inscription on the front of the College reminds us, the Royal Navy has for centuries provided the wealth, prosperity and peace, upon which Britain has depended to build an empire and spread international trade. In the course of providing the basis for Britain's international power the Navy has inevitably found itself required to go beyond the protection of sea-lanes of communication and play a critical, often decisive, role in the defence of the homeland. Though it may be a less than comfortable thought for those employed at the Royal Navy's College, whether staff officer, academic or student, the ultimate function of the Navy is to go to war in support of the nation's interests. The ultimate function of the Royal Naval College is therefore to educate Naval Officers for the prospect of finding themselves on the front line.

The first half of the College's history was to be punctuated by two world wars, each of which would have a very profound but very different impact upon the College and its population. In many respects it is no coincidence that the First World War broke out as the College began its tenth academic year. The founding of the shore-based College and Admiral Fisher's revolutionary new system of naval education that accompanied it were intricately linked to Britain's perceived need to counter the German Kaiser's growing naval ambitions.

The telegram received by the Captain of the College at 3.50pm on 1st August 1914, from the Commander in Chief Portsmouth, ordering the College to 'mobilise.'

The First World War

On Monday 27th July 1914, the College received a telegram ordering it to standby to mobilise. The next day Austria, having failed to secure the demands of its ultimatum from the Serbian government as recompense for the assassination of their heir to the throne and assured of German support, declared war on Serbia. But as relations among the great powers continued to deteriorate and the armies of Europe began to mobilise, life at Dartmouth carried on as usual. The end of term was approaching and final examinations were underway. By the end of the week hope was fading of the prospect that war might interrupt the College routine. Then at 3.50pm on Saturday 1st August, as a cricket match was being played on the playing field, Captain Victor Stanley received a telegram which simply read; 'mobilise.'

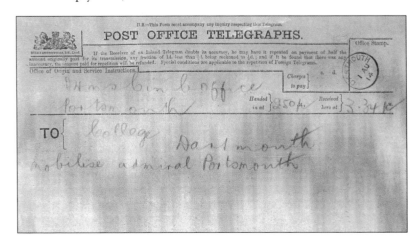

Cadets' sea chests at the back of B block packed and ready for transportation having received the order to 'mobilise' on Saturday 1st August 1914.

The earlier telegram meant that cadets' sea chests had already been packed and orders placed with local vehicle owners to transport the cadets and their belongings down to the railway pontoon. From there they would take the Great Western Railway's ferry boat, the *Mew*, to the railway station in Kingswear, where three trains were standing by to take cadets off to join their appointed ships in Plymouth, Portsmouth and Chatham. Cadets, officers and masters all helped with the loading of chests onto the various assembled vehicles. Soon the line of vehicles loaded with luggage covered almost the entire length of the northern embankment. Cadets marched to the *Mew* in their respective terms, cheered on by large crowds of residents. The first to leave were those with the longest journey ahead of them, the Third and Fourth Terms bound for Chatham. The Portsmouth train went next, carrying the Second and Fifth Terms. Finally the Plymouth train departed Kingswear at 10.46pm, taking the First and Sixth Terms together with nearly two hundred reservists from the ship's company. That night only the officers and masters remained at the College.

However, the speed and efficiency with which the College had mobilised seems not to have been repeated further along the line. The Portsmouth bound cadets had to be turned back, their ships unready

to take them. Their return to Dartmouth was, however brief. Having arrived back at seven o'clock on the Sunday morning they were excused church and that evening departed once again for Portsmouth. Meanwhile at Devonport cadets found themselves sleeping on the floor of the wardroom. The following day turned out wet, with nothing to do but wander around the dockyard admiring the ships, even the church service was cut short as a result of the impending war. But war could not interrupt the completion of naval education, on 3rd August Sixth Term cadets sat their final passing out exam at the Royal Naval Engineering College, Keyham. The next day neutral Belgium was invaded and Britain declared war on Germany.

Captain Stanley's response to the outbreak of war was swift, the College's miniature rifle range was to be open to the public from 10am to 1pm and 2pm to 6pm daily, while for those requiring a little extra tuition the following notice appearing in the town:

'England is at War. Every man should be able to defend his home and use a rifle. The Officers remaining at the College will gladly take drill classes at 3.30 and 6.30 today [5th August]. Volunteers should assemble in front of the College at either of these hours.'

The response was tremendous, the assembled crowd including

The GWR ferry the Mew, *which took Cadets from Dartmouth to Kingswear where they met the trains which would take them to join their appointed ships. This photograph is believed to show troops from the 7th Battalion London Regiment later in 1914.*

the Deputy Mayor, Alderman R. Row, and several other members of the town council, professional men, tradesmen, shop assistants, mechanics and others, all eager to defend their homeland. Captain Stanley addressed them:

> 'I am very glad indeed to see such a response to the appeal sent out this morning. I am not going to detain you long because I am of the opinion, and I expect it is the opinion of everyone here, that it is a time for deeds not words.' (Applause.) 'It is very easy to attain a certain amount of proficiency with a rifle . . . a very short time will suffice. There are a few officers of the College left – only two or three – and there are two or three masters and they are willing to show you how to handle a rifle, for the time may come for you to make use of one.' (*Britannia Magazine*, July 1964.)

By this time there were in fact few officers or masters left at the College. Of the naval staff only the Fleet Surgeon and one naval instructor remained, Captain Stanley himself was soon re-deployed to take command of the ex-Turkish battleship HMS *Erin*, to be temporarily replaced at Dartmouth by Rear Admiral Napier. The College itself, it seemed, might be made ready to act as a hospital for the Grand Fleet, to take care of the casualties of the impending great naval engagement that was expected. However, at the beginning of September it was announced that seventy-five Osborne cadets, and three Conway cadets, would be arriving on the seventeenth (*Dartmouth Chronicle*, 4/9/1914). Only the Headmaster, two heads of department and four other masters would be left to teach them and fill in the gaps left by the staff officers called up into the fleet. At both Dartmouth and Osborne masters took over the duties of term officers, wearing a sort of uniform/academic dress hybrid, consisting of blue suit and mortarboards on divisions (or when officers wore white cap-covers, straw boaters); a system which seems to have worked well. Of the rest

Memorial tablet to Midshipman H. L. Riley, lost in HMS Aboukir *September 22nd 1914, aged 15 years.*

of the academic staff, nine joined the services, including M. Charbonnier of Modern Languages who joined the French army, and eleven were sent to Osborne, which became the focus of naval education. Two more were co-opted to join a new organisation. Sir Alfred Ewing, a Professor of Mechanical Engineering at Cambridge University before being appointed as Director of Naval Education by Fisher, had been approached by Admiral Oliver, Director of Naval Intelligence, to set up an organisation to interpret German signals intelligence. To man this organisation, which became known as Room 40, Ewing turned to his colleagues in the Mathematics and Modern Languages departments at Osborne and Dartmouth. William H. Anstie and Denis Bond were the first recruits, followed in 1915 by A. G. Denniston from Osborne, who went on to become head of Bletchley Park during the Second World War, E. C. J. Green in 1916 and in 1918 by R. P. Keigwin. All these individuals' names were

Passing out photographs from RNC Osborne (these cadets were never to actually pass-out from Dartmouth so these are the only photographs), including twelve of those who died on HMS Aboukir, Cressy *and* Hogue *in September 1914.*

retained on the College Blue Lists, referred to as 'serving at Admiralty.'

At the outbreak of war 434 Dartmouth cadets had been sent, enthusiastically, to sea. They were not however, destined for the pride of the Grand Fleet but as not yet fully-trained naval officers were to find themselves on board older, less capable, more vulnerable vessels. Thus the realities of war were very quickly brought home. On 22nd September the three British cruisers, HMS *Aboukir*, *Hogue* and *Cressy*, were torpedoed in the North Sea by a German submarine, *U-9*. Among the 1,459 officers and men killed were thirteen cadets or midshipmen who seven weeks earlier had left Dartmouth. They were aged between fifteen and sixteen and a half years old. The *Osborne Magazine* records those who had been lost:[1]

1 Throughout the war the *Osborne Magazine* pays more attention to the war than its *Britannia* counterpart. This is perhaps natural as many of the boys sent to sea, who had completed their education at Osborne did not complete their time at Dartmouth.

2 J. A. Froude was the grandson of the historian James Froude of Salcombe and the great nephew of the engineer William Froude (1810–1879). William Froude joined the practice of I. K. Brunel in 1837. In 1844 he worked on the South Devon atmospheric railway, but moved to Dartington Parsonage in 1846 to look after his ailing father. Thereafter Brunel employed him on special projects such as the motion of ships and screw propellers. He went on the maiden voyage of the *Great Eastern* and did work on her stability.

H.M.S. *Aboukir*
Cadet J. D. Stubbs
Cadet G. Gore-Brown
Cadet G. B. Barchard
Cadet A. V. G. Allsopp
Cadet H. L. Riley
Cadet A. D. C. Robertson

H.M.S. *Cressy*
Midshipman C. P. Dalmege
Midshipman V. H. Corbyn
Midshipman F. G. Matthews
Midshipman J. A. Froude[2]

H.M.S. *Hogue*
Midshipman H. H. Ward
Midshipman G. C. Harold
Midshipman C. W. Holt

Amongst the controversy as to how these ageing vessels had been allowed to patrol unprotected and unprepared for engagement with the enemy, questions were also raised as to the rationale behind sending boys to sea. The case was taken up by Mr W. Joynson-Hicks, Conservative MP for Brentford, who wrote a letter to the *Morning Post* criticising the First Lord of the Admiralty, Winston Churchill: 'It must be understood that I am not speaking of Midshipmen who are not gazetted younger than 17 but of children who can do no possible good on board men-of-war in time of action . . . Their room would be much more valuable on board than their presence [for example, stories told of German prisoners having

to sleep, and die, lying under cadets' hammocks after the battle of Heligoland Bight].

Perhaps the Admiralty answer would be that it is desirable to harden boys but if Mr Churchill will only apply to the officers in command of cruisers where these boys are, I think he will be told that they would be better sent back to complete their education at Dartmouth, and that by so doing they will preserve the supply of officers for the navy of the future which is seriously endangered by the result of the disasters such as we are bound to expect in the course of a prolonged and difficult war.' (*Dartmouth Chronicle*, 2/10/1914.)

Other accounts, however, suggest a more positive contribution to the war effort. Cadets Riley and Stubbs of *Aboukir* had died while going to the assistance of a drowning man who had taken them under, while the newly-commissioned Midshipman Cazalet of the *Cressy*, using a whaler, had picked up eighty-eight survivors from the *Cressy* and *Hogue*, including the *Cressy*'s commander. The official Admiralty response was also unrepentant about the decision, made sometime before the outbreak of war, to discharge cadets from Dartmouth to help relieve the reserve fleet. As Churchill explained to the House of Commons, it was felt that these young officers would be very useful on board ship as part of the regular complement, and that they would learn far more of their profession at sea than they would at any educational establishment. As for their return to Dartmouth, that would depend largely on the duration of the war and was felt to be unlikely. Meanwhile, any future decisions to send cadets from Dartmouth to sea would depend upon the operational requirements of the fleet. Nevertheless, by the beginning of 1915 of those 434 cadets who had marched singing and cheering to meet their trains at Kingswear, forty-one had lost their lives, a greater proportion than any other class of naval officer in the fleet (*Dartmouth Chronicle*, 12/2/1915.)

Ironically, while at sea cadets and midshipmen were officially considered as undergoing continued naval training. Consequently their parents were still expected to pay a fifty pounds allowance to the Admiralty. When questioned in the House, Dr Macnamara replied on behalf of the Admiralty that;

'it would be prepared to give favourable consideration to applications for whole or partial relief where necessity exists, and further, that in the case of midshipmen killed in active service any sums deposited in advance in a period subsequent to the death are returned to the guardians upon the closing of the private allowance accounts of the officers concerned.' (*Dartmouth Chronicle* 26/2/1915.)

Those in this photograph had only just completed their first term at Dartmouth and many of them were barely fifteen years old. By the time the war was over most of the cadets from 1914 would have seen service in the Grand Fleet, being involved in the Gallipoli landings and the Battle of Jutland.

Midshipmen's Journals

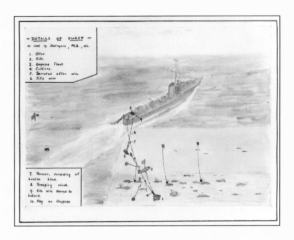

O n completion of their time at Dartmouth the newly commissioned midshipmen remained under training on board their first ship. During this time they were required to keep a journal, or diary, of the day-to-day life of the most junior officer in the Royal Navy. The College archive retains a selection of these journals, dating from the mid-nineteenth to mid-twentieth centuries. Of particular historical interest is the collection of Second World War journals, many of which chronicle some of the major events of the war at sea, from the Battle of the River Plate to the

D-Day landings. During the War it was necessary to impound journals completed by midshipmen during their training on board cruisers and destroyers of the fleet. Such journals would contain classified materials and information about Allied operations. The Naval College was one of the holding authorities of these impounded journals, some of which were not collected at the end of the War and therefore remained in the College archive. History aside these journals also demonstrate the dedication and in may cases real artistic and literary talents of their authors.

Midshipman P H Owen HMS Royal Oak, Scapa Flow, 14th October 1939

Mid. Owen had joined Royal Oak *on 25th August 1939, straight from Dartmouth. On the night of the 13th-14th October the ship was lying at berth in Scapa Flow, when she came under attack from a German U-boat. Owen's journal recalls the night's events:*

'It was about 0120…that the first tremendous explosion woke up the Ship's Company. The general assumption was that a bomb hit us and many men manned the A.A. stations; others went under armour; but very many turned over and went back to sleep again…

'The Midshipmen had just been shaken by the instructor Lieutenant when at 0140 three or possibly four shattering explosions occurred at about 3 second intervals and the ship immediately started listing to starboard…

'Twenty minutes after the ship had first been torpedoed no definite steps had been taken by anyone to save the ship or her company, and there was no more time as the final explosion had caused her to keel over very rapidly – she was uppermost 7 minutes later, according to witnesses in the *Pegasus*.

'As the ship started listing the lights went out, and the ladders grew progressively more difficult for everyman to negotiate – and virtually impossible for the 1100 odd men trapped below…

'The picket boat got away and picked up about 60 men and all went well until the officer in charge told these men to

paddle, causing the boat to roll on her beam ends, shaking off several people, who finally capsized the outfit by trying to climb back…The only man to reach the launch at her boom was the Midshipman of the boat, who unfortunately was not able to clear her before she was pulled under as she was moored up by too short a strop…

— H.M.S. JACKAL —

A POM-POM'S CREW IN ACTION.

'In the water there must have been about 600 men, of whom very many were picked up by the drifter off the port quarter and beam. Others met their fate with the picket boat and quite a number were picked up by the boats from the *Pegasus*. 15 men reached the shore and the remaining were drowned. The Flow was extremely cold and there was very little wreckage about; on the starboard side the oil fuel was very oppressive indeed and many men brought up solid fuel for hours afterwards.'

Midshipman G R Shaw HMS **Rodney**, *May 1941*

Mid. G R Shaw had joined Dartmouth in May 1939, two years later he found himself on board HMS Rodney *as she joined the chase to sink the* Bismarck.

'Tuesday 27th May – The Commander-in-Chief signalled he was going to work round to the westward and attack at dawn, while torpedo attacks by the destroyers were carried out under cover of darkness…

'The long wait throughout the night was somewhat trying, but soon after dawn I climbed the 6th D.C.T. and settled down. At 0800 the destroyers of the 4th Flotilla came in sight and at 0845 *Norfolk* could be seen on the horizon. It would only be a few minutes until we sighted *Bismarck*.

'The ADP reported her to be on the starboard bow, the aloft director was soon bearing, and a minute later the 16-inch opened fire. *King George V* on our starboard beam followed immediately with her main armament.

'A few seconds later the Captain altered course to starboard and I got my first view of the enemy through my glasses. She was steering towards us with an inclination of about 160 right and looked a huge ship. We saw our 16-inch fall round her, then two flashes as she opened fire at *Rodney*, at the same time altering course to starboard. We opened fire with the 6-inch at 20,000

yards and by this time it had ceased fire and her control top was burning momentarily. She looked very impressive – huge splashes coming up all round her, while she came on towards us the seas sweeping off the huge flare on her bows…'

'When we altered course for what turned out to be the last run on the port side, *Bismarck* was a grand but ghastly sight. Water poured from the numerous holes in her bows as she rose clear of the seas. Her guns were lying drunkenly at all angles, upperworks smashed and blowing, smoke pouring from the funnel, flames licking round her barbettes and numerous flashes denoting our shells were hitting, while 'shorts' and 'overs' threw up a cascade of water all around the doomed vessel…

'The enemy turned and sank when we were about three miles away and *Hood's* loss was avenged. Considering the odds against her and the disabilities she was already suffering from, *Bismarck* put up a great fight, and her builders were undoubtedly justified when they claimed her to be the most powerful warship afloat. She was the finest looking ship I have ever seen, and it was pitiful to see her in the final phase of the action beaten and battered but still giving the impression of immense power.'

— H.M.S. REVENGE —

All these illustrations are taken from the journal of Midshipman D. V. M. Moore. Clearly a gifted artist, Moore found himself in the North Atlantic and English Channel on board HMS *Revenge* between May 1940 and October 1941.

Meanwhile, back at Dartmouth, two Terms joined from Osborne in January 1915, bringing the College population up to 236. From April that year there were four Terms, rising to five in September 1916, when 121 cadets who had joined Osborne in 1914 moved up to the senior College. Despite this huge increase in numbers, reaching a peak of 535 in May 1918, cadets would only actually spend three terms (one year) in the College, rather than the pre-war six (two years), before being sent to sea.

In order to accommodate the projected rise in the number of cadets, work began as early as 1914 to build an extra accommodation block, to become known as D block. However, as the war effort continued labour around Dartmouth became increasingly scarce. In order to attract labourers it was therefore necessary to offer higher wages, a strategy that was met with hostility by local farmers who were unable to compete. D block was finally opened in 1917, just in time to accommodate the great increase in the number of students.

In June 1916 Dartmouth was to suffer yet another casualty of war. Since the shore based College opened HMS *Britannia* had continued to lie in the River Dart. In February 1915 she had been sold to Messers Hughes, Bolckow & Co. of Blyth. Work had begun to remove the top hamper and upper works; the figurehead was also removed to eventually find its resting-place ashore. A public outcry ensued, leading to the setting up of a 'Britannia Fund,' which secured the option to buy the old hulk for the nation and possibly turn it into an orphanage for servicemen's children. However, such were the demands of the war effort that finally it was decided that the old ship should be broken up so as to provide copper, iron and lead for conversion into munitions.

Throughout the war, for those who remained at the College, life had continued as normally as possible, save the occasional alert caused by the sighting of a German trawler[3]. Finally, on 11th November 1918 the College received news of the cessation of hostilities. The editor of the *Britannia Magazine* summed up the sentiments of the time:

' "The war is won," and the world will not forget the part the British Navy played. Nor shall we in our rejoicings forget those naval officers of every rank from Admiral to Cadet who have given their lives for the great Ideal.' (*Britannia Magazine*, December 1918).

The academic and naval staff of the College outside the canteen (now the pavilion) in the autumn of 1941. Notably many of the civilians are wearing uniform, principally that of the Home Guard. The Captain R L B Cunliffe is in the centre of the second row, with the Headmaster, E W E Kempson on his right. The second Director of Studies, G W E Ghey is also pictured, second from the right on the second row, as is the first woman on the staff, Second Officer Morris, the Captain's secretary, who is in front of the Captain.

3 See The Royal College Chapter 4.

The Second World War

Tragically the optimism that followed the end of the Great War was to be short lived. Just two decades later another generation of aspiring naval officers was to find itself, along with the rest of the world, dragged into a second, deadlier conflict. Once again, the Royal Navy would be called upon to fight, not just for the British Empire but for the preservation of civilisation.

The summer term of 1939 at Dartmouth had passed tranquilly enough, culminating in the royal visit of the King and Queen and their two daughters to the College. The visit was regarded as a great success and when the royal party left in the royal yacht *Victoria and Albert*, it was accompanied by cadets manning every boat the college could muster. The royal party was cheered heartily as they sailed out of the harbour. A dinghy was called alongside the yacht and a message lowered to it. It contained a signal from the King giving an extra four days leave at the end of the summer holidays, thus inspiring further cheers from the cadets. However, by the time they returned to the College in September Britain was at war.

The disruption and major changes that had marked the start of the First World War at the College were not repeated in 1939. College life continued much as it had done in peacetime and the changes were initially much more gradual. The German navy was unready for war in 1939 and did not have a large capital fleet ready for action. Consequently the regular Dartmouth cadets were not required to mobilise as the Royal Naval Reserve (RNR) and Royal Naval Volunteer Reserve (RNVR) could be relied upon along with the Special Entry cadets.

Unlike 1914 the College retained many of its officers, although the principle had been established that they would be drawn mainly from the retired list and from those medically unfit from the active list. The result was not unwelcome to cadets, who found the older 're-treads' more kindly disposed than the younger, keener house officers, being no longer concerned by the prospect of promotion (Holloway 1993, p.26). Captain Dalrymple-Hamilton was replaced after approximately two months of the first term of the war and the Commander a month later, thus ensuring some continuity of the senior officers and avoiding the situation that was inflicted upon the College in 1914 when the College was stripped of senior officers. The new Captain of the College was R.B.L. Cunliffe, the first Captain to have been a cadet at the shore based College, all previous commanding officers having been from the *Britannia*. The Commander and the First Lieutenant were both replaced by officers from the retired list, as were several other appointments. These were the first real changes, but one of the most obvious transformations was amongst the masters, many of whom began to wear the uniform of the Home Guard while others left to join the regular armed forces. Other noticeable changes included the blacked out windows, which at least meant curtains for the previously bare windows, and

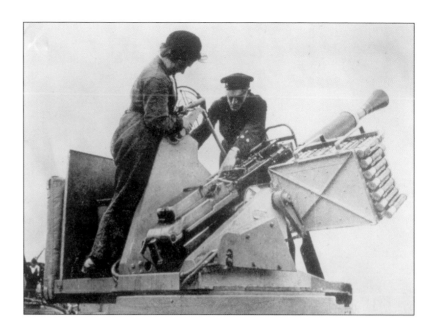

A Wren receives instruction on a two pound 'pom-pom' gun, thought to be on the top of D block.

Cadets filling sandbags outside D block, in anticipation of an attack.

as further air raid precautions the painted figurehead of *Britannia* on the parade ground, originally white, was painted black while the concrete parade ground itself was covered in asphalt. Those masters in the Home Guard formed their own unit in Dartmouth, and as befitted their position, were all made officers, one Captain and all the others Lieutenants. Their duties usually included guarding key sites such as the water tower on the hill above the town.

Meanwhile among the cadets, difficulties with the laundry led to shorts replacing white flannel trousers as part of the daily rig. Rationing also began to hit provisions in the Gunroom. A notice read that 'from Friday onwards milk will be rationed. It will be mixed with the tea and coffee. At breakfast 10 jugs of milk will be allocated to each table for use with porridge only. Milk is not available as a separate drink.' Worse was to come, as one line book entry commented despondently: 'lamb stew (staple food of the Cadets at the Royal Naval College) is now made out of leaves, as is borne out by the above (sic) specimen found in the portion of lamb 'stoo' assigned to Cadet Gettez'.

In February 1940 the recently re-appointed First Lord of the Admiralty, Sir Winston Churchill, visited the College while in the area to welcome home the damaged HMS *Exeter* after her success at the Battle of the River Plate. In a morale-boosting visit, he inspected the cadets and afterwards addressed them from the upper gallery of the Quarterdeck. During the visit the First Lord enquired of the history master, Mr Ted Hughes, how much history was taught. He was clearly pleased with the answer, replying 'I am very glad to hear that you teach so much history: it is the one guide to the future' he then paused and added, almost to himself, 'that and imagination'.

By the spring of 1940 the war was really starting to disrupt the College routine. The location of the College, the shipyard at Noss and the fact that Dartmouth and Kingswear were used as bunkering ports for the coaling of ships, made Dartmouth a prime target for air raids. Precautions had to be taken. The clock bells were silenced and barbed wire was placed around the buildings. Senior cadets were arranged into watches to cover fire parties and demolition and decontamination squads. These duties also continued through leave, with cadets divided in two, half of whom stayed on two weeks after the end of term and the others being recalled two weeks before the start of the next term. Routine was very much relaxed during these periods, although uniform was still worn. The summer leave, with its longer days of daylight was excluded from this procedure, which was eventually abandoned altogether. House officers were issued with ammunition and hand grenades to be kept in their rooms should there be an attack at night. A Special Service Company of local volunteers was formed, comprising sixty men who were trained in the use of revolvers and rifles, sten gun handling and grenade throwing. Cadets were also employed to make sandbags, which were deployed around the College, just as they had been in the autumn of 1938 in response to the Munich crisis. On that occasion the

preparation of College defences had been the cause of much excitement, as the Blake Line Book of the time describes:

'Parties were detailed off to do various jobs. Two groups of large cadets were marched off like 'iron guards' carrying picks and shovels at the slope. One lot went and filled sandbags; the others worked on the bank outside. A third party of smaller people carried and piled the bags into protective ramparts for A.R.P. stations. Intensive energy and excitement prevailed in all quarters, since we never knew whether we might be mobilised and rushed off the next day, or the College bombed within the next week.'

The buildings were also beginning to show signs that Britain was at war. The service passages beneath the building were utilised as air raid shelters, but they were cramped and carried the heating pipes and as such were not ideal for the new use, hence a number of shelters were built in the grounds. Some of these still exist and are used as storage areas. The upper dormitories were vacated and the ground floor boot rooms were cleared so that they could be used as sleeping areas.

At the outbreak of war the Admiralty had appointed a retired naval officer to the position of 'Naval Officer in Charge' (NOIC) of the port of Dartmouth, his jurisdiction extending along the coast from Salcombe in South Devon to Beer in East Devon. In early 1940 this position of NOIC Dartmouth was combined with that of Captain of the College. It was not long before the spaces vacated in the College began to be filled with the expanding NOIC's staff and a large contingent from the WRNS. The Wrens manned a telephone exchange, operations room and wireless transmitting station in the space under the terrace facing the parade ground. Huts were erected around the grounds for gunnery and torpedo training, the band practice room was commandeered as an aircraft recognition centre and even the beagles gave up their kennels so that pigs could be kept to help with the war effort.

Inevitably, the fortunes of the Royal Navy throughout the war had their impact on the cadets. On 14th October 1939, HMS *Royal Oak* was sunk by a German U-boat in Scapa Flow. Amongst the 809 men and twenty-four officers who lost their lives were midshipmen who had only left Dartmouth the previous summer; 'that did more than anything else to bring home to us what war was all about – killing and being killed' (Holloway 1993, p.27). An entry in the Exmouth Line Book of 1941 recalls that 'Philip Peck, cadet captain of the Exmouth House, and chief cheerer for the 'mumps' ward when the King and Queen visited [in 1939] has drowned while serving as a Midshipman in HMS *Wryneck*[4]. We are all saddened'.

In May 1940 the war really came to Dartmouth. One former cadet recalls walking onto the Quarterdeck and being struck by an unfamiliar smell. It was the odour of the 'unwashed human bodies, particularly feet' (Holloway 1993, p.33) belonging to soldiers of the British Expeditionary Force, recently evacuated from Dunkirk.

4 The destroyer HMS *Wryneck* was sunk off Greece in 1941

These photographs were all taken by Mr John Barlee MSc. a master and lecturer at the College from 1939 to 1976. Although at the time of the first bombing the College had not resumed from its summer break, Mr Barlee was working in one of the classrooms off the Quarterdeck, formerly known as the Great Hall, on the morning of 18th September 1942. He was almost half way between where the two bombs fell. After the second bomb he managed to vacate the classroom, where remarkably, only the soles of his shoes were damaged. He found a group digging frantically for someone buried in the rubble, "we are looking for Mr Barlee" they said as they had not recognised the figure of Mr Barlee, completely covered in dust, standing next to them. Being a keen photographer Mr Barlee collected his camera from the Common Room and took these photographs.

Right: The western side of the gallery destroyed, feet from where the second bomb fell.

Debris from the collapsed roof of the Quarterdeck, looking towards the corner classroom where John Barlee was when the two bombs fell.

During the following summer leave two companies of the Durham Light Infantry were housed in the College to be refitted and rehabilitated after their experiences. Meanwhile the River Dart was crammed with fishing trawlers from France, Belgium and Holland. Among them were two French tugs, which were taken over and commissioned with their own crews to work on the river. While these French ships were in Dartmouth a daily news sheet was organised, typed and distributed to them by cadets. In July 1940 it was decided that all French naval ships had to be taken over and their crews given the option of joining the Free French or being returned to France. Cadets provided the armed guards and the ships' companies were taken to the Guildhall where a statement was read to them giving them this option. According to Captain Cunliffe, writing in the *Britannia Magazine* in 1947: 'Not many volunteered to join the Free French but the incident passed off without any trouble but it was a terrible thing to have to do.' (*Britannia Magazine*, Easter 1947, p.6)

The French were not the only visitors to Dartmouth. In October 1941 twenty Norwegian Cadets were attached to the Special Entry. They were subsequently visited by HM The King of Norway and the Crown Prince, who spent a weekend at the College. Sixty years later HRH Crown Prince Haakon was to take the salute at Lord High Admiral's Divisions.

With the fall of France, the invasion of England appeared imminent. Beach defences, gun emplacements, search-lights, harbour booms and torpedo defences were constructed all along the south coast. In South Devon these were the responsibility of NOIC Dartmouth and consequently involved the College. The mobile naval battery was located at the College for a time and when the Dartmouth battery was ready, before the gun crew could arrive, a group of senior cadets took charge for a few days and fired several trial rounds, an exciting prospect for the cadets involved. Other cadets found themselves being deployed on the streets of Dartmouth to guard against fifth columnists, although quite what they were to do should they meet any was never elaborated upon! The College was also used for exercises, usually for the Commandos quartered in the neighbourhood to capture the College and port, as reported in the Exmouth Line Book:

'A mock battle took place, in which 800 soldiers took part with the College as the objective. Some of the attackers crossed the river in boats, others came from the direction of Norton, all were armed with Tommy guns, rifles, dummy grenades etc with blank ammunition. Various umpires gauged the progress of the fighting and with great difficulty allotted casualties. At the end of the afternoon it was decided that the hospital had been captured, but elsewhere the attackers had been repulsed with heavy losses'.

As Captain Cunliffe recalled, however, there was not always fair play: 'On one occasion the enemy was deemed to have cheated, as they drove through our patrols in a hearse, the coffin draped with a Union Flag containing machine guns and other lethal weapons.

On another occasion shortly after a similar exercise at Newton Abbot, where we were informed the Mayor had surrendered the town and collaborated with the enemy, an exercise was staged at Dartmouth. Our Mayor, being determined that there should be no similar occurrence, evaded capture by hiding together with the City Fathers and the Captain's wife, who was the W.V.S. Liaison Officer, under a bridge while the enemy went over it. The sight of this distinguished party must have been worth seeing but they lived to fight another day. The last full scale exercise was held in bitter weather early in 1942 and went on for 24 hours. It was so cold that the water froze in the Cadets' water bottles, and two regular soldiers died of exposure.' (*Britannia Magazine*, Easter 1947, p.8).

Two of the steamers on the River Dart were requisitioned in case of invasion and kept fully stocked with provisions to evacuate the Junior College up river if necessary, thus denying the invading forces of four year's supply of future officers. This threat was also taken seriously by the Admiralty, a memorandum dated 14th April 1942 from their Lordships to the Captain of the College informed him of alternative accommodation arrangements for the cadets should the need arise. It stated that the cadets and their teaching and domestic staff would be sent as follows: seventy-two to Shrewsbury School, seventy-two to St Chad's College, Denstone, Staffordshire, ninety to King William's College, Castletown, Isle of Man, and thirty-six to Trent College, Long Eaton Derbyshire. This amounted to 270 cadets, that is six full terms of forty-five. However, when the College was bombed, only five months after the issue of the above memorandum, the plan was not executed, perhaps because the school terms had already started and it would have caused too much disruption.

The Captain issued guidance to deal with the threat of daylight air raids, a copy of which still exists in the College Archive, as reproduced below.

PROPOSED TEMPORARY ORDERS TO BE BROUGHT INTO FORCE CONSEQUENT ON LOW FLYING DAYLIGHT BOMBING

1. Cadets are always to carry Steel Helmets when in the College building and grounds.
2. Divisions are to be cut as short as possible not more than 2 terms are to be fallen in together.
3. Meals – Dartmouth cadets and Special Entry cadets are to mess at different times in the cadets mess to avoid too large an assembly of cadets.
4. Church – Divine Service in the Chapel is to be conducted as at present with two services, Dartmouth Cadets and Special Entry Cadets at separate services.
5. Class Rooms – In the event of a snap raid cadets should take cover under the desks and wear steel helmets.
  No cadets are to take cover near a door or window.

The statue of King George V survives with minor damage from the destruction of the Quarterdeck. Photograph by John Barlee.

Officers and masters instructing cadets are requested to carry steel helmets and to wear them as necessary both for an example to the cadets and for their own safety.

6. Living spaces, classrooms, lecture-rooms etc., inhabited by cadets are always to have glass windows and roofs protected on the inboard side by wire.

7. Practice "take cover" for cadets is to be frequently exercised and times taken to improve times to a minimum.

8. It should be impressed on all that for this type of raid there is no warning, if unidentified aircraft are heard approaching, give the order to take cover at once, if it is a false alarm so much the better.

9. If a raid takes place with cadets:-
   a In the playing fields, cadets should dive into the nearest cover and to lie flat, if no cover lie flat and still.
   b If on the river lie still in the bottom of the boat. On no account look up.

10. This type of raid takes place with such speed and suddenness that it is not intended that cadets should take up A.R.P. stations until the raid is over.

11. Steps are being taken to distribute classroom instruction into more widely separated buildings such as the Hostel, the Cadet's Canteen, the Gymnasium.

Any further suggestions by officers and masters will be welcomed NOW.

(Sgd) E.A. Aylmer
CAPTAIN

These orders illustrate how real the threat of air raids was considered to be. Throughout the war there were hundreds of alerts, the majority passing without serious consequences. The area did however suffer attacks on at least nine occasions, inflicting some damage. Bombs also fell in the estuary and on the surrounding countryside. Dartmouth suffered two major raids, the first on 18th September 1942 and the second on 13th February 1943, when the town suffered considerable damage. In the second raid the College building, now abandoned by its staff and students, received a direct hit. The bomb fell on D Block crashing through one of the Hawke dormitories and finally coming to rest in the Common Room, but fortunately failed to explode. That particular bomb now stands outside Ashford House, inscribed 'a present from Adolf Hitler'.

September 1942 had seen the arrival of both a new Captain and a new Headmaster, but neither of them was to be afforded the luxury of a long honeymoon to acquaint himself with the ways of the College. Mr J. W. Stork had taken up his duties about two weeks prior to the beginning of the new term. After only one week in his new position he was in a meeting in the Commander's day cabin discussing arrangements for the new term. It was the morning of Friday 18th September and after discussing arrangements for the new term the meeting went on to discuss the provisions that had been made for the evacuation of the College, should the need arise. The group was sitting around the table when six Focke-Wulf aeroplanes attacked the College, approaching from the east down Noss Creek, so as to avoid anti-aircraft fire from the town's defences. The first bomb fell only feet away from the meeting, near the junction of O and B Blocks. When the second bomb struck the north-west corner of the Quarterdeck the group was already under the table or behind the settee. The large oak door to the Commander's cabin was blasted into the room smashing a chair that only seconds before had been in use. As the Commander remarked at the time, they had been discussing a most appropriate subject.

But while the occupants of the Commander's cabin had a lucky escape not every one was to be so fortunate. Wren Betty Joan Blake worked in the Confidential Book Office, together with her assistant, Ruth Blake:

'On the morning of September 18th 1942, Ruth and I had to toss a coin as to who should leave the office first to go to the Wren's loo! She won. A few seconds later I heard the all too familiar sound of German aircraft followed shortly by bombs smashing masonry. The office shook. I ran to the quarterdeck, which was adjacent to the classrooms, into a dense cloud of dust, and saw a gaping hole at the north east corner of the area. Because the cadets were away on summer leave the classrooms were empty. The quarterdeck floor was sagging outside the door to the plotting room. I shouted to them not to open the door. I believe they were later able to get out through the front windows. The Wren's loo was beneath the quarterdeck area and I feared for Ruth's safety. When I went down the staircase and saw a mound of stone and rubble against the loo I feared the worst. There was no answer when I called to her. Some College retainers heard me and came out to clear the rubble. At last we heard Ruth's faint voice say, "I am alive but I think the girl in the next cubicle is dead. There is a large stone block balanced across the partition above my head, so how will you open the door to get me out?" Very carefully the men released her. She was lucky to have survived and was surprisingly calm. But, the shock set in later. The girl who died was P.O. Ellen Victoria Whittall. She was crushed by masonry'.

Ellen Whittall was the only fatality from the bombing, but the casualty list could have been much longer. It has been suggested that the raid had been carefully planned to take place the day after the cadets had arrived for the start of term. This might have been the case except that every six years one extra week was added onto the summer leave to even out the terms. Luckily this was one of those years, had it not been, a generation of future naval officers might have been wiped out.

The Captain sent the following memorandum to the Commander-in-Chief Plymouth, detailing the attack and its consequences.

Photographs were taken from a photograph album belonging to Lt-Cdr Mellor RN, who was on the naval staff at the time.

The entry point of the second bomb and the damaged roof of the Quarterdeck.

Above: Closer view of the damage, the hole left by the first bomb having removed parts of the walls of both the front and rear of the B Block.

Right: Damage to the roof of the Quarterdeck after it had been made safe.

CONFIDENTIAL
TO C in C PLYMOUTH   FROM, N.O.I.C. Dartmouth

At 1131/18 six FW 190's attacked Dartmouth. They approached from the east down Noss Creek, height varying between 100 and 300 feet. Two bombs were dropped near R.F.A. BERTA damaging M.L.155 oiling alongside causing 5 slight casualties. Arrangements have been made to beach M.L.155 at high water. Two bombs burst apparently under the collier FERNWOOD, which sank with 4 or 5 casualties and slightly damaged H.M.S. SELKIRK coaling alongside. Two bombs fell in the river below lower hulks, no damage; two UXB's suspected in this area.

2.   R.N. College was hit by two bombs, substantial damage to Centre block. Casualties at R.N. College one Wren killed, one WT gunner serious and several slight.

3.   One bomb fell in machine shop Noss works, casualties about 20 to date.
     Detailed report follows.

4.   One plane seen to spin and dive seawards near Mansands.

5.   Amplifying signal will be made.

The amplifying message carried the following, detailing the damage.

DAMAGE TO R. N. COLLEGE, DARTMOUTH

CENTRE BLOCK Grand Hall roof 50% demolished remainder unsafe. 40% of gallery demolished. N.W. corner walls demolished. Bay immediately E of Main Entrance demolished, ceiling above and W. wall. 2 No. studies demolished, remainder windows and doors affected by blast, these can soon be made tenable.

'A' BLOCK   Very minor damage from blast, 3 No. windows out, quantity of glass broken.

'B' BLOCK   W. end of Block damaged, wall demolished and floors and ceilings at this end unsafe. Temporary shoring carried out. 60% of Block safe and tenable.

'C' BLOCK   Very minor damage from blast. 6 No. windows out, small quantity of glass broken.

'D' BLOCK   Glass broken by blast only.

General   Water services only slightly affected, Gas services and Drains unaffected.

That Dartmouth was a potential target had never been in doubt, as borne out by a copy of a Luftwaffe reconnaissance photograph in the College Archive collection. This photograph clearly shows the estuary and surrounding area with the College, the railway station at Kingswear, Noss shipyard, and the gasworks, all described in some detail. The enemy was doubtless aware that the College was training future officers, not only for the Royal Navy but for allied navies too, presenting it as a legitimate and important target. Nevertheless, for the first two years of the war the College was apparently a prohibited target, it can only be assumed that although its destruction would have helped the enemy, its continued existence would also have been useful to an invading force. What use Hitler might have had for the College is a matter of conjecture, but the College survived the first two years of the war intact. Nevertheless, low flying German aircraft passed over the College frequently, day and night, their continuous noise often making it impossible for a class to hear an officer or master unless he shouted (Hughes 1950).

The day after the raid, Saturday 19th September, both the Captain and the Headmaster went to see the Commander-in-Chief, Plymouth to discuss the future of the College. As a result of this meeting the Captain and the Headmaster, along with the Second Master, Mr Hughes, the Commander, the First Lieutenant, the Surgeon Commander and the Paymaster Captain travelled to Bristol for a meeting at the Muller Orphanage (later HMS *Cabot*). The meeting was to discuss the provision of accommodation for the junior cadets, who were due to join the College on Thursday 24th September, the orphanage having already been identified as a possible site for relocation.

Two blocks of the orphanage were to be utilised requiring some alterations to the buildings. The orphanage swimming pool and the grounds of the Gloucestershire Cricket Club were also requisitioned. Arrangements had to be made to move all the necessary equipment to Bristol and so it was not until 29th October 1942 that the transfer of the cadets could be made. The orphanage housed the seven junior terms and was known as HMS *Bristol*. A memorandum dated 6th October 1942 states that the orphanage would be commissioned as *Britannia IV*, but this name was not used, presumably to avoid confusion with the college at Dartmouth, which still retained the name HMS *Britannia*. The cadets settled in quickly and were soon organised into their daily routines (including fire watches) as had been the case at Dartmouth. One Dartmouth house officer, while visiting HMS *Bristol*, was reminded of Osborne, the keenness of the cadets there capturing the spirit of the former junior college.

It was only the juniors that went to Bristol, the four senior terms joined Dartmouth later in the autumn term and resumed their studies under difficult circumstances. The canteen (today the Pavilion) was utilised as classrooms for the cadets, who were required to take cover during air raid warnings, even during passing out examinations. By this time a number of staff who had formerly been masters at

The entry point of the first bomb, the temporary steelwork supporting the walls and roof, clearly visible. The pile of rubble is all that remains of the toilets where PO Wren Ellen Whittall was killed.

The only known photograph of the College at Muller's Orphanage, Ashley Down in Bristol, showing divisions in the winter of 1942 — 43.

Osborne and Dartmouth were brought out of retirement to help overcome the staff shortages. Amongst these were Messrs Darby, Harrison, Hughes-Games and Warner. The disruption to College life was borne well and with high spirits among the cadets and the staff. Nevertheless it must have been with some relief that both junior and senior colleges learnt that they were to be reunited, in early 1943, at the Duke of Westminster's ancestral home at Eaton Hall in Cheshire.

In 1942 the Hall was in use as an Army rehabilitation centre which had built a number of huts in the grounds, but it was obvious from the initial visit by the Captain and an inspecting party that more were needed. The Hall and grounds were let upon payment of a peppercorn rent coupled with a full repairing lease, a lucrative arrangement for the Duke as the wiring and lead plumbing were in constant need of attention. The re-location would naturally have required a great deal of planning. Everything that had been taken to Bristol had to be moved to Eaton Hall, while what was to be taken from Dartmouth, where the senior terms had remained, depended largely on the space available at Eaton. A memorandum dated 8th November 1942 from the Commanding Officer HMS *Bristol* to the Captain HMS *Britannia*, reporting on a visit to the Hall, makes interesting reading. The edited version appears below.

Accommodation
The College would require the following.
1. Quarters for the Drakes and Drake HO – arranged.
2. Matron's Quarters arranged.
3. W.R.N.S Officers sleeping quarters and sitting room arranged.

Through the magnificent iron gates are visible the temporary huts of the Royal Naval College at Eaton Hall.

4. (a) Senior Officers & Masters	–	9 single, 1 double room.
(b) Other Officers & Masters	–	26 in Hall.
Officers	–	7 in Huts.
Masters	–	8 over stables.
Masters	–	4 in Agent's House.
		56
Required		15 rooms for Masters.

Houses available for Captain, Headmaster, and remaining Masters:-
1. Eccleston Hall - one and a quarter miles from Hall (N) 13 bed.
2. Alford Rectory - one and a quarter miles from Hall (S) 5 bed.
3. Footsmans Block -   6 bed.

Stokers, nine in number, can be accommodated in North Wing attics.

Hospital has not yet been found, possibilities:-

1. Saighton Grange.
2. Boldsworth Castle
3. Build for R.N.C.

W.R.N.S accommodation will be in Huts. The Superintendent of W.R.N.S. and S.C.E. will arrange site and layout.

It can be seen from the above that much work remained to be done to prepare Eaton Hall for the arrival of not only the cadets but also the W.R.N.S. There was a telephone switchboard but only two outside lines and fourteen internal extensions, though at the time no one actually knew where these were located. A larger switchboard was obviously necessary and the work put in hand. Fourteen extra huts were to be built in addition to the six already

The Hawke Term huts add a regimented dimension to the formal gardens of the Eaton Estate.

The Captain and an unknown Admiral take the salute at the march past at what appears to be a passing-out parade in front of Eaton Hall.

A group of WRNS Officers mix with other members of the College staff, including on the left, the legendary Miss Bulla.

there. These would be the gunrooms, classrooms, sleeping huts and washing blocks. The existing sleeping huts were to be modified by putting in fitments for basins and an Elsan, no running water or drains were to be provided.

Once the accommodation had been taken care of, the training needs of the cadets also had to be considered. While at Dartmouth the close proximity of the River Dart for all river activities and seamanship training could be taken for granted. The fact that Eaton Hall stood beside the lower reaches of the River Dee, which was fairly wide and not too swiftly flowing, was therefore a major consideration in the choice of the site. Negotiations were made with the local boatman at Eaton, a Mr Probyn, who had been hiring out boats. He agreed to take the position of Head Boatman and gave up his business putting his boat shed, landing pontoon and bank moorings at the College's disposal. The site was not ideal, being liable to flooding in the winter, but it would offer boat training for the cadets, and so was made ready to receive the boats from Dartmouth in early 1943.

Formality meets the formal as divisions take place in the grounds of Eaton Hall. The group in the lower left-hand corner are WRNS personnel on administrative duties.

Naval additions, including the bell from the battleship HMS Britannia and the College's ensign, to the impressive entrance hall of the Duke of Westminster's residence.

The move north to Cheshire required a co-ordinated effort. The Great Western Railway, just as in the First World War, competently and without fuss moved everything needed. The boats were taken either entirely by rail or to Ellesmere Port from where they were moved via the Manchester Ship and the Shropshire Union Canals to the River Dee. However, the official move did not include 'Britannia V', the cow belonging to the Captain's wife, Mrs Aylmer. At her own expense she hired the GWR to take the cow to Chester Station, where she met the train and then proceeded to walk her bovine pet to the Hall at Eaton. The move to Eaton Hall was not completed until late January 1943. The following from the Captain signalled the official commissioning.

MEMORANDUM
The Royal Naval College has officially commissioned as from to-day, 1st February, 1943.

From this date it will be known as HMS *Britannia* (Royal Naval College, Eaton.)

The establishment is at all times to be referred to as the Royal Naval College and not as Eaton Hall, or any other name.

E. A. AYLMER
CAPTAIN

A stately home Eaton Hall may have been, but on arrival the cadets were to encounter a rather depressing place, with the grounds flooded and the inevitable mess left by the workmen who had undertaken the alterations. The accommodation was largely in huts and the washing and toilet facilities were a far cry from those at

Sketch of Eaton Hall by a cadet, from the Blake Line Book of 1946.

Dartmouth that they had known. However, once the floods retreated, the College cleaned and the first of the spring daffodils started to bloom in the grounds the spirits of the cadets appeared to rise, as borne out by a personal message to the Captain from the First Sea Lord after an Inspection by him on 27th June 1943.

TO CAPTAIN E.A. AYLMER, D.S.C, R.N.
FROM FIRST LORD

PLEASE CONVEY TO ALL CONCERNED MY APPRECIATION OF THE ARRANGEMENTS MADE TODAY AND OF THE SMART TURNOUT OF THE CADETS. I WAS MOST FAVOURABLY IMPRESSED BY THE WAY IN WHICH ALL OFFICERS, MASTERS AND CADETS HAVE ADAPTED THEMSELVES TO THEIR NEW SURROUNDINGS AND I FEEL SURE THAT THE GREAT TRADITIONS OF THE ROYAL NAVAL COLLEGE WILL BE FULLY MAINTAINED. THE TASK OF TRANSFERRING THE COLLEGE WAS A HEAVY ONE AND I CONGRATULATE YOU AND THE HEADMASTER ON THE EFFICIENT MANNER IN WHICH IT WAS CARRIED OUT.

Indeed, the cadets and the staff soon settled back into college routine in its new location. While at Dartmouth the cadets had kept 'house' gardens, gardening being one of the more popular hobbies encouraged by the masters. At Eaton Hall the tradition continued and the cadets planted flower gardens in front of their huts and vegetables in plots behind. Vegetables were also grown in what in peacetime had been herbaceous borders in front of the Hall and the produce used to supplement the galley requirement. The Commander detailed parties to tend the gardens, under the supervision of Mr E. T. Warner, one of the retired masters brought back to help out for the duration of the war, a task in which the cadets took great pride. The Duke often used to walk in the gardens of the Hall with his gold–topped tall walking cane, stopping to chat to the cadets.

The Duke was also adapting to his new house guests, becoming a familiar figure to the cadets and the staff at the College. On arrival at the Hall the Commander had instructed assembled cadets that if they saw an old man walking around followed by dachshunds that they were to salute him. The Duke himself did not seem to understand the constraints of the working day, it was not unknown for him to telephone John Barlee, one of the young masters, while he was in a staff meeting to ask for help with a crossword clue. When he was at home he would occasionally invite academic staff and officers to 'coffee and liqueurs', when he would recount his own exploits in the First World War in Russia when he had his own Rolls Royce armoured car troop manned by estate employees.

The Wardroom Mess, which was shared with the Masters, the nursing sisters and the WRNS officers was at first housed in a steward's room in the basement, but later it occupied the Duke's dining room. The sports facilities were excellent, the Duke already having a good cricket ground and pavilion, two hard tennis courts, a squash court and a nine-hole golf course. The Duke's polo ground was made into a number of pitches for rugby, soccer and hockey. The estate also boasted an airfield and a private narrow gauge railway connection to the GWR at Balderton station some four miles away. The River Dee at this point was too dangerous to be used for swimming so the cadets were taken by bus to swimming baths in nearby Chester. The cadets also went to Chester for their engineering training, which was held in workshops that had been used for the training of munitions workers.

In addition to classes and sport, entertainment was provided, everything from guest lectures, such that given by Field Marshal Viscount Ironside on 'Europe', to regular film shows and chamber music concerts. Cadets also made their own entertainment, as outlined in one of the line books:

'The storm broke at 6.15 when the juniors put their Cadet Captains Read and Baillie-Hamilton through the mill. Having tied Read up and hoisted Baillie-Hamilton to the roof they proceeded to barricade their huts. Then the senior year were rudely awoken by screaming hordes of juniors outside. Only Dewing managed to get in their hut and he was soon ejected. This rather riled the senior year who proceeded 'en masse' to rescue the tortured C.C.s. However Hut I proved to be impregnable and even a battering ram had no effect, so Hut II

An outdoor service at Eaton Hall. All the participants seem to be paying attention except for one cadet in the back row who seems more interested in the photographer.

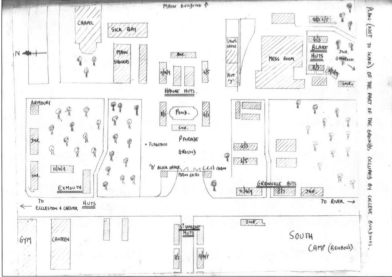

Lay out of College buildings within the grounds of Eaton Hall, as drawn by a Blake Term cadet.

Boats towed up stream on the River Dee prior to the start of a race.

was stormed and taken and its occupants forcibly removed. Then the senior year went back to protect their beds, which were being wrecked by the juniors, and a pitched battle took place on our carefully tendered lawn, which wasn't very good for it. Eventually Hut I was entered and after a fight was wrecked. Unofficial reports say the devastation was unprecedented. At last, at 7.30 everyone retired to wipe the sweat from their brows and invent accounts of their deeds. Considering the size of the operation, damage was considerably small.'

The greater battle, however, was never far from the minds of the Cadets, as the Exmouth Line book of 6th June 1944 illustrates: 'At one o'clock the BBC confirmed the German reports by announcing that D-Day had arrived and that Allied troops had landed in Normandy, a fleet of four thousand ships having been used for ferrying the troops across. It was announced

Divisions at the College, as HMS Effingham, *for the visit of the Chief of Combined Operations, Vice Admiral the Lord Louis Mountbatten, 23rd October 1943. The unrepaired damage to the front of the College is clearly visible, as are the huts under the ramps and cabling used for the telephone exchange, operations room and wireless transmitting station.*

The Women's Royal Naval Service

Although many believe that the origin of the WRNS dates back to the beginning of the Second World War, the Service actually has its origin towards the end of the First World War. In November 1917 the First Lord of the Admiralty outlined his ideas for a women's naval service in a letter to King George V, in his capacity as a naval officer. In his letter the First Lord suggested '…substituting women for men on certain work onshore directly connected with the R. N. …' The newly formed group would be known as 'The Women's Royal Naval Service,' the WRNS. A WRNS college was set up at Ashurst near Crystal Palace and it was originally thought that ratings would be immobile, living from home, but this did not work.

The war over, an Admiralty Fleet Order went out in February 1919 announcing 'the gradual demobilisation of WRNS, as the requirements of the Service permit'. Shortly afterwards the Association of Wrens was formed as a forum to keep ex members in touch with each other. Their magazine The Wren was first published in February 1920. It is from this time that the Service became known as the Wrens. The mid 1930s brought the fear of war back to Britain and Dame Katherine Furse GBE (the first Commandant of WRNS back in 1917) wrote to the Board of Admiralty offering the services of the Association of Wrens should the need arise. By 1937 the Admiralty was in an advanced stage with its plans to re-form the Service, finally receiving Treasury approval early in 1939. By December 1939 the strength of the WRNS was over 3,000 a figure that steadily rose to a peak of 74,620 by 1944. Their wartime aim was to 'replace Naval officers and Ratings in wartime on certain duties in Naval Shore Establishments'.

Wartime measures required a vast range of skills that the WRNS readily adapted to. They proved themselves to be a most capable workforce, often operating under difficult and dangerous conditions. Their resolve was unquestionable, they often worked very long hours and justifiably earned a reputation for very high standards and loyalty to the Royal Navy. A change from the early years was that women in the WRNS could be classed as 'immobile' and work from home if their circumstances required.

At the Naval College one of their duties was to act as stewards, serving meals to the cadets thus relieving men from the role in the early years of the war. One such 'immobile' was Marjorie Pillar who joined the WRNS in 1941. She recalls how she started work at 6 o'clock to serve breakfast in the Senior Gunroom, had a few hours free in the middle of the day and then was on duty again for the evening meal. After the move to Eaton Hall she worked in the Wardroom and remembers seeing General Montgomery and General Eisenhower walking through the College only to be told by one of the officers to forget whom she had seen. All the WRNS fully understood and adhered to the strict security measures in force. She also recalls serving Lord Louis Mountbatten with two eggs for breakfast, he looked up at her and said 'I say, is this really legal?' the ration at the time being one egg per week!

If any of the new recruits had any experience of boats their skills were soon put into use on the River Dart where they manned the motor launches, which were in frequent use taking personnel from the quayside to ships moored in the river. Elizabeth McGeorge had an interest in boating and sport and this led to her joining the WRNS. Her billet at Dartmouth was in the canteen (now the Pavilion), but most WRNS were in the main college building. She became a despatch rider, based at the College from May to September 1941. There were six in the group and they worked twenty-four hours on and twenty-four hours off. She recalls:

WRNS Officer uniform of 1917.

A college photograph used as an official guide as to the correct wearing of No.5's uniform, taken shortly after full integration in 1990. The caption to the original photograph reads:-
No.5's. Reefer jacket and trousers, white shirt, stiff detached collar, black shoes, black tie, cap, wear name tally. When worn. Ceremonial occasions, Sundays, Officer of the Watch 1 and 2. As an official guide.

Ladies they may be, but they are not averse to competing with the men in a game of cricket, the photographer captures them walking to the cricket square.

'I was really lucky to be based at the College – it was a fantastic time for me. I spent all my spare minutes in the college boats based at Sandquay, rowing and sailing. I also belonged to the Naval Base cricket team (ten sailors and me!). We were allowed to use all the college facilities – gym, swimming pool, cricket nets, shoe repair shops, canteen for the base staff, and join sailing boat activities. We would go to the film shows for the cadets, and to their parades and prizegivings. We hardly visited the town, because of the limitless activity at the college'.

As a despatch rider she would take despatches to ships in the harbour as well as to the Commander in Chief Plymouth and to the resident Naval officers at the various bases such as Teignmouth, Brixham, Exmouth, Torbay and to the army bases at Slapton Sands and on Dartmoor. (Freeman, 1994).

What the cadets thought of the arrival of the WRNS is not recorded but an influx of females at the College must have caused some comments amongst them. After the move to Eaton Hall they were billeted in the former cadet's dormitories as Clare Hanscombe recalls in A Wrens-Eye View of Dartmouth.

'We slept in dormitories of about 32 girls. At the foot of each double bunk (two tier) was a four drawer chest of drawers, a mirror behind the bunks, a shelf and a rail on which to hang garments and store suitcases. I would say the average age was about 21-22 years, so you can imagine the fun we had at times. Our dining hall and galley was in a separate and I think temporary buildings close to the Wren's block'.

The importance of the work carried out by the WRNS, in Dartmouth in particular and for the war effort in general cannot be praised too highly, they were an integral and vital part of the war effort. At the end of the war many of the WRNS were demobilised and returned to civilian life, however this mammoth task required a large number of them to be retained to administer it. By June of 1946 the WRNS numbers were down to 15,000 and declining but a Government White Paper in May 1946 on the future of all the Services announced the retention of the Service. In February 1949 the WRNS became a permanent service, separate from but integral with the Royal Navy. The 1950s were a period of consolidation for the Service and permanent training headquarters were established. In July 1974 HRH The Princess Anne became Chief Commandant WRNS and one of her early duties was to take the salute at the final WRNS OTC passing out parade in March of 1976 at The Royal Naval College Greenwich. They had been trained at Greenwich since October 1939, except for short time when the College was evacuated because of bomb damage. Initially this training was a basic two weeks but had been extended over the years to three months.

In September 1976 the first WRNS officer training course arrived at Britannia Royal Naval College, and remained three months (one term) in length. The decision to move to Dartmouth was taken because by this time the training had broadened to encompass wider naval responsibilities and there was a limit as to what could be achieved when isolated from the main officer training establishment. A separate division was set for them, Talbot Division, named after Mary Talbot (Director of WRNS 1973-76). This one term pattern of training remained until in January 1992 the first totally integrated intake of women into the Royal Navy began.

The Women's Royal Naval Service thus ceased to exist, those women entering the Navy now undertaking exactly the same training as their male counterparts. They hold the same ranks or rates, go to sea, are promoted or advanced in open competition, paid the same salary and most of all are subject to the same code of discipline and conditions of service. Gone were the blue stripes of the WRNS, officers now wearing gold as the men had done before them. All roles are now open to them except service in submarines.

Her Royal Highness The Princess Anne in her uniform as the Chief Commandant of WRNS. The blue braid was replaced with gold upon full integration in 1990.

that HM King would be broadcasting to the Empire and the United States of America at nine o'clock and so Exmouth did their prep at 1945-2030 so that we could listen to the speech in pyjamas.'

The College was to remain in its northern home throughout the war, as only makeshift repairs to make the structure safe were undertaken at Dartmouth. It was at Eaton, therefore that the end of the war was celebrated, as recalled in the 'Blake' Division Line Book of 1945:

'The Term began on the 11th May, just as everyone was recovering from the "VE-Day" celebrations. On the first Sunday of term there was a Victory Parade through Chester, to which Terms 11, 10, 9 and some of the Ships Company were invited. As the only representatives of the Royal Navy, we marched at the head of the procession led by our own Marine Band, which shared the task of providing the music with the A.T.C. Band. After marching past the G.O.C. Western Command we completed a two-mile round course and back to our buses in Frodsham Street. Although there was a nasty moment just before the Saluting Base, when the Cheshire Regiment Band broke into the wrong tune, but all went well, and we acquitted ourselves quite well, especially as we had no marching practice for a month.'

Once again the cadet's training had come to the fore, a training that had helped to sustain them and their predecessors throughout the darkest days of the war.

Although a year was to pass before the College could return to Dartmouth, the College buildings had been far from dormant throughout the war. As the staff and students of the Royal Naval College had been carrying on with their routine in their alternative surroundings, so the buildings they had left behind, initially known as HMS *Dartmouth III*, were to take on a new role, which would ensure they continued to play a very active part in the Allied war effort. In this role the building did not require restoration after the bomb damage so only temporary repairs to make the building safe were carried out, the major repair work being carried out between September 1945 to August 1946. Initially the College, re-named HMS *Effingham* in July 1943, was taken over by Combined Operations, for the training of Royal Marines in the art of amphibious warfare. Then on 27th December 1943, having already been in the area for a month, the Americans arrived to take over the College on behalf of the US Naval Advanced Amphibious Base (USNAAB). USNAAB was just one of the many Allied bases to be used along the south coast for training and preparations in the run up to the D-Day invasion of Europe in June 1944. American forces stationed throughout Devon and Cornwall were known as *U Force*, being destined to land on Utah Beach on the Cherbourg peninsula, which closely resembled the South Devon coast.

First impressions of the College for the American forces were not good. An official American report on USNAAB, recalls that plumbing, heating and other comfort-giving facilities appeared to have been neglected, in contrast to the customs and traditions of the Royal Navy, which had been vigorously maintained. Indeed, one RN Commander who stayed on after the change over was horrified to see the Quarterdeck become a storage room for boxes of cigarettes and worse, to witness a match being struck on the base of the statue of George V to light an American cigar (Freeman 1996, p.10). For the newly arrived Americans, however, the priority was to make the College liveable. Space was limited, with classrooms having to be transformed into living quarters. Housekeeping materials, beds and toilet paper were all at a premium, the previous owners having being careful not to leave anything behind, each Royal Marine taking with him a light bulb in addition to the rest of his kit.

As D-Day approached USNAAB became increasingly busy, its principal task being the repair of ships and landing craft for the preparation and execution of the invasion. By the beginning of 1944 over 4000 USN personnel were billeted in the Dartmouth area, along with various army units, British liaison groups, war correspondents, high ranking army and navy officials and members of observation tours. The College was filled to capacity and a tent city was set up in the College grounds. Finally, on 1st June US troops and their equipment were loaded on to their transport craft for the last time and set sail on June 4th, taking shelter in Weymouth Bay on the 5th until the storm that swept the English Channel had abated, before reaching Normandy on the 6th June.

For the next few months USNAAB was to be fully occupied repairing landing craft but as the Allied forces advanced into France so its importance began to decline. It was too far west to be used to supply forces in France or receive casualties. As a final act, on 29th April 1945, as the war in Europe was drawing to a close, the St. Columba Window was presented to the College Chapel on behalf of members of the United States Navy resident at the Royal Naval College. Commodore Korns USN, who was Commander of the Amphibious Base, United Kingdom made the presentation. In making the gift Commodore Korns acknowledged that while at the College he and his men had constantly striven to preserve the College and its traditions, and that he had personally derived much inspiration from the use of the chapel. Captain Warner accepted the gift on behalf of the College and said that it would be appreciated throughout the Service, as it expressed the deep feelings of friendship that existed between the United States Navy and the Royal Navy. Moreover, after their return to Dartmouth, this handsome gift would help them to recall the critical contribution that sea power had made to enable the Allied armies to invade France and precipitate the liberation of Europe.

Combined Operations during Sunday divisions at HMS Effingham *in 1943. The impact of the war is evident with the figurehead of* Britannia *having been painted to camouflage her and the barbed wire around the parade ground to guard against attack.*

The still war-scarred College as United States Naval
Advanced Amphibious Base in 1944.

CHAPTER 6

Education Since 1945

The end of the Second World War in 1945 heralded the beginning of a new era, one in which the role and position of Britain, the Royal Navy and Dartmouth would all be fundamentally challenged and changed. As Paul Kennedy observes in charting *The Rise and Fall of British Naval Mastery,* with the end of the war, long-term trends, 'the relative weakening of the British economy, the rise of the super-powers, the disintegration of the European empires, the decline of sea power in its classical form *vis-à-vis* land and air power, the growing public demand for increased domestic rather than foreign expenditure – now combined to overwhelm a British naval mastery that had long been in question.' (Kennedy 1983, p. 383). The combination of the decline of British power and the change in society, reflected in the administration of the post-war Socialist government and its successors, was to have a profound effect on the way in which appropriate officer training would be conducted at Dartmouth. Between 1945 and 1960 there were to be no less than five fundamental reviews of the Naval College, including its transformation from public school to naval academy. In contrast to the first forty years of relative stability, the latter sixty years in the life of Britannia Royal Naval College have been permeated by change, culminating in some of the most fundamental reforms to the structure and delivery of training and education at Dartmouth as the College approached its centenary.

Return from Eaton Hall and the Beginning of an Era of Change

Following the bombing of the College in September 1942, only patch-work repairs had been possible, given the wartime shortages of labour and material. It was, therefore, to be another year after the end of the war before the College was fit for cadets and staff to return. In addition to the repair work a number of improvements were made to extend the library and science laboratories; fluorescent lighting, an automatic telephone system and a loud-speaker system were installed. A competition was held by the Captain to find a new design to replace the electroliers that had been destroyed along with the quarterdeck roof and work began on a new block (F-block) to provide extra classrooms for the new additions to the curriculum – music and art. Nevertheless, on the College's return there were too many cadets to be catered for altogether, necessitating the conversion of staff quarters into a dining room with a separate servery on a different floor to the galley. Two sittings were required for breakfast, dinner (mid-day) and supper and serving staff had to be organised into watches to cope.

The Royal Naval College returned to Dartmouth in September 1946. Officers and cadet captains had joined in advance to reconnoitre and draw up plans, which were posted up to indicate to staff and students alike where they were in their strange new surroundings. Meanwhile scores of workmen finished off their refurbishment work, restoring the building to its former glory, as a master at the time observed; 'the gallery of the Quarter-deck had been restored so well that it was hard to see the join between the old and the new' (Hughes p.158). Despite these upheavals College life continued much as it had at Eaton, including wartime additions such as visits from guest lecturers. In the winter of 1947 one such lecture was given by Viscount Mountbatten of Burma who spoke about the difficulties of jungle warfare and joint and combined operations. At the end Mountbatten made a presentation to the College of two Japanese swords, one of which is still displayed on the wall outside the quarterdeck. Other visitors that year included the King and Queen. On inspecting the statue of George V on the quarterdeck His Majesty noticed it had been damaged during the bombing and expressed the wish that it should not be restored but remain, as it does, a memorial.

However, while continuity reigned at Dartmouth the seeds of reform were already being sown. In July 1945 the 'Noble Committee on Entry into the Royal Naval College, Dartmouth,'(ADM 1/17293) was set up to consider whether there were grounds to improve the current system. Since 1941 there had been two modes of entry for boys aged thirteen, when a scholarship scheme was introduced to encourage boys from grant-aided secondary schools through a system of reduced fees for those from families on lower incomes. There were thus two systems of entry based on the Common Entrance Examination for Public Schools. For the old or 'ordinary cadet' system a pass mark of 55% followed by an interview to determine intelligence, capability, character and personality were required. For the 'scholarship cadets' a pass mark of 65% and a more straight-forward suitability interview was required. However, as the Noble Committee was to report in 1946, while the ordinary entry continued to satisfy the requirements for successful naval cadets the scholarship system had introduced a 'small tail of weak candidates' into the system. Of even greater concern, however, was the steady decline in numbers competing for both entries, a decline felt to be in excess of a reaction against a service career following a major war or even the reduced birth rate of the 1930s. The findings of the Committee therefore concluded that the selection process for both forms of entry should be more rigorous and that a publicity programme should be initiated by the Admiralty, to appeal particularly to the boys and headmasters of grant-aided grammar schools. However, it also recognised that a 'radical transformation in national education is about to take place,' and that consequently it was 'difficult to see how the Royal Naval College in its present form can hope to conform with such a national system.'

That there should be a further investigation into the system of entry to Dartmouth was therefore inevitable, although as he wrote prior to its announcement in the House of Commons in May 1947, Prime Minister Attlee was at pains to make 'clear to the country that the changes I am making do not result from any dissatisfaction with the past.' As he went on to tell the House;

'It cannot be too strongly emphasised that we have every reason to be satisfied with the quality of the naval officer produced by the entry of boys at about 13 years of age and the subsequent

education at Dartmouth. The Royal Navy can justly claim that its officers have stood the supreme test of war . . . The best tribute to Dartmouth is the distinction with which the product has served the country.' (ADM 1/20918)

The need for change, it was emphasised, was brought about as a result of changes in the system of national education that had taken place over the past forty years. Moreover, 'inevitably, entry was the privilege of boys whose parents were able to afford to send their children to preparatory schools,' where the natural age of advancement was thirteen – an important consideration for the Socialist government as it strove towards social equality in education. The new system was announced in January 1948, its twin objectives to ensure that no boy should be disqualified from a career as a naval officer on the basis of social status, financial situation or schooling, while providing the Navy with officers of the highest academic standards, character and leadership qualities. This was to be achieved in dramatic fashion. In consultation with the Admiralty and Ministry of Education, together with opinions from other educational authorities and eminent Naval Officers, it was decided the thirteen year old entry would to be phased out over the next two years, the last such entry joining in May 1949. In its place there would be three entries per year to the Executive, Engineering and Supply Branches at the age of sixteen to sixteen years and four months old, the first joining Dartmouth in September 1948. Tuition and boarding fees were abolished and the cost of uniforms would be subsidised when necessary. The entrance exam would be devised so as not to disadvantage boys from any particular sort of school, and candidates would also undergo tests of intelligence, aptitude, character and personality before a board consisting of naval officers, a psychologist, a representative from the state system of education and a headmaster on rotation from the state and public school systems. The Special Entry at eighteen years of age was to continue, with the ultimate aim of recruiting twenty-five per cent of commissioned officers by promotion from the lower deck and of the remainder half each from the sixteen and eighteen year old entry (Statement to the House of Commons, 28/1/1948, ADM 1/22690).

By democratising the entry it was hoped that the Royal Navy would be able to continue to recruit the best officers from a decreasing available population, in terms of numbers and inclination, while shaking off any allegations of anachronistic snobbery. However, the sixteen-year-old entry was by no means universally acclaimed and also raised questions about the continuing suitability of Aston Webb's College for its task. Consequently, in March 1949 a committee was appointed to assess the best use of the accommodation available at Dartmouth.

The problem, as reported by the 'Dartmouth Accommodation Committee' (ADM 1/21773) in July 1950, was that the raising of the age of entry to Dartmouth would lead to a reduction in the number

Viscount Mountbatten of Burma speaking to cadets in the gymnasium about his wartime experiences in early 1947.

of cadets from 500 to 280. Overhead costs, however, would not decline as buildings and facilities still had to be maintained. The net result was that whereas in 1939 the average cost per cadet was £130, by 1950 it had risen to £500 and was estimated to increase to £800 by 1953. Meanwhile accommodation itself was also becoming available, with a surplus of boarding school accommodation in the main building for 220 boys, sleeping and messroom space for a hundred in the old ship company's block, and spare capacity for fifty-six in sick quarters (as sixteen year old boys suffered less sickness that thirteen year olds). A number of suggestions for using this spare capacity were suggested, including: the transfer of the Upper Yardmen's College and Admiralty Interview Board from HMS *Hawke* at Exbury; making Dartmouth a junior naval university, with Greenwich as the senior, through the transfer of the Sub-Lieutenants' General Education and War Course from Greenwich; or turning the College into a boarding school providing a normal course of education, with a naval bias. Of these suggestions only the first two were finally recommended. The proposal to move the Sub-Lieutenants' course was ruled out, partly due to a lack of accommodation and appropriately qualified staff, but also because it was felt that, 'it would be a psychological mistake to send Sub-Lieutenants back to the school atmosphere of Dartmouth, with its strict and almost monastic discipline . . .' (Ibid.). The suggestion to turn the College into a boarding school was not, however, ruled out but declared to be beyond the remit of the Committee. Nevertheless, it was noted that Naval members of the Committee 'consider the only suitable way to fill Dartmouth would be to adopt the proposal to convert the College into a boarding school.'(Ibid.). Finally it was agreed that unless means could be found to make further economies and utilise all available capacity, that 'the Admiralty may have to move the training of naval cadets from Dartmouth to a smaller and cheaper establishment.' (Ibid.).

Inevitably, therefore, the system that had been introduced in 1948 was soon under review. In July 1951 a report was commissioned into the sixteen-year-old entry and the quality of candidates from secondary grammar schools (ADM 1/22463). The findings were not encouraging, concluding that the best grammar school boys were simply not applying. As a result boys from independent schools continued to perform better than their state school counter parts in competing for places at Dartmouth.[1] Clearly it was far too soon after the introduction of the sixteen-year-old entry to assess its success in producing naval officers of the highest quality. However, it was already clear that it was failing to achieve the supposedly secondary objective of enabling equal opportunities for boys from all backgrounds.

Instruction in the classroom.

Thus in July 1952 a 'Committee on Cadet Entry' was appointed, under the chairmanship of the Judge Advocate of the Fleet, the Honourable Ewen Montagu. This time, however, the findings of the Committee were to be made public so as to encourage the widest possible debate. The Montagu Committee reported in May 1953 in a blaze of publicity, focused upon accusations of 'snobbery' in the selection process. These allegations had been fuelled by press reporting, such as a 1952 report in the *Daily Express*, following a top grammar school boy who had passed the written exam four times but each time had been rejected by the interview board. Indeed, the report recognised that if they passed the written exam boys from a public school stood a sixty-eight per cent chance of success in the oral examination, compared to a twenty-eight per cent chance for a grammar school boy. Despite having been designed to catch boys leaving school on completion of their general certificate of education, school-masters in public[2] and grammar schools were reluctant to lose their best pupils, who could be primed for university. Public school boys therefore continued to take the

---

1 For example, between May 1949 and February 1951, 449 boys from independent schools sat the entrance exam, of whom 144 passed. Of those, 106 passed the Admiralty Interview Board (AIB) and 97 were accepted. In contrast, 1366 grammar school boys sat the exam, of whom just 311 passed the exam and 96 passed the AIB, with 90 candidates finally being accepted.

2 The Headmaster of Eton wrote a letter to *The Times*, criticising the sixteen-year-old entry (7/7/1953).

Ballroom dancing classes were a regular and memorable feature of the social education of cadets, until recent times. As this photograph demonstrates cadets provided both the musical accompaniment and the 'female' partners.

The Passing Out Parade

*T*he culmination of the Young Officers' training at Dartmouth is the Passing Out Parade. Traditionally these were held three times a year at the end of each term. The 'Passers Out' would be inspected on the Parade Ground, followed by a slow march up the steps and into the front door of the College. The door would be slammed shut, and the Young Officers who have passed out toss their caps into the air to a resounding loud cheer.

Since the introduction of the six phase multiple entry system in May 2003, the passers out are jointly inspected along with those officer cadets who having just completed the first seven weeks (Phase One) of their training, and are regarded as 'passers in'. Thus the parades are now known as Passing Out/Passing In Parades.

All the Parades follow a similar format and begin with the march on of the Divisions to the Band of Her Majesty's Royal Marines. This is followed by the march on of the Queen's Colour through the front door of the College and down the steps to the parade ground where follows the Trooping of the Colour. The Commander then calls the 'Britannia Royal Naval College' to

Mayoral Divisions. Commander David Vaughan reports the parade to the Mayor of Dartmouth, Councillor Richard Rendle, June 2003.

The Queen's Colour.

attention before reporting the Parade to the Guest of Honour at main door. The guest proceeds to take the Royal Salute on the Bridge. The Guest of Honour accompanied by the Commodore reviews the faces of both ranks of the Guard of Honour, the front rank only of the Royal Marine Band and the faces of all ranks of Platoons of Officers Passing Out. If there are any awards to be presented they are awarded at this stage on the Parade Ground[1].

On completion of the inspection the Divisions will follow the Queen's Colour and the Guard and march up the ramps, where the salute is taken again by the Guest of Honour, before returning to the parade ground. The Queen's Colour and Officers Passing Out Platoons Advancing in Review Order slow march up the steps and into the College with due ceremony.

Lord High Admiral Divisions[2]

*T*he post of Lord High Admiral has in the past been held by James, Duke of York (later King James II) from 1660 to 1673; King Charles II (1685); King James II (1685); Prince George of Denmark (Consort of Queen Anne) from 1702 – 1708; and from 1827 – 1828 William, Duke of Clarence (later King William IV).

In 1964, the Admiralty became the Admiralty Board of the Defence Council and Her Majesty Queen Elizabeth II graciously consented to assume the title of Lord High Admiral. In 1970 Her Majesty approved Admiral of the Fleet Earl Mountbatten of Burma's proposal that each year one of the passing out parades at the Britannia Royal Naval College should be called the Lord High Admiral's Divisions. In addition the salute at these Divisions should be taken by the Lord High Admiral or by his personal representative, this nearly always a member of the Royal Family. Lord High Admiral's Divisions are usually held at Easter, although there have been exceptions to this tradition.

The Flag of the Lord High Admiral

*T*he flag of the Lord High Admiral is hoisted in addition to the Royal Standard on occasions when the Sovereign is presented with any body of the Royal Navy or Royal Marine forces, afloat or ashore, and on such other maritime occasions as Her Majesty may command. The fourteen feet by six feet flag is of crimson silk with a golden anchor and cable. Until 1815 it was often depicted foul of the shank of the anchor, as it was in the seal of the Board of Admiralty, and still is in naval uniform buttons and badges.

Passing Out Platoons slow-march up the stairs for the last time.

The Queen's Colour of the Royal Navy

The Queen's Colour is a silk White Ensign with a Crown and Royal Cypher embodied. It has a red, white and blue silk cord with gold tassels and is carried on an ash staff, surmounted by a gilt badge consisting of the Admiralty anchor on a three-faced shield with a Crown superimposed. King's Colours were carried only by military forces, but in 1925 King George V approved the use of King's Colours by the Royal and Commonwealth Navies. The Queen's Colour is never paraded on foreign territory. It is paraded on shore only on the following occasions, by a) Guard of Honour mounted for the Sovereign or a member of the Royal Family, or for the Head of a Foreign State; b) at Parades held to celebrate the birthday of the Sovereign; c) on important ceremonial occasions as directed by the Admiralty Board. When paraded the Queen's Colour is awarded the same respect as if Her Majesty were present. When carried uncased it is at all times saluted with the highest honours. In addition to being presented to the principal Naval Commands, the Queen's Colour was presented

Field Marshal Montgomery inspects the Guard.

Presentation of the Queen's Sword, April 2002.

to the Britannia Royal Naval College on 28th July 1958 by his Royal Highness The Duke of Edinburgh, on behalf of Her Majesty the Queen. This colour was laid up in the Brett Ince Chapel when Her Majesty the Queen presented a new Colour on 7th April 1988.

In 2009 HRH The Earl of Wessex took a passing out parade for the first time in his role as Commodore-in-Chief of the Royal Fleet Auxiliary.

The Colour Party.

1 HM The Queen graciously makes a number of awards annually to Young Officers, which recognise outstanding performance during training. The principal award is the Queen's Sword, this is awarded to the Young Officer who has achieved the highest and most outstanding level of overall performance whilst under training during the last year. Her Majesty also awards binoculars to Young Officers who have performed outstandingly whilst under training during the last year. Five pairs of binoculars are awarded for officers of the Royal Navy; two pairs of binoculars to officers of the foreign and Commonwealth countries.

2 See Chapter 4 The Royal College, for a more detailed account.

majority of places in the sixteen-year-old entry. Jim Callaghan, former Parliamentary Secretary to the Admiralty, told the House of Commons during a three and a half hour debate: 'Snobbery is robbing the Navy of many first class potential officers . . . There has been an unconscious bias in favour of the public school boy with the smooth manner, the polish that is put on at the public school, as against the boy from a secondary grammar with a provincial accent and rugged manner.' (*Daily Telegraph, 7/7/1953*)

The Montagu report itself was to fuel rather than quell the debate. Amongst its less controversial recommendations were; the exemption from written examination for the sixteen and eighteen-year-old entries on the basis of performance in school examinations, thus eliminating the need for special 'cramming,' which was seen to mitigate against the grammar school boy; and a liaison committee was established between the Admiralty and school and local education authorities. However, on the issue of recruitment the report recommended three ages of entry; half of all cadets would be recruited at eighteen, a quarter at sixteen and a further quarter at thirteen. Of those who entered at thirteen there would be a quota of sixty percent reserved for grammar school boys. Dartmouth would come under the authority of a civilian headmaster and boys would not commit themselves to a naval career until they were eighteen. Thus the College would become more like an ordinary public school, albeit with a strong naval character, so as not to disadvantage those that opted for civilian life.

The solution offered was a compromise, not least between senior naval officers who supported the re-introduction of the thirteen-year-old entry and educationalists who regarded it as anachronistic. The quota system failed to satisfy either side, however, as it implied that an able boy could lose his chance to a less able one on the basis that his parents paid for his education. The half-retention of the sixteen-year-old entry railed against the report's own criticisms of the entry, whilst the weight given to the eighteen-year-old entry suggested that a period of intense training on completion of public or grammar school education produced officers of equal quality to those who had gone through five or two years of naval education.

Meanwhile, back at Dartmouth, those entrusted with delivering the Navy's education, felt compelled to voice their opinion in support of the original thirteen-year-old entry. As stated in their letter to the Admiralty (BRNC Archive), 'the masters of the College feel that they too have the right to be heard, and that their knowledge of the actual working of the system, both before and after the changes brought about in 1948, can make a valid contribution to the issues raised by the report.' They found issue with a number of the Report's findings, arguing that it was possible to select suitable candidates at the age of thirteen and that a thirteen-year-old boy was capable of knowing his own mind. They refuted any class bias, as thirteen year old boys 'in uniform, from every kind of home, can mix and grow up together,' in a unique naval community. To remove naval control of the College would 'irretrievably impair that special element in Dartmouth which inspires its spirit and defines its aims.' Moreover, it was inappropriate to consider 'that the College, which exists for a specific purpose, should be made subservient to the requirements of the general system of education, where no such common purpose as that found at Dartmouth is needed.'

The reservations of many Naval Officers were encapsulated in a letter from the Commander-in-Chief Plymouth to the Admiralty (9/5/1953, BRNC Archive). The report itself was considered to be based not so much on concern to provide the Navy with the best officers but appease public opinion:

'There can be only one sound criterion in deciding upon the future methods of cadet entry and that is "what is best for the Navy". Yet although this is given as the "prime aim" in the terms of reference, I can find only one reference to it in the Report, where it is stated, "all of us are agreed that the Royal Navy cannot be content with anything below the highest quality." The whole Report is coloured by the fear of so called public opinion and the apparent desire to enter as an officer, the boy from the state school, not in equal competition with, but at the expense of the boys from the independent school.'

This was not to suggest that there should not be arrangements to prevent financial considerations being a bar to entering the service, but competition should be based entirely upon merit. If that happened to mean a preponderance of public school boys were admitted then that merely proved that such schools were most suited to providing suitable officer material. As for the idea of non-commitment until eighteen, it was thought unnecessary to change the existing procedure under which parents could ask to remove their sons from naval training. To advertise such an option would merely encourage students who had little or no interest in joining the Navy to go to Dartmouth. On the issue of age it was recognised that, 'educational opinion appears to be almost unanimous in regarding 16 as the wrong age at which to either leave school or to change school.' Although the low birth rate might justify the retention of this entry for the next five years, after that there should be a return to the thirteen-year-old entry, supplemented by the Special Entry:

'The bulk of the intake should, however, be at 13 years old. Naval life is community life and the best preparation for this is the boarding school. It is universally accepted that 13 is the age at which boarding school life of the higher standard, as opposed to preparatory standard, should commence. Moreover boys from whatever class of the community, provided they possess inherent potential can be properly moulded in 5 years.'

Opposition was not confined to the Navy. Mr F. Barraclough, Chief Education Officer for the North Riding of Yorkshire and a

After hours: prep and a game of cards

member of the Montagu Committee produced his own minority report, recommending the eventual move to an all eighteen entry to reflect the growing trend in national education. In November 1953, the government decided to accept Barraclough's report, abolishing the thirteen and sixteen year old entries and the old Special Entry within the next two years. The overriding objective, Parliament was told was; 'to establish a system of Cadet entry into the Royal Navy which not only gives the Navy adequate numbers of cadets of the required standard but conforms beyond dispute with the general trend of educational policy and is entirely beyond the field of controversy.' (ADM 1/30995) The Montagu Report could not, therefore, be accepted on the basis of the conditions it had placed upon itself, i.e. that its findings should be acceptable to public and educational opinion. As First Lord of the Admiralty, J.P.L. Thomas, wrote to Lord Mountbatten (ADM 1/30995):

> 'I hope you are not too disappointed about the cadet entry decision. There was really no alternative and the Sea Lords all agreed that they did not wish to return to the 13 entry with all the conditions attached to it by the Montagu Report; and everybody was agreed that the 16 entry was producing unfortunate results. It was therefore felt that the bravest thing to

do was to go right out for 17 – 19 . . .
> 'I really believe that we have now placed cadet entry above party politics and I hear from Jim Callaghan that we have taken a decision which no political party would wish to upset.'

The fact that reform of the Royal Naval College attracted so much public debate and involved personalities from the Prime Minister down, is testament to the regard in which the Royal Navy was held in the aftermath of the Second World War. Nevertheless, the system of naval education established under Fisher, revolutionary in its own time, had inevitably succumbed to what today would be termed political correctness. The armed forces have long claimed to reflect the society they serve; in 1950s Britain this was a society in which age-long class barriers were finally being broken, in a new era of equality of opportunity. Simultaneously, the very rationale behind Britain's Navy was also being eroded, the Empire that it had served was contracting and the future wars that it might fight looked like being very short and extremely destructive in the new atomic age. Against such a background of change within Britain and Britain's place in the world it was therefore inevitable that an institution such as Dartmouth would need to reform if it was to survive into its second half century.

From Public School to Training Establishment

In January 1954, the Committee on Officer Structure and Training (COST) was appointed under the chairmanship of Vice Admiral Sir Aubrey Mansergh. Its remit was to report on the officer structure of the future, but owing to its urgency the first matter to be investigated was the initial training scheme of young Naval Officers, both to meet the new conditions and reflect scientific and technological advances. In accordance with the Committee's recommendations three working groups were set up: 'A' to work out the curriculum and syllabus for the new scheme and the staff required; 'B' to consider the composition of the Training Squadron; and 'C' to consider the necessary works and buildings at Dartmouth. The length of the course would be seven, thirteen-week terms, divided into three phases. The first phase consisted of two terms of naval training and academic levelling, during the second phase cadets spent one term in the Dartmouth Training Squadron (DTS) learning about life at sea[3], after which they were promoted to midshipmen. The third phase consisted of four terms academic and professional training interspersed with short periods with the DTS and a visit to a naval air station.

It was recognised that as the students would be young men who had left school it was proper to reduce the amount of regimentation that had permeated the old system, while maintaining high levels of discipline and paying the greatest attention to training in leadership. Students would be encouraged to think for themselves, work for themselves and use their leisure time profitably. Inevitably, this would require a period of adjustment for the staff, even for the inimitable Miss Bulla, who prescribed extra milk rations to one Cadet (later Captain) Wixon when he appeared somewhat pale at breakfast, unaware that he had spent the previous evening at the Floating Bridge public house.

On the academic side the tutorial system would be adopted where possible, time being divided between lectures, private study and tutorial periods consisting of two or three students and a lecturer. It was assumed that new entrants would be of or above the necessary intellectual level but would have studied a wide variety of subjects. Everyone would therefore have to be brought up to a minimum standard in mathematics and science in addition to naval history and modern languages where possible. In professional training the emphasis would be on teaching principles that could be built upon as a foundation at a later date, without the need for separate specialist training, allowing all cadets to learn about each other's jobs[4]. This theoretical work would then be put into practice during periods at sea.

One of the most immediate implications of introducing a new system concerned the future of the civilian masters. As mentioned above, despite their obvious qualifications to advise on the subject of naval education, the Dartmouth academics had been largely

The front cover from the Britannia Magazine, *midsummer 1949. The first magazine was published in 1884. Its aims were to provide a vehicle for cadets and staff to voice their opinions and a record of sporting and other notable events. It is the source of much valuable material for the researcher and there are some very talented pieces of artwork within its pages, but most importantly it gives an often humorous, sometimes sad, but unique insight into College life over the past one hundred years.*

3 The DTS consisted of three Type 15 anti-submarine frigates and two minesweepers: HMS *Vigilant, Venus, Carron, Jewel* and *Acute*.

4 In 1954 the distinctive colours for the various branches in the RN were abolished and in 1956, in line with COST and the introduction of the 'General List', the supplementary (E), (S) and (L) to the rank of Engineer, Supply and Electrical Officers were removed as these officers were now to have common entry and training with Seamen Officers (no longer called Executive).

The reward for all that practice; dancing with a Rear Admiral!

overlooked in the public debate over their future. It was acknowledged in the House of Commons on 25th November 1953 that some of the masters, 'have devoted most of their lives to the education of naval cadets.' However, it was not possible 'to speak about their prospects of further employment after Dartmouth ceases to be concerned with cadets of school age.' (ADM 1/30995). Before the official announcement had been made Second Master G. Ghey had written to the Admiralty, on behalf of all the masters, pledging their collective loyalty but asking in return for some security of tenure. Nevertheless, when the announcement was finally made, as the Captain of the College, W.G. Crawford noted, it 'naturally left the Masters completely in the air.' (BRNC Archive). Ultimately, however, eighteen of the twenty-four masters on the staff in 1954, survived the changes to 1956 and beyond. The post of Headmaster became Director of Studies[5], with an Assistant Director of Studies, Heads of Departments (Science, Mathematics, Modern Languages and History and English – as under the old system), Senior Lecturers and Junior Lecturers. Under this new structure, based upon the lecturer system at Sandhurst, the academics became Civil Servants and full members of the Wardroom Mess. Overall the new scheme saw an increase in both academic and naval staff, which together with the increased number of cadets, who being older required more personal space, led to extensive building works to adapt and expand the College buildings.[6]

As Davies and Grove commented in their history of the College's first seventy-five years; 'the conversion to tertiary college was in principle more radical than the changes of 1905.' (1980, p.20). The rise in age of entry to eighteen meant not merely changes in curriculum and teaching methods but denied to the Navy the

opportunity to mould its future officers at a younger, more impressionable age, as Captain Pack observed: 'There were still those who argued that the best training ground was in a ship at sea, and the younger they went to sea the more quickly would cadets become able naval officers.' Nevertheless, it was recognised that as ships became technologically more complex all officers would require a sound understanding of their working; 'with the onset of the technological age there is an inherent conflict between the requirement for deeper professional study and the wish to learn on the job.' And in an uncanny prediction for the future; 'The best training scheme can only be a compromise . . . The result is that we encounter a recommended shake-up every five years instead of the fifty envisaged half a century ago.' (1966, p.265).

Indeed, the new system was barely up and running before yet another review was announced, due in part to the recommendation in COST, which set-up the 'General List' (GL) of officers from various specialisations. A committee was appointed in April 1958, under the chairmanship of Sir Keith Murray, Chairman of the University Grants Committee. The Committee found two serious shortcomings in the existing system:

'Firstly, the standard of entry of most of those who are now going to Dartmouth appears to us to be too low to meet either the demands made upon them by the existing syllabus or the future needs of the Navy. Secondly, the phasing of the present scheme seems to us to make impossible achievement of the full development, within the time limits imposed, of those qualities of character which a naval officer must possess.' (BRNC Archive)

While it was recognised that the COST system had yet to produce any sub-lieutenants for the fleet an immediate review of both the existing method of entry and training programme were considered essential. Ideally the Committee was, 'convinced that the 13 year old entry, if it could be reintroduced, would be the best for the Navy,' but it was also appreciated, 'that for political and social reasons it is impossible to put back the clock' (BRNC Archive). The eighteen-year-old entry was to remain but to attain a higher quality of cadet a minimum of two 'A' Levels was required, preferably including mathematics and physics. For the first year the emphasis was on developing leadership qualities. The first term of basic naval training would smooth the transition from civilian to service life; the second term would be spent in the DTS acclimatising to life at sea; the third term of introductory naval

---

5 The last to fill the post of Headmaster and first Director of Studies was J. W. Stork CB, CBE, MA. Mr Stork had arrived at Dartmouth as Headmaster just two weeks before the College was bombed in September 1942. He had then overseen the removal of the College up to Eaton Hall and back again. After the war he oversaw the end of the 13-year-old entry, the introduction and abolition of the 16-year-old entry, and finally the end of Dartmouth's days as a school with the introduction of the all 18-year-old entry.
6 See Chapter 2 on Architecture.

i.

ii.

iii.

courses would give cadets preliminary appreciation of the functions performed by naval officers, together with basic instruction in navigation and naval history, discipline and physical training. The whole of the second year would be spent at sea as midshipmen, before returning to Dartmouth as acting sub-lieutenants for a year of academics. The only exception from this pattern was for engineers, who went to the Royal Naval Engineering College, Manadon for two years on returning from sea. The remainder at Dartmouth received academic courses of first-year degree level, as the Murray Committee acknowledged:

> 'Apart from the argument that the Navy has no right to good calibre minds that it is not prepared to educate further, it is called for because without it the subsequent professional and sub-specialist training can never have full value.' (BRNC Archive)

In addition to mathematics, science and engineering the curriculum included English, foreign languages, social studies (i.e. the study of contemporary society, in which the Navy works and from which it draws its personnel) and Naval History – considered to be 'important in its own sake.' That Dartmouth should remain the location for the new scheme was supported by the Committee, on the basis that, 'Naval tradition, the buildings, the river, and the general training facilities all provide strong arguments for keeping Dartmouth as the central naval officer training establishment.' (BRNC Archive)

Navigation training. i. HMS Sealark, *the bridge trainer (simulator). ii. Bridge trainer in use by Young Officers. iii. Practical navigation training at sea.*

Navigation training. Bridge trainer in use by Young Officers.

The River

One of Dartmouth's greatest assets is the sheltered harbour that is offered by the estuary of the River Dart. This was the primary reason for the mooring of Britannia and Hindostan in the river in the 1860s and it has always offered a safe haven for the many varied waterborne activities. The workshops at Sandquay not only provided the engineering workshops for the College, so vital to the success of the Selborne Scheme, but also the skilled workforce who maintained and built many of the smaller craft.

Left and below: Cadets enjoying the River in the 1930s.

Seamanship instruction on the previous training vessel *Hindostan* and a picket boat.

Blowing the cobwebs away in a RIB (rigid inflatable boat).

Dinghy sailing in the College Bosun craft.   Safety first!

After the storm: picket boats alongside at Sandquay.

Sail Past in College motor-whalers, followed by an STC (sail training craft).

Hindostan, old and new.

Aerial view of the Sandquay workshops, showing the latest *Hindostan* (seamanship training vessel) and other College craft.

Academic instruction in;- i. Oceanography; ii. Meteorology.

The first Murray scheme cadets arrived in 1960, however it was becoming evident that the new, higher entry requirements were preventing some boys with suitable character and leadership qualities from joining the service. A 'Supplementary List' (SL) was therefore formed, to complement the 'General List,' firstly for aircrew and then seamen and eventually engineer officers, requiring lower entry grades. SL cadets spent two terms of academic and professional training at Dartmouth before going on to flying training, DTS or Manadon respectively. Other courses were also starting to arrive. The Upper Yardmen Course, for officers promoted from the ranks arrived from HMS *Temeraire* in 1960, taking up residence in what had been the hospital until 1958, when the Admiralty Interview Board used it for a short time. The course lasted two years before they went to sea as midshipmen. In 1962 a special course for 'New Commonwealth' and foreign officers was offered as an alternative to the RN academic course for those that were sufficiently qualified. By 1967 a specific package had been developed for all 'Internationals', with a third term of academics followed by an 'International Senior Term' for more advanced study.

Despite all the efforts to transform naval education after 1945, to make it socially inclusive and more appealing as a career to intellectually gifted school leavers, by the mid-1960s Dartmouth was once again suffering as a result of changing patterns in national education. The 1960s were to see a major expansion in higher education, thus potentially denying the navy and other armed services of its best potential officers as they chose to go to university instead. In 1963 five cadets were nominated to go to university instead of the third year at Dartmouth. A year later the first of what were to become known as the 'Direct Graduate Entry,' (DGE) arrived. In 1965 the 'University Cadet Entry' (UCE) scheme was established, whereby the Navy would sponsor school leavers with university places. On graduation UCEs would go to Dartmouth for professional training and a course in technical subjects for arts graduates. While once again allowing Dartmouth to conform with national trends, the introduction of graduates into the College had the potential to undermine the tradition of unquestioning obedience expected from cadets. The contrast was summed up in the *Britannia Magazine* of Christmas 1964 (p.13):

> 'Traditionally there appears to be a feeling of antagonism between the services and the Universities: this is a mixture of mutual mistrust and jealousy, giving rise to secondary feelings of disdain. The young officer regards the undergraduate as scruffy, while the undergraduate regards the young officer as being incapable of thinking for himself . . . prepared to obey orders without thought.'

The Murray Scheme was finally superseded in 1972 by the 'Naval College Entry' scheme. Under the revised system new entrants would undertake a period of 'Naval General Training,' in professional and character and leadership courses. One term would be spent at

iii.

iv.

v.

the College, the second on the Dartmouth Training Ship, which replaced the squadron.[7] After that engineers would go to RNEC Manadon or the University of Cambridge and some suitably qualified seamen and supply officers without university places would be 'nominated,' to a university. Non-graduates on the General List would go on to do two, later extended to three, terms of academics at Dartmouth, while SL seamen and supply officers did one term. Meanwhile UCEs were encouraged to defer taking up their places at university in order to undertake the Naval General Training course first. In 1974 the first Special Duties Officers (older ratings commissioned from the ranks) arrived from Greenwich to undertake their one-term professional and academic course, as a separate 'St. George' Division.

It was not just the educational system that was changing in Britain in the 1960s and 1970s. In the spring of 1973 the first female officers to train at Dartmouth arrived, consisting of eight QARNNS sisters who formed the first short introductory course. In 1976 the WRNS moved their entire officer-training course of one term's professional and academic training to Dartmouth from Greenwich, forming a separate 'Talbot' division. As the Royal Naval College entered its seventy-fifth year in 1980 it had undergone numerous changes since its staff and students had returned from their northern exile in 1946. Much of this change had been brought about by necessity, a most fundamental necessity – to continue to supply the Royal Navy with sufficient numbers of suitably qualified and able officers. In the process the College had been transformed from a public school into a training establishment, where the number of

Academic instruction in;- iii. Engineering Science; iv. Modern Languages v. Strategic Studies and International Affairs.

7 The first to act as Dartmouth Training Ships were HMS *Fearless* and *Intrepid.* They were supplemented in 1982 by HMS *Peterel* and *Sandpiper*, and in 1987 by HMS *Fife, Apollo, Euryalus* and *Juno.*

staff officers was now twice that of the academic staff and with the first graduate entrants the average age of cadets had begun to rise by a decade. Indeed, the transformation of Dartmouth since the end of the Second World War had been of a more fundamental nature than that which had occurred with the move from *Britannia* to the College and the introduction of the Selborne Scheme. But as Davies and Grove were to conclude:

> 'The College's aims, the inculcation of a broad view of the naval profession, the development of the conduct and sense of duty required of an officer and the preparation of officers for further training, remain what they always have been. They are grounded in three-quarters of a century of tradition, for change at Dartmouth is always tempered by stability.' (1980, p.24).

Naval Education for the 21st Century

The 1980s saw the continuation of the tradition of change at Dartmouth. The decade started bleakly for the Royal Navy. The previous twenty years had already witnessed the withdrawal of British forces from 'East of Suez' and the last of the true aircraft carriers, HMS *Ark Royal*, had been decommissioned in 1978 to be replaced by the smaller Invincible class carriers. Against a back drop of the economic and political decline of Britain and the deterioration of East-West relations, further defence cuts were envisaged by the defence review conducted by the newly elected Thatcher government, under Secretary of State for Defence Sir John Nott. The Nott Review of 1981 threatened to reduce the Navy to a comparatively small specialist anti-submarine force within NATO, with drastic cuts in platforms and personnel. However, the Falklands conflict of 1982 was to prove a dramatic reminder that Britain retained crucial interests outside the North Atlantic and that the Royal Navy was still required as a tool of foreign policy, to transport and supply forces across the globe, and to deploy and protect amphibious forces. The success of the campaign served to boost Britain's standing in the world and critically saved the Royal Navy from some of the more draconian measures that had been proposed, but thankfully not yet implemented, in the Nott Review. Moreover, a new generation of Dartmouth graduates had found themselves successfully tested in the theatre of war.

One of the most evident changes felt at Dartmouth, however, was a reflection of the transformation of the educational system with the introduction of comprehensive schools and the expansion of the universities from the late 1960s. The increase in the number of university graduates lead to a steady rise in average age of officers under training, so that by 1988 the average age had risen to twenty-three years and 73% of full career officers either had a degree on joining or would have obtained one by the end of their training. Thus the Navy

was recruiting more graduates, but it was still those who entered straight from school that were more likely to remain in the Service and to make the Navy their chosen career. The Navy had encountered a problem of retention that had been slowly growing since the 1960s, as graduate entrants were far more likely to see the Navy as a stepping stone to another career later in life, and only sign up for a short career commission. To combat this situation the Navy considered the introduction of an in-service degree, as many school leavers were actively being encouraged to go to university before embarking upon a career.

This inevitably required the training methods at Dartmouth to be scrutinized, and the establishment of a new ethos at Dartmouth appropriate to a tertiary training establishment. Having staved off the suggestion to close the academic department completely it was decided in 1988, under Captain John Brigstocke, to introduce a new degree. This was the College's first foray into degree level work, through which Dartmouth would teach the first year and the final two years would be completed at the Royal Naval Engineering College, Manadon. Students would then be awarded the new degree of BA in Maritime Defence, Technology and Management, often referred to as the 'Dartman' degree. The Council for National Academic Awards (CNAA) awarded the final degree but it was Director of Studies Ian Jones who undertook much of the groundwork. One of the requirements of this transformation was that time be made available for the staff teaching on the degree programme to engage in subject development and research. A number of new appointments were made in the academic faculty to bring in those with research experience and a background in academic publication, in particular a new Director of Studies with a background in university teaching, Dr Alan Machin, was appointed in 1988 to demonstrate Captain Brigstocke's 'determination to signal that BRNC was into tertiary not secondary education'[8]. The degree was launched in 1990 and continued until Manadon closed in August 1995.

The overall effect was to finally cull those elements of the public school atmosphere that had continued to linger in the College since the mid-1950s. Meanwhile some of the more childish rules and activities were eliminated and 'all night leave' was finally to be granted to Young Officers. The bells signalling the changeover between periods were abandoned and in order to fit the maximum amount of material into the limited time available the fifty-five minute teaching period was reduced to forty-five minutes, although as one lecturer at the time recorded, this transition was not without its difficulties:

> 'Unfortunately, the implementation of these new arrangements coincided with the replacement of the original electro-mechanical master timing system, which required a complicated and time-consuming placing of pegs in holes in order to sound

Previous pages: Aerial view of the College in 2002.

8 Personal communication from Admiral Brigstocke.

The first female officers course, consisting of eight QARNNS, to train at Dartmouth in the spring of 1973.

the bells, with a modern, electronic, instantly-programmable device. The fact that the new timer was not to be used for its intended purpose was too much for the College clocks, which all failed and were to remain out of service for more than three months. The effect of all this was to introduce elasticity into the period length and the allocated five-minute changeover interval. Realising that most lecturers were unsure about the accuracy of their wristwatches, the officers-under-training were quick to seize the advantage by offering to keep note of the time. This resulted in them managing to extend lectures in popular subjects, such as oceanography, and delaying their arrival for classes, which were less to their liking, such as statistics.'[9]

Once again international affairs were exerting a major impact on the College. In 1989 the Berlin Wall fell, revolution swept Eastern Europe, Communism collapsed and the Iron Curtain retreated, within two years the Soviet Union itself would cease to exist: the Cold War was over. The consequent opportunity for a 'peace dividend', coupled with the rapid pace of change in electronic technology combined to produce another series of defence cuts, which were to encompass the closures of both Manadon and the Royal Naval College at Greenwich. By the mid-1990s the future of Dartmouth as a single-service initial officer training establishment looked precarious.

Change was not confined to the grand-strategic. In 1990, women became fully integrated within the Navy, with the sole exception of the submarine service. Women could now serve at sea, although those who joined previously and did not wish to follow this path were allowed to remain in shore jobs. From September 1990 all officer cadets, both male and female would receive the same training and follow the same career structure. The WRNS were disbanded and their blue braid was replaced by gold, their rank structure was abandoned and they received the same rank as the men. Consequently at Dartmouth the separate Talbot Division was disbanded as they were integrated into the existing College Divisions and both men and women had Divisional Officers of both sexes to train them.

The year 1992 also saw a large number of changes to the way in which Dartmouth trained its young officers. HMS *Bristol* had for a number of years been the flagship of the Dartmouth Training Squadron (DTS), where young officers went to sea for a term; upon her retirement Initial Sea Training (IST) was introduced. This was still undertaken in the second term, by two groups per term, spending a period of five to six weeks each, in Batch 1 Type 22 frigates, led by Captain IST in HMS *Brilliant* and joined by *Battleaxe* and *Brazen*. As part of this re-organisation of training the New Officer Training Structure (NOTS) was introduced and phased in over a number of terms. Under this 'new' scheme young officers were sent to sea for a period of nine months or so, immediately after their second (IST)

term at Dartmouth. They then returned to Dartmouth after their Fleet Board as Fleet Seniors for their one or two academic terms. This scheme was similar to the Murray Scheme seen earlier, which earned it the nickname of 'Son of Murray Scheme'. There were a number of reasons for the introduction of this scheme, the main one being financial as too many were failing their Fleet Board after Dartmouth, this at least would have saved two terms of training. It was unpopular with the Young Officers, mainly because they had been living in the Wardrooms while at sea and then had to return to the College to become an officer under training again and with the loss of their Wardroom status. The scheme was abandoned after a few years and reverted to the old system of Dartmouth before Fleet Board.

The other major educational innovation of this time was the recognition by the University of Plymouth of the two term Naval Studies course at Dartmouth (taken by senior non-graduate students) as the equivalent of the first year of a degree course. Successful completion of the course earned transferable degree credit points and the award of a Certificate of Higher Education.

As a result of the reduced sea training time that was introduced with NOTS a bridge trainer (simulator) was acquired and installed in F Block in September 1992. HMS *Sealark*, as it was called, was to give Officer of the Watch and coastal navigation training. It employed sophisticated computer imagery to give a realistic moving picture through 'bridge windows' and called for equally realistic responses from the bridge team. The 'bridge trainer' still continues to give invaluable 'bridge' experience and was replaced in 2002 with *Daring*, a state of the art modern simulator that provided movement with an increased sea-state.

The number of civilian academic staff remained constant throughout this period, with thirty-three lecturers in 1973 and thirty-three in 1998. The main difference was in the number of Instructor Officers within the academic faculty, from six in 1973 to none in 1998. The academic departments also changed, with the Department of Strategic Studies and International Affairs replacing History and English and History and Economics, the Mathematics Department becoming Maths and Computing, the Science Department sub-divided into Marine Environment, Ship Technology and Radar and Telecommunications, and the emergence of a separate Department of English.

However, by the mid-1990s numbers remained low and Dartmouth was still perceived to be failing to deliver an appropriate package for the modern navy. Commodore Roy Clare was therefore appointed with a mission, the first of a series of reformers to command the College. Under his command, over the next eighteen months, the naval training of officers was subject to comprehensive reform and the groundwork put in place for his successors to lead the parallel changes to the academic faculty.[10] The dawn of a new millennium therefore saw yet more changes, marshalling in the

9 The observations of former lecturer Brian Parker.

10 Personal communication from Rear Admiral Roy Clare.

ii.

i.

iv.

iiii.

i. The Rt. Hon. Tony Blair MP arrives at BRNC on the 11th January 2007 to be met by Commodore Tim Harris and Commander Richard King. Mr Blair was the first serving Prime Minister to visit the College. Winston Churchill had visited the College in 1940 when First Lord of the Admiralty.

ii. Mr Blair observes students under instruction in the bridge trainer.

iii. Mr Blair is presented with a copy of this book by authors Dr Jane Harrold and Dr Richard Porter.

iv. Mr Blair departs to continue his tour of West Country naval establishments.

beginning of the end of the Academic Faculty. A review of training and education was conducted in 2000 under Commander Steele. This led to the removal of the fourth term of academic instruction for non-graduates, which had previously amounted to a Certificate in Higher Education, and the total integration of graduates, school leavers and Upper Yardmen into a three term course of professional training, education and initial sea time. The Academic Faculty itself was trimmed with the Director of Studies post disestablished and down graded to that of Head of Faculty. Ashford House, the Director of Studies' (formerly Headmaster's) House was taken over by Flagship Training for the teaching of English as a foreign language.

The overall syllabus was re-cast to give greater focus to front line training and more emphasis on maritime leadership. A new 'squadron' structure, consisting of Cunningham and St. Vincent Squadrons, was introduced to facilitate the supervision and administration of training and the former hospital building was reallocated from student accommodation to house the BRNC Royal Marine Band. These revisions, however, were to prove transitionary, and indeed less radical, than those to occur between 2003 and 2004. In May 2003 the Multiple Entry System introduced six entries and passing outs per year, instead of the traditional three, in order to provide a more even flow of Young Officers out into the Fleet. While this naturally required a revision of the delivery of courses at the College, further changes were then introduced by a review of the Academic Faculty. Consequently when the last Head of Faculty retired in September 2003 she was not replaced. The eight academic departments were merged into three (of five) 'pillars' (the other two being Naval departments), placing all lecturers under the management of the newly entitled Commander of Naval Training and Education.

Concurrently, in a continued effort to attract younger cadets straight from school, the 'Foundation For the Future' in-service degree was launched in January 2001, whereby non-graduate Warfare and Supply Officers can register for a foundation degree (two-thirds of an honours degree) in Naval Studies with Plymouth University. The degree is awarded on successful completion of the training pipeline from entry at BRNC to the end of the Junior Warfare Officer's Course (JWOC) or Junior Supply Officer's Course (JSOC). On completion of the Foundation Degree the Officer has the option of proceeding to an honours degree via distance learning with Plymouth University. A similar scheme, named 'A Flying Start' is also available offering an in-service degree to aircrew through the completion of Open University Accredited initial officer training at BRNC and RN flying courses at levels one and two, before completing an honours degree from Plymouth University.

Meanwhile the structures introduced in 2003-4 were soon judged unsustainable and in 2009 a three term entry was reintroduced. Under Initial Officer Training (IOT 09) cadets were to spend their first fourteen week term at Dartmouth before going to sea for Initial Fleet Time (IFT) and returning to BRNC to pass out at the end of their second fourteen weeks. Meanwhile financial stringency led to the abolition of one of the academic pillars, thus removing Modern Languages, Maths and all but the most basic English from the curriculum. In June 2008 all lecturing staff came under the employ of Plymouth University, rather than being Civil Servants, as part of a partnering agreement which saw the management of lecturers return to a senior academic.

As naval education at Dartmouth approaches its 150th anniversary IOT 09 is to be replaced by Initial Naval Training (Officer) in an attempt, once more, to accommodate the changing demands of the Fleet; in this instance the declining number of RN ships following the Strategic Defence and Security Review of 2010. This will see the introduction of four smaller entries per year and closer alignment with ratings training currently delivered at HMS *Raleigh*. Nevertheless, the College's mission remains to produce the Royal Naval Officers of the future. Admiral Fisher established a system of education at Dartmouth in 1905, which in order to achieve its objective produced a revolutionary system of education, through which the qualities of character and leadership required of an officer were instilled through the acquisition of knowledge, delivered to the highest possible standards compared to the outside world. In the post war world this system had to change but it did so under the scrutiny of a highly interested public, which still identified the Royal Navy, and by association Dartmouth, as one of the great British institutions. The Royal Naval College is currently undergoing one of the most fundamental changes in its history. This time there are few questions in Parliament and little public debate beyond Dartmouth itself. The armed services are no longer held in the same regard that they were one hundred or even fifty years ago, which reflects Britain's changing position in the international system. Nevertheless, the country remains an active participant in world affairs, for which the government relies upon a deployable Navy led by the most able officers. These officers will, as have the majority of RN officers since 1863, begin their career at Dartmouth. The future of the Royal Navy depends upon the future of the Royal Naval College; it is a heavy burden, which for 150 years Dartmouth has not failed to carry.

CHAPTER 7

College Life

In many respects the world, and the Royal Navy have changed immeasurably over the past century. Technology and the rise and fall of nations have transformed the environment in which Dartmouth's cadets live and train, adapting to the development of submarines and aircraft, nuclear propulsion, radar, sonar, computers, satellites, the increasingly complex politics of state and non-state threats to security and indeed the changing nature of such threats. Yet Dartmouth's purpose remains essentially the same. The average age of cadet may have risen by a decade, the length of training shortened, the subjects taught been adapted but the basics of command and leadership, seamanship, intellectual and personal development remain constant, as the following extracts will demonstrate.

Arrival of the New Entry cadets. Traditionally the New Entry travelled to Kingswear by train, until the closure of the branch line from Paignton, by British Rail in 1972. This re-enactment, using a vintage steam hauled train shows the raw recruits upon arrival at Britannia Halt (opened in 1877 for the arrival of Princes Albert Victor and George). Today new arrivals are met by College transport at Totnes station.

New Entry cadets arrive on the Parade Ground.

Fitness test, burpee jumps.

A Young Officer's cabin (study-bedroom).

An account of the life of a young officer towards the end of the so-called 'Murray Scheme' was recounted by two Sub Lieutenants (R. Clare and A. Piska) who in 1971 had recently passed through Dartmouth under that regime. Although this account is now almost thirty-five years old it still gives a good impression of the life of a Cadet in the College. Those who have more recently passed through BRNC will recognise much of what is recounted and come to realise that although there may have been major changes over the past thirty years, the overall routine is similar. After all the end product is the same, as the authors state in their introduction, 'to train young men to Act and React Instinctively as Officers'

'The Cadet of 1971 spends on average six months at the College in which to acquire a sound theoretical knowledge of the departments of a modern warship. The syllabus is broad; seamanship, navigation (including astronavigation), gunnery, underwater warfare, communications, man management, supply and secretariat, naval history, warfare, amphibious operations, damage control, and parade training – being just some of the headings. It is still realised that the self-discipline, personal pride and self- confidence acquired on the parade ground make parade training a very valuable and essential part of the syllabus. To achieve the required standard of drill new entry cadets spend at least one hour a day on the parade ground and at the end of their fourth week they are examined by the Parade Training Officer; success qualifies a Cadet for his first shore leave at the end of the sixth week – few fail.

Much of the Cadet's training is done, perhaps sub-consciously, by the Sub Lieutenants in their third year of training in the Navy. They have completed their year in the Fleet as Midshipmen and return to Dartmouth as Seamen or Supply officers on the General List to study mathematics, general

Rounds. Cabin cleaned, clothes pressed and folded, boots polished, drawers tidied and open for inspection.

science, history, economics and languages at a tertiary level. The science course broadens the Sub Lieutenants' knowledge of the principles behind much of the complicated electrical and mechanical equipment in service with the Fleet and topics include oceanography, meteorology, 'computers' and nuclear physics. The humanities choices of subjects open to Officers under training includes; 'A Study of Peace and War', 'Naval History', 'Contemporary Affairs' and a choice of one of seven Foreign Languages – from Russian to Malay.

They (the Sub Lieutenants) bring with them a newfound experience and self-confidence, which combined with the small age gap tends to make them better equipped to teach the

Practice divisions marching on after a storm.

Essential maintenance: Top: The clock receives a face-lift.
Bottom: Stonemason works on the Royal coat of arms on the clock tower.

Man overboard.

Cadets by example than any one else in the College. Every cadet is therefore allocated to a 'Guiding Sub Lieutenant' or 'Sea-Daddy'. They will discuss with the Cadet their general progress at regular intervals and by pointing out their faults they can make the new entry feel at ease and will almost certainly be able to contribute to the Cadet's general naval training.

Every Cadet is allocated to one of five Divisions, named after a famous Admiral; Jellicoe, Blake, Hawke, Cunningham and St Vincent. Each Division is headed by a Lieutenant Commander, he supervises the Cadet's training and administrative needs and will ensure that every cadet does his bit for the Division – on the sports field, on the river or in some other useful way: always watching for signs of weakness so that early steps may be taken to reject unsuitable characters – he will go out of his way to assist a Cadet who finds some part of the course difficult to master.

Each Cadet is allocated a Civilian Tutor who will assist him if he finds problems with academic training. The Tutors report on the Cadets in their 'tutor sets' – so providing a double check on the Cadet's progress. Most Tutors are permanent staff so they fulfil the valuable task of continuity, since Divisional Officers remain in the College for only two years. The most important Sub Lieutenant, as far as the new entry is concerned, is the 'Divisional Sub Lieutenant' who is chosen for his qualities of leadership and personal bearing. He is responsible for organising the Division and ensuring that the Cadets meet high standards in such matters

A rare sight; wet weather divisions on the Quarterdeck.

as kit stowage and smartness of turnout.'

Clare and Piska go on to describe a typical day in the life of a New Entry Cadet of 1971.

'At 0600 awake and attend 'Early Morning Activities' (EMA's) every morning except Sunday, for the first six weeks. These include morse flashing, physical training, swimming and parade training. Followed at 0700 by breakfast. This meal will often be a hurried affair snatched in the modern cafeteria style dining hall, (the Junior Gunroom – JGR) after which the Cadet hurries to make his bunk, square off his cabin and be ready to begin 'After Breakfast Activities' at 0745. On three days a week this will be 'Divisions' – a traditional ceremony in the Navy, akin to the Army's Parade – when the Cadets fall in by divisions on the parade ground to be inspected by their Divisional Officers. Then prayers are said and the ceremony of 'Colours' takes place when the White Ensign is hoisted on the main mast, the strains of the National Anthem played by the Royal Marine Band. Finally the divisions march past, smartly in line, heads swivelled to the right in salute to the Captain. At 0830 the Cadet begins the day's instruction, six one hour

periods every day, except Wednesday and the weekends, including one or two periods of physical training, make up the formal training time. Breaks in routine occur at intervals: several days are spent flying in the College Flight's Wasp Helicopter or in one of the 'Chipmunk' Trainer aircraft maintained at Roborough Airfield, near Plymouth. Two or three days are spent at sea in the minesweeper attached to the College – to give Cadets their first experience of practical navigation and seamanship. Day visits are arranged to such places as The Plymouth Planetarium – for a look at the best-known navigational aids; to a small arms range; and to the fire fighting school in HMS *Raleigh*. The Cadets will later find pertinent questions in their examination papers on matters they should have noted during their visits.

The less formal part of a Cadet's general training will be covered by his Divisional Officer during specially nominated periods. Subjects covered include; 'Behaviour at Cocktail Parties', 'Service Letter Writing', 'Dress Ashore' and 'Leadership'. Cadets are also expected to prepare and deliver talks lasting between ten and fifteen minutes on subjects of their choice.

Parading the scroll granting the College the freedom of the Borough of Dartmouth in February 1956

Divisional Officers also keep a close watch on the Cadets' 'Activity Logs' which are completed weekly and contain brief descriptions of their sporting or river activities for every day of the week They give Cadets the chance to express their thoughts and opinions in writing and so prepare them for the task of Journal writing that they will encounter in the Fleet as Midshipmen. Not all the Cadet's training takes place within the College: essential character building exercises on the moors and in the countryside around Dartmouth are included in the syllabus and occur at regular intervals. Every weekend one of the Divisions embark on an expedition (often travelling by boat up the Dart) to 'defend' some imaginary installation from attack by 'aggressors', or to practise map reading in an orienteering exercise. Cadets are chosen to lead teams of five or six of their contemporaries during the exercises, so 'taking charge' of a group of men and attempting to achieve an objective for possibly the first time in their lives.

Remembrance Day parade through the town of Dartmouth in 1999.

After a full day of professional training the Cadet is almost worn out by 1645, when the recreational period begins! Such are the facilities at College that a Cadet may take up any sport or activity he cares to mention. However, there is seldom-sufficient time to take up more than one or two, because of the requirement to spend a minimum of two afternoons a week on the River Dart in one of the many boats maintained by the College for practical seamanship training. Only by constant practice will he gain sufficient expertise to be able to pass a demanding handling test in each class of boat. When he later joins the Fleet he will meet most of the types of boat in use at the College and it is important that a young man of the sea should be proficient in their use. Those Cadets who are fortunate to be good enough, may find that they have been selected to play for one of the College sports teams – an honour indeed, but hard work. They will be expected to train on two afternoons a week and will then defend the high reputation of the College against crack West Country teams on Wednesday and Saturday afternoons. Clearly the remaining two afternoons have to be devoted to river work and so fond hopes of skiing in Norway, cruising in one of the College yachts to France, flying in a 'Chipmunk' to gain a pilot's licence or joining the famous Britannia Beagles on a fast-moving chase across the countryside nearby, are finally dashed.

Divisional life is taken seriously at the College – both to extract the right spirit from the individual and to demonstrate to them the value of the Navy's 'Divisional System'. [1] Competition is fostered whenever possible, as, for example, in the case of the Inter-Divisional Sports Trophy which is awarded at the end of each term to the Division that has been the most successful at a number of sports and activities – ranging from the Rugby knockout to the Bosun Dinghy racing series. Other mass events such as the Sailing Regatta and 'Away all Boats' are popular and victories are celebrated with much gusto in local taverns. Once a term each Division holds its own mess dinner, to which a distinguished guest is invited – usually a senior Naval Officer – and for possibly the first time the Cadet realizes that there is a gentlemanly side to his chosen career! [2] Apart from these occasions, social life is virtually nil as there is not sufficient time in a Cadet's routine for any other organised functions during the term, except for the end of term Ball.

1 The 'Divisional System' was first introduced by Captain Kempenfelt in 1779 as being 'The only way to keep large bodies of men in order by dividing and sub dividing them, with officers over each to inspect and regulate their conduct, to discipline and form them'.
2 See Box 'Mess Dinners'

College picket boats coming alongside.

The Dartmouth Training Squadron

With the introduction of the Selborne Scheme all cadets on completion of their education at Osborne and Dartmouth would join a special cruiser that had been fitted out as a Cadet Training Ship. This ship was part of the Training Squadron formed for the seagoing training of naval personnel. The first vessel to be used for this purpose was HMS Isis, which began her task in 1902. The Isis spent most of her time in the Mediterranean with a great deal of her time in harbour. Excursions were arranged for the cadets and a good 'run ashore' would be a well-organized paper chase, of which there appear to have been many. The Training Squadron produced its own magazine, but unfortunately few survive, but an entry for Monday 18th March 1907, read 'Went into Arosa Bay at daylight and anchored in our billet off Villefranche at 1730. General drill took place and consisted of exercising at turning and being towed. Cadets landed in the afternoon to have a look round. It is doubtful if they found much to do, the strong point of Arosa certainly not being its stodge shops'. The Mediterranean remained a popular location for the Training Ships with occasional cruises to the West Indies, the warmer climes being more healthy and requiring less expenditure for heating, until the outbreak of war when the operations were suspended.

The need for a cadet's training ship was again recognized after the end of hostilities and the cruisers Cornwall and Cumberland were recommissioned as Cadet Training Cruisers. With the introduction of the eighteen year old entry in 1955 the Squadron continued, but with the use of three frigates in place of a single ship. Since 1955 the sole function of the Squadron was to take Cadets and latterly Young Officers under training to sea for practical experience.

They would take 'flag-showing' cruises to such destinations as Scandinavia or the Mediterranean. The young officers lived on mess decks identical to those used by ratings, – in fact the DTS ships were under-complemented with seaman ratings, and they were involved in chipping and painting, running the boats and indeed everywhere on the ship where they would learn, through experience, the basic practical aspects of their future in the Navy.

The Dartmouth Training Ships

1902 – 1906	HMS Isis	Protected Cruiser
1907	HMS Cumberland	Belted Cruiser
1908 – 1910	HM Ships Cumberland and Cornwall	Belted Cruisers
1911 – 1912	HMS Cumberland	Belted Cruiser
1913 – 1914	HMS Cornwall	Belted Cruiser
1915 – 1918	Training ships suspended, First World War	
1919	HM Ships Cornwall and Cumberland	Belted Cruisers
1920	HMS Temeraire	Dreadnought Battleship
1921 – 1923	HMS Thunderer	Super Dreadnought Battleship
1924 – 1925	Training ship concept scrapped for economic reasons	
1926 – 1932	HMS Erebus	Monitor, used in the harbour only
1933 – 1936	HMS Frobisher	Cruiser
1937 – 1939	HMS Vindictive	Cruiser
1940 – 1943	Training ships suspended, Second World War	
1944 – 1946	HMS Frobisher	Cruiser
1947 – 1952	HMS Devonshire	Heavy Cruiser
1953 – 1955	HMS Triumph	Aircraft Carrier
1956	HM Ships Vigilant and Venus	A/S Frigates
1957	HM Ships Vigilant, Carron and Roebuck	A/S Frigates
1958	HM Ships Vigilant, Venus and Roebuck	A/S Frigates
1959	HM Ships Vigilant, Roebuck and Carron	A/S Frigates
1960	HM Ships Vigilant, Carron and Urchin	A/S Frigates
1961	HM Ships Roebuck, Wizard and Venus	A/S Frigates
1962	HM Ships Urchin, Roebuck, Wizard and Vigilant	A/S Frigates
1963	HM Ships Tenby, Wizard and Torquay	A/S Frigates
1964	HM Ships Tenby, Torquay, Eastbourne and Scarborough	A/S Frigates
1965	HM Ships Tenby, Eastbourne and Scarborough	A/S Frigates
1966	HM Ships Scarborough, Torquay and Eastbourne	A/S Frigates
1967 – 1968	HM Ships Scarborough, Eastbourne and Tenby	A/S Frigates
1969	HM Ships Tenby, Eastbourne and Torquay	A/S Frigates
1970	HM Ships Tenby, Torquay and Scarborough	A/S Frigates
1971 – 1972	HM Ships Eastbourne, Tenby and Scarborough	A/S Frigates

Life in a DTS ship, HMS Hermes, March 1979.

On 26th July 1972 The Dartmouth Training Squadron, with ships specifically dedicated to the training of cadets from BRNC, was disbanded. The DTS did continue for another twenty years but the College had to bid for sea-time for the cadets and a variety of ships were used, although the two LPD's (the Assault ships Fearless and Intrepid) were commonly in use for the purpose. However with a shrinking Navy the RN could no longer afford ships dedicated to training and the ships became dual role while under the Captain DTS. Below is a list of some of the vessels used, but a scarcity of available information means that the list is incomplete.

1973	HMS Intrepid	Assault Ship
1974	HMS Fearless	Assault Ship
1975	HMS Intrepid	Assault Ship
1976	HMS Fearless	Assault Ship
1979	HM Ships Fearless, Intrepid and Hermes	Assault Ships and Aircraft Carrier
1980	HMS Intrepid	Assault Ship
1981	HMS Londonderry	Fleet Trials Ship
1983	HM Ships Fearless and Rothesay.	Assault Ship and A/S Frigate
1984	HM Ships Plymouth, Berwick and Londonderry	Fleet Trials Ship and A/S Frigates
1985	HM Ships Fearless and Glamorgan	Assault Ship and Type 42 Destroyer
1986	HM Ships Fife and Juno	Destroyer and A/S Frigate
1987	HM Ships Bristol, Euryalus, Juno, Fife and Rothesay	Destroyer and A/S Frigates
1988	HMS Bristol	Destroyer
1989	HM Ships Bristol, Euryalus and Achilles	Destroyer and A/S Frigates
1990 – 1991	HM Ships Bristol, Ariadne and Minerva.[1]	Destroyer and A/S Frigates
1992	The Dartmouth Training Squadron was replaced by Initial Sea Training (IST) which was principally undertaken by Batch 1 Type 22 Frigates, initially led by HMS Brilliant.	

HMS *Cumberland* from an old postcard.

HMS *Isis* from an old postcard.

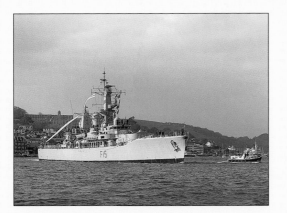

HMS *Euryalus* visiting Dartmouth in April 1989, flying the paying-off pennant in her final deployment. Her commanding officer was Commander J. P. Cardale who subsequently joined the College as The Commander.

HMS *Bristol* visits the College in 1991 prior to paying off. Her Captain, Richard Hastilow took up his next appointment as Captain of the College.

Cadets on board HMS *Isis* (c. 1902-1903).

1 At the start of 1991 saw the ships *Bristol, Ariadne* and *Minerva* all sailing for the Western Mediterranean to take on the primary task of patrol ships for that area after the escalation of hostilities in the Arabian Gulf. This meant that their training role, though still an important aspect of their work was to become a secondary consideration.

Cadets are expected to perform various College duties each term, as members of the Divisional Guard, as coxswain of the Duty Motor Cutter on the river, as members of the Colours and Sunset flag party or perhaps as the Commander's Messenger.[3] However trivial the duty two things are important: firstly, for many the duty will be their first taste of responsibility, with penalties to be awarded for failure; secondly, the prestige of the Division is at stake if things go wrong – very often the scorn of his fellows is the worst punishment a Cadet could suffer! Throughout the Cadets' training they are learning to carry out simple tasks correctly so that the greater responsibilities that they will have in the Fleet will be second nature to them.

To be able to relax for short periods becomes vitally important to Cadets after they have concentrated hard on their studies during the long days at Dartmouth.[4] Culturally the Britannia Society of Music and Arts, caters for most tastes by arranging regular performances by well known artists in such widely differing fields as folk music and ballet; an annual College Play that is entered for the Inter-Command Drama Competition; an annual College Revue and the provision of facilities for giving music lessons on instruments from piano to the guitar. It is very easy for Cadets to forget the world outside after the first few days within the organisation[5]. A NAAFI canteen is provided for the use of Cadets in the evening, but only beer is sold, but a television and snooker table is provided.
With the basic theoretical knowledge under his belt the Cadet is ready to put ideas into practice at the end of his second term at the College and he joins one of the three frigates of the Dartmouth Training Squadron[6]. The sole function of the Squadron is to take Cadets to sea for the whole of their third term. With the first year of training behind them the Cadets become Midshipmen and leave Dartmouth for the Fleet.'

This is the routine that both HRH The Prince of Wales and HRH The Prince Andrew would have been trained under and much of it is still recognisable by those who have passed through more recently, and as such it provides a valuable insight into the life of a junior officer under training at Dartmouth.

The smell of floor polish is one of the most evocative memories of the College.

One of the major changes at Dartmouth, which will be obvious from the account above of 1971, is that women have been for the past fifteen years an integral part of not only College life, but also of life in the Royal Navy. Another major change is that the rank of Cadet is no longer in existence, it having being abolished in 1972, when all junior officers training at the College would become Midshipmen. Although the term, not rank, Officer Cadet is still in use for those who join BRNC. In 1973 BRNC opened its doors for the training of female officers for the first time in its history, the first group being a number of QARNNS (Queen Alexandra's Royal Naval Nursing Service). This heralded the way for further training of females at the College as the WRNS officer-training course moved form Greenwich to Dartmouth in 1976 and 'Talbot' Division[7] was formed to house them. The first females to train in the all male dominated BRNC must have found life quite strange; the following account was written by Surgeon Lieutenant Susan F Good, who joined the College in 1973.[8]

3 Little has changed here except that the Duty of Commander's Messenger has disappeared. Duties with rather more responsibility are given to senior Young Officers today, such as the Assistant Duty Commanding Officer (ADCO) or Duty River Officer, the former assisting the DCO and the latter organising the river activities.

4 To this end a young officer will snatch sleep whenever he can, often on coaches going to a sports fixture and occasionally during an academic period. One of the authors (RP) remembers taking a group of young officers to RNAS Culdrose some years ago and once in the minibus all thirteen of them were asleep by the time the bus had reached the top of 'College Way'.

5 Everything that the Cadet should need is provided, such as a cobbler, tailor, hairdresser and even a cash dispenser.

6 See box relating to the DTS. Today a junior young officer will spend about six weeks on board a ship as part of his 'Initial Sea Training'(IST), this system having replaced the DTS in 1992.

7 Named after Mary Talbot, Director of WRNS 1973-76. Talbot Division lasted until January 1992 when women were totally integrated into the Royal Navy.

8 First published in the *Britannia Magazine*, Christmas 1973.

Handing over the staff of office, Commander Richard Marshall hands over to Commander David Vaughan in 2002.

A regular sight in recent times, a Merlin HM1 helicopter 814 Naval Air Squadron landing on the Parade Ground.

Defence diplomacy: Commander-in-Chief of the Ukraine Navy Admiral Yezhel visiting the Engineering Science laboratory in November 2000.

'I should imagine that the idea of a female Royal Navy Officer passing through the male dominated corridors and classrooms of The Britannia Royal Naval College would bring shudders of horror to the more traditionally minded officers. Nevertheless I had the honour to be the first – a Surgeon Lieutenant (D) in the NEO Class of 17th September to 12th October 1973.

On arrival I committed the great sacrilege of parking on the parade ground. After reporting my presence, I was escorted to my cabin by a Midshipman and helped to unload the car – advantage number one of being female. The following day I mustered for introductory talks with members of the QARNNS and with other the female new entry, Constructor Midshipman Claire. Amongst other things we were told about the swimming test. In theory this was not compulsory for Midshipman Claire and myself, but a challenge was thrown

down in such a away that neither of us could really refuse. The idea came as rather a shock as I had played no games for about eight years. In fact I had little difficulty either with swimming or the treading water test (in spite of the large boiler suit). However, I could not pick a brick up from the bottom of the pool and so became a 'backward swimmer'.

Normally groups only attending the College for short periods do not do 'early morning activities' unless they are 'backward swimmers'. Then they have to report to the pool every morning at 0630 until they pass the test. I did not have to do this – just another of the very many occasions when being a girl was a definite advantage.

To avoid having to apologise for bad language and blue stories, my colleagues elected me an 'honorary gentleman', though after medical or dental school they need not have worried. It was really quite amusing in lectures for the class to be greeted by a 'good morning gentlemen' with the addition of 'Oh' I do beg your pardon, when I was noticed. Certain members of the staff persisted in calling me 'Sir' because of the gold stripes.

Operation Fresco. College personnel stand in during the fire-fighters strike in 2002.

Dr. Alan Machin, Director of Studies, enjoying International Day in the Senior Gun Room, an opportunity for international students to display the culture of their country.

Outreach. A class from Dartmouth Primary School visit the meteorological station in 2002.

Our gym sessions proved to be the next problem. I was quite prepared to join the men for gym, in spite of my unfitness, to give everyone a good laugh at least. I did not have any kit but was assured that this could be supplied. However, for some reason the gym lessons did not materialise, though I did join the men for a session in the pool with a life raft. After it had been turned upside down, I was allowed to be the first to right it. Could this be preferential treatment? The coffee with the instructor most certainly was.

Accommodation was an interesting problem. Originally I had been allocated to Hawke Division and was supposed to share a cabin with one of the doctors. After it was realised that my name was Susan, this mistake was rectified and I was transferred to C Block with the QARNNS and Midshipman Claire. In this wing we do not appear to be subjected to 'rounds' or inspection. At meal times the stewards occasionally

Fleet Air Arm day, Lynx Mk 8 when local schools are invited to the College.

come round with second helpings and, when I caught a heavy cold, the bar stewards supplied me hot toddies to take to bed.

I have enjoyed our various excursions. During our fire fighting course at HMS *Raleigh* the nurses and I were led round the inside the smoke chamber by lads working in that department – a comfort that I am sure the men in the group neither had nor would have appreciated. We have had two days at sea – one in HMS *Undaunted* and the other in HMS *Walkerton*. On *Walkerton* I was entertained in the Wardroom whereas the men had to go to the Mess-deck. I actually succeeded in hitting the lock hard enough the first time to enable the anchor to go. I had been warned previously about having to buy a round of drinks if I missed!

Another item worthy of note is Parade Training. I had never done anything like it before. Our Parade Training Instructor was

a bit surprised to find out about me but seemed to accept me very well. I took part in the Tuesday and Thursday Divisions and also in the weekend Ceremonial Divisions. I did not double with the men, nor did I carry a sword[9], though I was allowed to practise some sword drill, which was very amusing.

The most interesting social function I attended was the Senior Gunroom Ladies Night. I think that I was probably the only member of the Mess to take a male guest!!

The final escapade on which I was somewhat spoiled was Divex (Divisional Exercise) on Dartmoor. Originally I had been told that it would be a gentle stroll across part of the moor, staying in a tent overnight. I agreed to go thinking that it would

9 The carrying of swords by female officers would not come about until their full integration into the Navy in 1992.

Visiting cadets from the Japanese National Defence Academy with Modern Languages lecturer Dr. Ian Roberts in 1998.

i.

ii.

iii.

iv.

v.

vi.

vii.

On the Moor. *i. Arrival by a Merlin Mk 3 helicopter from 28 Squadron RAF in Bosnian livery. ii. Typical Dartmoor weather. iii. Nearly there! iv. Blisters. v. Mustn't fall in! vi. Cold and wet. vii. Final debrief.*

Mess Dinners

*O*ne aspect of life in the Royal Navy is the Mess Dinner, where officers dine formally together. This may be to celebrate a special occasion such as Trafalgar Night or Taranto Night, or it may involve the 'dining out' those officers who are leaving, although the Navy does not need a special excuse to dine formally. At Dartmouth there is one combined mess dinner a year held to celebrate Trafalgar Night, where the Wardroom and Senior Gunroom messes dine together in the Senior Gunroom. The Young Officers will also have the opportunity to attend their Squadron Dinner and New Entry dining in, held after their initial training phase. At Dartmouth these dinners are regarded as training events and the young officers will receive a 'brief' prior to the dinner on etiquette and the format of the evening. They will probably be required to host a member of staff and although the event is part of

their training the aim is that it should still be an enjoyable evening as they begin to realise that they have joined a rather exclusive and prestigious 'club'.

The 'rig' for the evening will be announced beforehand, and is Mess Dress, which comprises miniature medals, a stiff shirt and white waistcoat, usually worn if Royalty or Flag Officers are being dined, but Mess Undress (soft pique shirt, with blue waistcoat and miniature ribbons) is more usual.

The format of most Mess Dinners follows a set procedure, which will only vary in slight detail. A bugle is sounded ten minutes before dinner and when ready the Senior Steward reports to the Mess President (The Commander at BRNC) who takes the Guest of Honour, and precedes the Officers, into the dining room to the sound of the band playing Roast Beef of Old England. The Chaplain, if present will, say Grace before which nothing on

An early photograph of the dining hall, laid for a formal dinner.

A chef prepares chocolate 'ships of the line,' for a Trafalgar Night Dinner.

Candle light in the Senior Gun Room.

A Divisional Dinner for staff and students in the Senior Gun Room.

the table must be touched. The mess silver adorning the table must also be left untouched. The meal is served in the usual order, and everyone present takes their lead from the President. After the last course, the tables are cleared (including all glasses, whether empty or not) and the final Grace is said. The stewards place glasses and decanters of port on the table and the stoppers are removed. A decanter of madeira or another drink may also be offered. Once the stoppers are removed the port is passed clockwise around the table, the port should not leave the table, which means that it is passed by sliding it to the left along the table (some take this too literally and pour a glass of port with the decanter still touching the table, not an easy task when nearly empty). The port always leads the way and it never travels backwards, acknowledging Portugal as Britain's oldest ally. When the President orders the Loyal Toast, 'Mr Vice, The Queen' the National Anthem is played. The Vice President then replies with the Toast 'Ladies and Gentlemen, The Queen', all present raise their glasses repeating 'The Queen'. It is naval tradition to drink the Sovereign's health while seated, unless she is present, then all stand and face her for the toast.[1] One of the most enduring sounds of a mess dinner is that of dozens of port glasses being placed on the table after the toast, in an otherwise silent room. The only other time that officers stand is if foreign officers are present, a toast to their country's leader is made first and all the guests stand and remain standing for the Loyal Toast that follows. Daily toasts may be made after the Loyal Toast. Traditionally these are:

Monday	our ships at sea
Tuesday	our men
Wednesday	ourselves (as no one else is likely to concern themselves with our welfare)
Thursday	a bloody war and sickly season (leading to early promotion for us)
Friday	a willing foe and sea room (a good fight and room to manoeuvre a sailing ship)
Saturday	wives and sweethearts (may they never meet)
Sunday	absent friends

On Trafalgar Night the toast to Lord Nelson is proposed by the President, or whoever is making the speech, the Loyal Toast having been proposed earlier. The toast is Ladies and Gentlemen, the immortal memory of Admiral Lord Nelson. The toast is then drunk in silence.

After the dinner the officers and guests retire to the anteroom, where 'mess games' may be played. These are often rowdy and their format is best left to the imagination.

1 The origin of the custom of naval officers sitting for the Loyal Toast has four possible origins. Three of these relate to the monarch bumping his head when on board. The first is that in 1660 Charles II bumped his head when rising to reply to a toast while returning from Holland in HMS *Naseby*, the second that William IV, when Duke of Clarence, did the same, the third that it was George IV, who said to his officers as they rose 'Gentlemen' pray be seated. Your loyalty is above suspicion'. The fourth is that in the Restoration Navy, formed of gentlemen volunteers, these gentlemen were not used to being at sea and had not yet found their 'sealegs' hence the need to remain seated to avoid the embarrassment of falling over if they were to rise.

be great fun. After I had committed myself, I learnt that amongst other things we had to cross a river on a rope and to go hurtling around in the middle of the night. I then started to get cold feet, not literally at this stage that was to come!! Anyway the great day arrived and we had to trundle off in a troop lorry – the coach being too large to negotiate the narrow lanes and bridges. After arriving at our starting point, we were divided into teams and set off down a river to our allocated crossing points. Unfortunately rainfall had been very heavy since the area had been first examined and the gentle stream with stepping-stones had become a dangerous raging torrent. After much deliberation it was decided that in fact we would cross as planned, but that one group would have to man a safety line further downstream. I was petrified! My team was absolutely marvellous and hooked me on to the rope with so many belts etc that I could not have fallen off even if I had tried. After a meal and a chance to thaw out at base camp, the men went on an orienteering exercise. I was allowed to trundle round in the Land Rover with the staff, stopping for liquid refreshments and to pick up and rescue members of the expedition. The following day was very strenuous for the men, but pretty easy for me. I just strolled up to one of the markers for the hike with the staff and was given some lessons on how to use a hand compass.

I should like to conclude with a very big thank you to everyone at BRNC for all their kindness and courtesy and for making my time there so enjoyable. I hope that all my successors are trained in comparable fashion.' (*Britannia Magazine*, 1973)

It would appear that Surg. Lt Susan F Good enjoyed her time at the College and as one of the first women to be trained at BRNC was treated with some degree of care and given what some would describe as a fairly easy time. Today it is somewhat different as the women enter BRNC under a fully integrated scheme that has been running for well over ten years and the same training programme is followed by both sexes and the same level of commitment is expected of them all.

Since the days of the old *Britannia* and *Hindostan* the Royal Navy has trained cadets from the Commonwealth countries and continues to do so, there has therefore always been a percentage of foreign cadets at the College. In addition to the Commonwealth, cadets from other navies have also been trained, for example in the early 1960s both Thailand and the Sudan sent cadets to Dartmouth where they joined the Royal Navy General List cadets for the normal four years of training and cadets from the Imperial Ethiopian Navy spent one term at Dartmouth at that time prior to going to Portsmouth for naval short courses. Today International Officers include individuals from Bahamas, Brunei, France, Ghana, Jamaica, Jordan, Kenya, Kuwait, Qatar, Oman, Romania, Senegal, Singapore, Syria, Tanzania, Trinidad and Tobago, United Arab Emirates, USA and Ukraine, who

Minister for the Armed Forces, Dr. John Reid greeted on arrival in Twin Squirrel from 32 The Royal Squadron RAF by Commodore Roy Clare and Commander Philip Ingham.

follow courses that are largely similar to that of the short career officers, they study courses in maritime technology and computing with the addition of English for those who do not have English as their first language. Some International Officers return to the College for further studies, possibly leading to the award of a degree. They are fully integrated into College life and run an International Day for the benefit of the rest of the College where they proudly show the culture of their home country. There are also regular visits from the students and staffs of sister academies in Germany, France, Spain, USA and Japan, indeed official twinning agreements have been signed between BRNC and the French, German and Spanish academies while exchange officers from the USA, France, Germany and Australia serve on the naval staff. In 2004 a group of officers from the Iraqi Coastal Defence Force visited the College for a short course as part of the Coalition's programme to rebuild post-Saddam Iraq. The contingent included senior officers who had previously attended Dartmouth back in the late 1980s. The presence of both Iraqi and Kuwaiti students proved unproblematic, indeed on meeting an Iraqi Commander in the Mosque one Kuwaiti YO commented that he found the knowledge that Iraqis were also receiving a Dartmouth training reassuring. Proof that Dartmouth still commands tremendous respect internationally.

It is perhaps appropriate to end this chapter from the perspective of a Young Officer in the new millennium, Sub-Lieutenant Chris Easterbrook. His account makes an interesting comparison to that of 1971 and indeed of that of life on board the old *Britannia*. In many ways there is a thread of similarity throughout, after all the final product remains the same, 'to stimulate, inspire and teach a new generation to act and react instinctively as naval officers in the front line.'

Field gun crew practising on the Parade Ground.

The College decorated for the end of term Ball. The Ball offers
another opportunity for town involvement in the daily life of the College.
The Dartmouth Flower Club has for many years provided splendid floral
displays throughout the building and few will forget the past leadership
of the indomitable Mrs. Iris Webb.

'A Young Officer in 2003'

'The rate at which time passes, as many YO's will attest, is not constant. In my initial weeks at the College each day would last an age, each PT session an aeon and three terms may well have been an eternity. But now that my training is approaching its end, the weeks slip by without being noticed and, unlikely, as it may have seemed when I was in New Entry, I almost feel as though I'll miss the place.

I may just be being sentimental, and time has almost certainly numbed the pain of all those period zeros[10], but my time here seems to be not quite so bad. It was however undoubtedly tough at times. New Entry was dominated by periods of manic haste, when it seemed that you would never be ready in time for rounds, and then battles of self-control, as it was always when you were exhausted that a lecture would be held in a warm, badly ventilated lecture theatre. A happy consequence of this part of training being so difficult was the sense of achievement after you completed it. Although few of us would have wished to spend time on Dartmoor in November where sleep and dry clothes drift into distant memory, everyone knew they had achieved something when it had finished.

The heart of the second term is the six weeks every YO spends living alongside Junior Rates at sea. At the end of this lengthy deployment the Officer Cadets return to the College as wise old men of the sea, call everyone 'shippers' and spend a lot of time brushing the salt from their shoulders. Initial Sea Training consists of a good deal of cleaning, learning about life afloat and constantly trying not to get caught in a 'wind-up' by the Senior Rates, who revel in sending YO's to non-existent departments. This year the Lord High Admiral's Parade came at the end of my second term, so we provided the Guard of Honour for his Royal Highness, Vice Admiral The Prince of Wales.

The senior term is remarkably different from the previous two. By now it is assumed that the parade training, early mornings and lots of inspections have done their job and more emphasis is now placed on academic subjects. The senior term brought with it membership of the Senior Gunroom. As well as being able to eat in much grander surroundings, the SGR mess functions are almost legendary. The Socials Reps outdid themselves with everything from horseracing to heroes and villains fancy dress nights. The summer was also now upon us and it is difficult to resent instructing on the river in such good weather. It was not all fun and games however; the stress of constant inspections is replaced by the stress of imminent examinations. The stress level becomes apparent when lengthy conversations are heard in the SGR about whether Flight eat more than their fair share of sandwiches.

BBC Question Time on the Quarterdeck in 2003. Other television and radio programmes recorded at the College include the Antiques Road Show, Mastermind, Songs of Praise, Just a Minute and Any Questions?

Pudsey Bear takes the salute at charity divisions for Children in Need in November 1997.

This term was the first term of the new six entry scheme, so as well as an entry at the beginning of term, there was also one half way through. As one of the legacy entries, our training was not particularly affected. All we had to do was to get to grips with what the different Phases of training equated to in the old system.

10 The period beginning at 0600, before breakfast.

Commodore Tony Johnstone-Burt 'Splices the Mainbrace' in honour of HM The Queen's Golden Jubilee in 2002.

As I write this our Passing Out Parade is just over two weeks away. The day we all thought would never arrive is just in front of us. After this we will disperse amongst the Fleet for Common Fleet Time, or go to the first stage of flying training. It will have been almost a year since we arrived through the gates on the coach from Totnes station and, for one reason or another, I expect it will be a year that none of us will forget quickly.' (*Britannia Magazine*, 2003).

Any history of the College will, as this has, relate largely to the training of Young Officers by the Naval and Academic staff but of the 350 people employed by the College, 250 of them are local residents that rely on the College for their livelihood. These are the people that keep the College running on a day-to-day basis by providing essential services such as buildings and grounds maintenance, catering, transport, cleaning services, administrative and secretarial support. Much of this work was in the past done by permanent staff employed by the College on a permanent basis, but as the world changes so do attitudes towards business. The catering was privatised in 1986 and that heralded the way forward. The cleaning services followed some time later, but the next major privatisation was that of the maintenance services at Sandquay to Vosper Thornycroft Marine Services, (VTMS). Today the commercial partner, 'Flagship Training Ltd'[11] an organisation founded in 1996, supplies much of the Service Provision. In 1996 'Flagship Training Ltd' signed a fifteen-year agreement with the Ministry of Defence to enter into a unique partnering arrangement with the Royal Navy's Recruiting and Training Agency (NRTA), and in doing so ushered in a new era in naval, industrial and management training. One of the aims of the agreement was to increase training opportunities for non-Royal Navy students within the Royal Navy training organisation. Flagship markets Royal Navy training expertise and courses to overseas navies, related naval markets and to UK industry as a whole. Royal Navy or 'Flagship' personnel working to the highest standards set by the Royal Navy deliver any training purchased through 'Flagship'. Every aspect of training, from course design to delivery is subject to an internationally proven quality control system which has been in use and continually refined in all Royal Naval training establishments for many years. The commercial partner provides two main pillars of support for the College, firstly and perhaps the most important, is the 'service provision' whereby it has taken over and now runs most of the essential services mentioned above, although today much of the general maintenance and grounds work is contracted out, and secondly to provide an income generation potential by utilising any spare capacity that the College may have.

As Britannia Royal Naval College enters its second century much has changed to affect its daily life; the age of cadets, the shifting emphasis from academic to professional training, the total inclusion of women, the application of technology and the contracting out of essential support services. The previous one hundred years have proved that without the ability to change and reflect society Dartmouth could not have survived as a Naval College. However, while the means have continually changed over the past century there remains continuity in the aims and objectives of the College: to maintain the highest qualities of command, leadership, intellectual development and humility, which combine to produce an Officer of the Royal Navy. Although composed in 1955, John Masefield's words still resonate[12]:

In all the waters that are Britain's walls
The seamen face the issue as it falls
Against all Death that shatters and appals.

Often the issue is at touch and go
Between a few ships and a foreign foe,
How close the issue only seamen know.

Through fifty years of strain and overstrain
Within these precincts men have come to train
That Right may stand, that Britain may remain.

Well have they struggled both in peace and war,
Through grimmer tests than aught prepare them for,
To keep the Seven Seas and hold the shore.

Long may such Courage guard, such Wisdom guide
The men who sail all seas on every tide
To save the Queen,
That she may prosper, and Her realm abide.

11 Flagship Training is a Vosper Thornycroft joint venture company, (in collaboration with BAE Systems).

12 This poem penned by the Poet Laureate for the fiftieth anniversary of the College, appears in the *Britannia Magazine* for July 1955.

POSTSCRIPT

A Future Built on Ethos and Heritage

I t seems incredible that this excellent book, originally produced to mark the centenary of the College in 2005, has reached its third edition to be published in Her Majesty's Diamond Jubilee year. The College has been at the heart of the Royal Navy throughout Her Majesty's reign, and indeed played a most personal part in Her early life, and thus the timing seems particularly pertinent.

The College has never been far from debate and controversy, from early concerns as to whether Naval Officers could be trained on land at all, to more recent discussions on whether the building is still relevant to a 21st Century Navy of immense technological complexity.

To this I offer a quiet certainty that the essential nature of the Naval Officer is an enduring one. We inhabit a very particular environment where those we lead are part of a tightly knit team who remain close at hand – literally all in one boat. When I commanded HM Ships *Brecon*, *Sheffield* and *Cornwall*, I needed similar leadership capabilities to that required in a Sloop, Frigate or Ship of the Line from two centuries before. Leadership is about people and people do not change very much in the essence of their character.

Dartmouth shaped my Naval Career in a fundamental way. I remember very clearly the first sight of the College as we arrived by coach from Totnes. The place has a presence; it exudes historical significance and then, as now, wrapped a feeling around me that I had something to live up to. There is a powerful sense that this is where it all starts, and a knowledge that all the great leaders of the current Navy began their career here. To me , as the Commodore, the College acts almost as an extra member of staff, helping me inculcate a sense of the core values of the Navy as an enduring, historically proven bulwark of our Nation's capability.

The River Dart offers a unique maritime training ground, providing all the complexity required to first train and then test young Naval Officers in the vicissitudes of wind, tidal stream and changing depths. The people of Dartmouth assist at every turn, the town taking pride in its international reputation for Naval excellence. As the 21 different nations who send their cadets to BRNC would agree, the term 'Dartmouth trained' has a cachet which is second to none.

The College today has a central role in generating the Royal Navy of the future. Training has evolved to meet the needs of the modern fleet and the responsibilities of the Commodore now includes both Officers training at BRNC and Ratings training at HMS *Raleigh*, together with the 14 University Royal Naval Units around the country. Also under command is the Royal Navy Leadership Academy, with a responsibility for through-life leadership development. The Officer and Ratings training model has been rationalised and improved, and the first 10 weeks training for both covers much of the same ground, although the officer challenge is kept significantly more taxing.

My role in all of this is to hand the baton of the Future Navy to the next generation, with the hand of history on my shoulder as I look out to the Navy of 30 or 40 years hence. The College remains the cradle of Naval leadership for the future, as relevant today as in 1905, producing courageous leaders with the spirit to fight and win.

Richard Porter and Jane Harrold have produced that very rare thing – a definitive reference that is also a fascinating and highly readable book which captures the rich history of the Royal Navy training at Dartmouth. I am delighted that their sedulous research and elegantly structured presentation has met with such success.

Commodore Simon Williams ADC Royal Navy
Commodore, Britannia Royal Naval College

The Britannia Association

The Britannia Association is a registered Charity "uniting all the alumni of Britannia Royal Naval College." If you are a serving or retired officer in the Royal Navy or Royal Marines, or a wardroom member of staff at BRNC, you are eligible to join the Britannia Association.

BA accepts donations and legacies, and provides grants in support of non-publicly funded College activities and the wider Naval Service. It helps and encourages members to stay in touch with BRNC enabling them to make a contribution to the formation and welfare of successive generations of young officers, promoting military efficiency, fostering their *esprit de corps*, comradeship and welfare and preserving College traditions. It is unique among other naval and military associations in providing a focus for the Royal Naval College, Dartmouth.

His Royal Highness the Prince of Wales became patron on the Association's formation in 2001, believing that the College should become a real and meaningful point of convergence for all those who have been connected with its history and training provision during their lives. During 2011 The Britannia Association celebrated its 10th Anniversary in style, with a magnificent dinner for 330 members and their guests in the Painted Hall of the Old Royal Naval College, Greenwich. All generations of Naval Officers were represented from those who passed out some sixty or seventy years ago to those who passed only weeks before the event, thus acknowledging the growth and vibrancy of the Britannia Association.

BA has made a variety of grants from managed funds. It has provided a J80 yacht and three Cornish pilot gigs for use on the river; these have proved very popular among staff,

Photo taken by Kevin Pyne.

Cornish pilot gigs Leander *and* Bacchante *at the Isles of Scilly World Championships in 2004.*

cadets and members. There are plans afoot, after the J80 World Championships on the River Dart in 2012, to replace the yacht with two Hawk Day boats which will be accessible to a wider range of sailors.

Recent BA contributions have enhanced College life by the provision of some beautiful works of art currently on display in the main passageway, and the purchase of the Prince of Wales Cannon from the old Britannia moored in the river. The cannon now stands at the entrance to the Quarterdeck providing a link between the young cadets of yesteryear and the present day. Some of them may be seen rubbing it for luck as they pass just as their predecessors did. The Association has assisted with funding for the creation of The Bridge Wing (a "dry" recreational space) and the recent refurbishment of the Senior Gunroom Anteroom. Each year, support is also available for BA members who may undertake Merchant Navy liaison opportunities. Financial support is available for adventurous training, where an officer cadet's ambition is beyond the public purse. Recently the Association has supported diving in Belize and has provided the opportunity for a group of cadets to train a number of Officers and Ratings of the Sierra Leone Military.

A well-established and growing website (britanniaassociation.org. uk) continues to highlight information and services provided. A key feature is the opportunity for members to locate old friends and to network on a business level. The website also provides details of the ever-growing list of membership openings around the country, as well as college news and notification of forthcoming events.

A BA membership card allows access for members and their guests to the College, Passing Out Parades and College Balls, and the Wardroom welcomes use of the 'pay as you dine' facility.

In recent years a number of reunions have taken place in BRNC. BA members can access College archives to help with their planning of such events and the Britannia Association Office is willing to assist wherever it can. One word of advice is always to plan well ahead as date availability is at a premium.

The BA Office operates during office hours. Its business is managed by the Association Secretary, Mrs Liza Cadby with support of two part-time administrators. The team provides a focus for the BA within the College and is always happy to hear from members.

Contact details:
T: 01803 677565 / 69   E: admin@britanniaassciation.org.uk

Photo taken by Mrs J. Moores.

Past and present Captains and Commodores of BRNC in attendance at the Britannia Association 10th Anniversary Dinner at The Old Royal Hospital, Greenwich. 20th May 2011. (Commodore Jake Moores, Commodore Simon Williams, Rear Admiral Martin Alabaster, Vice Admiral Sir Richard Ibbotson and Rear Admiral Robin Shiffner)

Photo supplied by Midshipman Katy Henderson Royal Navy.

BRNC Cadets instructing members of the Sierra Leone Military. August 2011.

Centenary Celebrations 2005

1

2

3

4

5

8

6

7

1. The publication of this book launches the College's celebrations on 7th April. Chief of the Defence Staff General Sir Michael Walker GCB CMG CBE ADC receives his copy of the book from authors Dr Jane Harrold and Dr Richard Porter. Publisher Richard Webb and wife Gilly hard at work in the background selling books to some of the two hundred guests.

2. Centenary Lord High Admiral's Divisions, taken by General Sir Michael Walker, with Commodore Ibbotson, on 8th April.

3. A watercolour by HRH The Prince of Wales is admired on the Quarterdeck. The Prince's picture provides the centre piece of an art exhibition held in May, organised by the Britannia Association as part of the centenary celebrations.

4. The time capsule, placed under the foundation stone by King Edward VII in 1902, is recovered from its watery resting place by (from left to right) Commander Richard King, Commodore Tim Harris and Chief Petty Officer Nick Carter.

5. HRH The Duke of York unveils Centenary Lord High Admiral's Divisions, a specially commissioned painting of the College by Mandy Shepherd during his visit of 20th July.

6. HRH The Duke of York prepares to place his own contribution, in a sealed envelope, into the new time capsule, also on 20th July.

7&8. The Duke fails to escape being presented with a copy of the College's definitive history, inspiring an unscheduled visit to the Wardroom to view his signature on the ceiling.

9. The Centenary Band Spectacular. The parade ground becomes the venue for an amazing open-air concert, demonstrating the full range of the HM Royal Marine Band's musical repertoire. For the grand finale music and fireworks combine to tell the story of the Battle of Trafalgar, narrated by BBC South West weatherman David Braine, an officer in the Royal Naval Reserve.

10. HRH Prince Michael of Kent, together with Commodore Tim Harris and former commanding officers of the College, gathered for a centenary reunion dinner on 29th September.

11. Competitors in the International Regatta for Young Naval Officers from around the world, held at Dartmouth on 27th July.

12. HRH Prince Michael of Kent unveils a plaque to the memory of PO Wren Ellen Whittall, 63 years after she was killed when the College was bombed, as part of his visit on 30th September.

13. Academic Staff past and present meet to mark their centenary. Aged from 33 to 92 years old, those gathered represented nearly 70 years of the College's history.

14. Tree planting in the Trafalgar 200 Britannia Wood. Friend of the College Mrs Margaret Skipp plants her contribution, a Coast Redwood (Sequoia sepervirens) to Dartmouth's wood commemorating the other great naval anniversary of 2005, the Battle of Trafalgar.

APPENDIX I

Chronology

1843	The term 'Naval Cadet' used officially for the first time, though the term had been in common use for many years previously.
1857	Admiralty decides officer cadets should serve on board a training vessel, initially HMS *Illustrious* at Haslar Creek Portsmouth.
1859 1st January	*Illustrious* replaced by HMS *Britannia*.
1860	HMS *Prince of Wales* launched (later HMS *Britannia*)
1863 30th September	*Britannia* arrives in the Dart.
1864	HMS *Hindostan* arrives.
1869	Second *Britannia* arrives in the Dart (previously HMS *Prince of Wales*)
1874	Committee set up and chaired by Ad. E. B. Rice to look into health and general training of cadets.
1875	Rice Committee reports that a college should be built on shore.
1876 July	Committee under chairmanship of Ad. G. G. Wellesley formed to look into the acquisition of a site and considers thirty two sites.
1877	Prince Albert Victor and Prince George (later King George V) join as cadets.
1878	Passing Out photographs first taken.
1878	First Beagle pack founded.
1884 February	*Britannia Magazine* first published.
1884 May	The *Wave* arrives, (barque rigged vessel of 300 tons)
1885	Yet another committee suggests moving training to The Solent.
1895 15th November	Admiralty Board proposes to revise existing cadet training scheme.

1896 March	First Lord of the Admiralty announces that a new college will be built at Dartmouth.
1900 18th April	Admiralty accepts tender from Higgs & Hill to build the college for £220,600 in three and a half years.
1902 7th March	Edward VII lays the Foundation Stone.
1902 September	Sick Quarters opened, three years ahead of the main College.
1902 25th December	'Selborne Memorandum' on officer training published.
1903	Cyril Ashford appointed as first Headmaster of RNC Osborne.
1903 September	RNC Osborne opens. Introduction of the Selborne Scheme.
1903	Prof. J A Ewing appointed as Director of Naval Education from University of Cambridge.
1904	Battleship HMS *Britannia* laid down and the old ship became known as HMS *Britannia* (hulk).
1905 14th September	College opens.
1906	Swimming bath opened.
1906	Masters' Hostel opened.
1906	Rifle range under arches in use.
1907	First introduction of the new six term scheme. (Blake, Drake, Grenville, Hawke, Rodney (later re-named Exmouth) and St Vincent.
1907	E Block opens.
1907	Swimming bath covered in.
1909 May	Prince of Wales (later King Edward VIII) joins as an 'Exmouth' term cadet.

1910	New squash courts completed.
1910	Visit of their Royal Highnesses the Prince and Princess of Wales.
1911 January	Prince Albert (later King George VI) joins as a Grenville cadet.
1911 February	Epidemic of measles and mumps kills two cadets and is also caught by Prince Edward and Prince Albert.
1911 March	HRH the Prince of Wales passed out.
1913	New entrance to grounds, from North constructed.
1913	Special Entry begun for boys who had completed their education at public school, not based at Dartmouth initially.
1914	Construction of D Block begins.
1914 1st August	Telegram to mobilize.
1914 September	College re-opened.
1916 July	The old *Britannia* is towed out of the Dart, her copper plating going to help the war effort.
1917 May	New studies connecting D Block completed.
1917 September	HRH Prince George joined.
1917 September	D Block opens.
1918 9th November	HMS *Britannia*, battleship sunk off Cape Trafalgar by German U-Boat.
1920 March	HRH Prince George passed out.
1920	First hard courts behind D Block completed.
1920 May	Admiralty decides to close RNC Osborne.
1921 20th May	Closure of RNC Osborne. Five new terms at Dartmouth from Osborne; Anson, Benbow, Hood, Rodney and Duncan.
1924 23rd November	Dedication of War Memorial Shrine.
1926 May	Parade Ground laid out.
1927	New rifle range opened.
1927	Presentation of yacht *Amaryllis*.
1930 January	New pavilion opened.
1937	'House' system replaces terms; Blake, Exmouth, Grenville, Hawke and St Vincent. (Drake was the House for the two junior terms)
1937 May.	The mast of the yacht *Britannia* erected on the pavilion.
1938 5th-6th July	Ninth Infantry Brigade under the leadership of Brigadier B. L. Montgomery, accommodated at the College.
1938 15th October	Montgomery visits the College and presents a statuette in gratitude for the help given on 5th-6th July of that year.
1939 22nd-23rd July	King George VI, Queen Elizabeth, and the Princesses Elizabeth and Margaret visit the College.
1942 18th September	College bombed.
1942 3rd October	College moves to Bristol to become HMS *Britannia IV*.
1943 1st February	Cadets of HMS *Britannia* re-assembled at Eaton Hall, Cheshire.
1943	HMS *Effingham*, The Combined Operations Headquarters under Mountbatten move into the College buildings.
1943 December	The US Navy occupies the College.
1946 19th September	RNC returns to Dartmouth.
1948 September	Cadets enter Dartmouth age 16 years. Fees for tuition and boarding abolished.
1949 May	Last of the 13 year old entry.
1949 Winter term	The Chapel of Remembrance is opened.
1953 1st July	Following commissioning of Royal Yacht HMY *Britannia* the College becomes HMS *Dartmouth*.
1954	Committee on Officer Structure & Training (COST) reports on 18 year old entry training scheme.
1955	COST scheme necessitates many internal alterations to the College.
1955 May	First 18 year old cadets join.
1955	Director of Studies replaces post of Headmaster. House system replaced by five 'divisions'; Blake, Drake, Exmouth, Grenville and St Vincent. Dartmouth Training Squadron (DTS) operational.
1955 July	BRNC celebrates its Golden Jubilee.
1955 November	College receives the Freedom of the Borough of Dartmouth.
1956	Royal Marine Band arrives.
1958	Queen's Colour is presented to the College.
1958	Murray Committee increased minimum entry to BRNC to two 'A' levels.
1959	First Upper Yardmen entry at BRNC.
1960 September	Murray Scheme Introduced. First year professional training at BRNC (inc. DTS), second year at sea as a midshipman and third year at Dartmouth as acting sub-lieutenant for a one year academic course of first year degree standard.

1962	First special course for 'New Commonwealth' and foreign officers.
1963	Centenary celebrations of HMS *Britannia* at Dartmouth.
1963	First five cadets selected for university entry instead of third year at BRNC.
1963	Hawke Division re-established in the old hospital quarters.
1964	Casper John Hall opens.
1965	First Direct Graduate Entry.
1966	First University Cadet Entry (sponsored cadets).
1968	Cunningham replaced Exmouth and Jellicoe replaced Grenville as divisional titles.
1968	Work begins on the building of College Way.
1970	Drake Division abolished.
1971	Last Pay Parade on the Quarterdeck.
1972	'Naval College Entry' replaces Murray Scheme.
1972	Rank of Cadet abolished, all junior officers under training become Midshipmen.
1973	HMS *Walkerton* joins as Navigational Training Tender.
1973	First women officers under training as QARNNS.
1973	Last of Murray Scheme cadets Pass Out.
1974	Special Duties Officers' Pre-Qualifying Course (St George) comes to Dartmouth.
1976	Women's officer training course moves from Greenwich to Dartmouth to form separate 'Talbot' Division.
1979	HM Ships *Sandpiper* and *Peterel* join to form the Dartmouth Navigation Training Squadron and replace HMS *Walkerton*.
1986	Catering at the College is privatised.
1990 25th January	Mast of racing yacht *Britannia* lost from the Pavilion (canteen) during a severe storm along with twelve trees in the College grounds.
1990	Integration of male and female officer training.
1990 August	Seamanship Training Vessel *Hindostan* arrives at Sandquay.
1990 12th December	HMS *Sandpiper* and HMS *Peterel* (Dartmouth Navigation Training Squadron) decommissioned.

1995 September	Integration of Foreign and Commonwealth Young Officers within Naval Studies course.
1996	Special Duties Officers' Course moves to BRNC on the closure RNC Greenwich.
1996	Contract with the commercial partner 'Flagship Training' initiated.
1997	Blake Division abolished.
1998	Three Divisions replaced by two Squadrons, 'Cunningham' and 'St Vincent'
1999 May	Senior Upper Yardmen replace Special Duties Officers.
1999 July	Britannia Museum opened by HRH Prince Philip.
2000	Steele Report published.
2000 December	Post of Director of Studies abolished.
2001 January	First Head of Faculty appointed.
2001 December	Learning Centre opened.
2003 May	Six term entry introduced.
2003 September	Post of Head of Faculty abolished.
2004	Academic faculty merged with professional training and creation of five 'pillars'.
2005	BRNC celebrates centenary.
2007 11th January	The Rt. Hon. Tony Blair MP is the first British serving Prime Minister to visit the College.
2007	Establishment of The Britannia Museum Board of Trustees.
2008 1st July	The University of Plymouth takes over responsibility for academic provision and staff.
2009 April	New Initial Officer Training scheme introduced, returning to three term entry.
2009 May	BRNC Royal Marine Band disbanded.
2012 February	Initial Naval Training (Officer) introduced with four entries over three fifteen week terms. Closer alignment with ratings training at HMS *Raleigh*. Discussions over co-location of officer and rating training continues.

APPENDIX II

Captains and Commodores of Britannia Royal Naval College

1905–2012

1905	W.E. Goodenough	**1963**	J.E.L. Martin, D.S.C.
1907	T. D.W. Napier	**1966**	I.W. Jamieson, D.S.C.
1910	H. Evan-Thomas	**1968**	D. Williams
1912	Hon. Victor Stanley, M.V.O.	**1970**	A.G. Tait, D.S.C., A.D.C.
1914	T.D.W. Napier, M.V.O.	**1972**	J.M. Forbes, A.D.C.
1914	E. Hyde-Parker	**1974**	M.A. Higgs, A.D.C.
1915	N.C. Palmer, C.V.O.	**1975**	S.D.S. Bailey
1916	W.G.E. Ruck-Keene, M.V.O.	**1976**	P.W. Greening
1919	E. La T. Leatham, C.B.	**1978**	N. Hunt, M.V.O.
1921	F.A. Marten, C.M.G., C.V.O.	**1980**	J. Oswald
1923	The Hon. H. Meade, C.B., C.V.O., D.S.O., A.D.C.	**1982**	T.M. Bevan, A.D.C.
1926	M.E. Dunbar-Nasmith, V.C., C.B.	**1984**	G.M. Tullis
1929	S.J. Meyrick	**1987**	J.R. Brigstocke
1931	N.A. Wodehouse	**1988**	J.R. Shiffner, A.D.C.
1934	R.V. Holt, D.S.O., M.V.O.	**1991**	R. Hastilow
1936	F. Dalrymple-Hamilton	**1993**	S. Moore
1939	R.L.B. Cunliffe	**1995**	A.P. Masterton-Smith, A.D.C.[i]
1942	E.A. Aylmer, D.S.C.	**1998**	R.A.G. Clare
1943	G.H. Warner, D.S.C	**1999**	M.W.G. Kerr, A.D.C.
1946	P.B.R.W. William-Powlett, C.B.E., D.S.O.	**2002**	C.A. Johnstone-Burt, O.B.E., A.D.C.
1948	Faulkner, C.B.E., D.S.O.	**2004**	R.J. Ibbotson, D.S.C.
1949	N. Vincent Dickinson, D.S.O., D.S.C.	**2005**	T.R. Harris
1951	R.T. White, D.S.O.	**2007**	M.B. Alabaster
1953	W.G. Crawford, D.S.O.	**2008**	J.K. Moores
1956	W.J. Munn, D.S.O., O.B.E.	**2011**	S.P. Williams, A.D.C.
1958	F.H.E. Hopkins, D.S.O., D.S.C.		
1960	H.R. Law, O.B.E., D.S.C.		
1961	W.J. Parker, O.B.E., D.S.C.		

i In 1996 the post of Commanding Officer BRNC became that of Commodore.

APPENDIX III

Headmasters, Directors of Studies & Heads of Faculty

Britannia Royal Naval College 1905-2003

Headmasters Britannia Royal Naval College, 1905-1955	Directors of Studies Britannia Royal Naval College, 1955-2000	Heads of Faculty Britannia Royal Naval College, 2001-2003
1905 C.E. Ashford, K.B.E., C.B., M.V.O., L.L.D., M.A.	**1955** J.W. Stork, C.B., C.B.E., M.A.	**2001** P.R. Street, B.Sc., Ph.D.
1927 E.W.E. Kempson, M.C., M.A.	**1959** G.W.E. Ghey, M.B.E., M.A., A.M.I.E.E.	**2001** A.C. Walton, B.Sc., Ph.D., P.G.C.E.
1942 J.W. Stork, C.B., C.B.E., M.A.	**1967** H.G. Stewart, C.B.E., M.A.	
	1978 C.H. Christie, M.A.	
	1986 C.I.M. Jones, M.A., F.B.I.M.	
	1988 A.W. Machin, B.Sc., Ph.D.	

APPENDIX IV

Dartmouth recipients of the Victoria Cross[i]

Name	Rank	Where serving	Date	Dates at Dartmouth[ii]
Guy B. J D.	Midshipman	HMS *Barfleur*, China	13/7/1900	*Britannia*, 1897-98
Ritchie H. P.	Commander	HMS *Goliath, Dar-es-Salaam*	29/11/1914	*Britannia*, 1890-92
Holbrook N. D.	Lieutenant	HMS/M *B11* Dardanelles	13/12/1914	*Britannia*, 1903-05
Robinson E. G.	Lt Commander	HMS *Vengeance*, Dardanelles	26/2/1915	*Britannia*, 1897-98
Malleson W. S. A.	Midshipman	HMS *River Clyde*, Gallipoli	25/4/1915	Osborne/BRNC 1912-14
Boyle E. C.	Lt Commander	HMS/M *E14*, Dardanelles	27/4-18/5/1915	*Britannia*, 1897-99
Dunbar-Nasmith M. E.[iii]	Lt Commander	HMS/M *E11*, Dardanelles	19/5/1915	*Britannia*, 1898-1900
Cookson E. C.	Lt Commander	HMS *Comet*, Kut-el-Amara	28/9/1915	*Britannia*, 1897-98
Firman H. O. B.	Lieutenant	SS *Julnar*, Kut-el-Amara	24/4/1916	*Britannia*, 1901-03
Bingham E. B. S.	Commander	HMS *Nestor*, Jutland	31/5/1916	*Britannia*, 1895-97
Jones L.W.	Commander	HMS *Shark*, Jutland	31/5/1916	*Britannia*, 1894-96
Campbell G.	Commander	HMS *Q5*, Atlantic	17/2/1917	*Britannia*, 1902-03
White G. S.	Lt Commander	HMS/M *E14* Dardanelles	28/1/1918	*Britannia*, 1901-02
Carpenter A. F. B.	Commander	HMS *Vindictive*, Zeebrugge	23/4/1918	*Britannia*, 1896-97
Harrison A. L.[iv]	Lt Commander	HMS *Vindictive*, Zeebrugge	23/4/1918	*Britannia*, 1901-02
Bradford G. N.	Lt Commander	HMS *Iris II*, Zeebrugge	23/4/1918	*Britannia*, 1902-04
Sandford R. D.[v]	Lieutenant	HMS/M *C3* Zeebrugge	23/4/1918	Osborne/BRNC, 1904-08
Crutchley V. A. C.	Lieutenant	HMS *Vindictive*, Ostend	9-10/5/1918	Osborne/BRNC, 1906-10
Agar A. W. S.	Lieutenant	HMCMB 4, Kronstadt	16-17/6/1919	*Britannia*, 1905-06
Dobson C. C.	Commander	HMCMB 31, Kronstandt	18/8/1919	*Britannia*, 1899-1901
Roope G. B.	Lt Commander	HMS *Glowworm*, Norwegian Sea	8/4/1940	Osborne/BRNC, 1918-22
Lee B. A. W.	Captain	HMS *Hardy*, Narvik	10/4/1940	Osborne/BRNC, 1908-12
Fegen E. S. F.	Captain	HMS *Jervis Bay*, Atlantic	5/11/1940	Osborne/BRNC, 1904-08
Wanklyn M. D.	Lt Commander	HMS/M *Upholder*, Mediterranean	25/5/1941	BRNC, 1925-28
Peters F. T.	Captain	HMS *Walney*, Oran Harbour	8/11/1942	*Britannia*, 1904-06
Sherbrooke R. St.V.	Captain	HMS *Onslow*, Barents Sea	31/12/1942	Osborne/BRNC, 1913-17
Linton J. W.	Commander	HMS/*M Turbulent*, Mediterranean	4/5/1942	Osborne/BRNC, 1919-22
Place B. J. G.	Lieutenant	HMS/M *X6*, Kaafjord	22/9/1943	BRNC 1935-39

i The main source for this list is Winton, J 1978: *The Victoria Cross at Sea*, (Michael Joseph Ltd, London.)

ii Dates for HMS *Britannia* are approximate, as cadets were not listed in the Navy Lists of the time.

iii Captain Dunbar-Nasmith VC was captain of the College between 1926-29

iv Harrison's VC is displayed inside the main entrance of the College.

v Sandford's VC is also displayed inside the main entrance of the College.

APPENDIX V

References and Bibliography

Anon. 1961 – *From Dartmouth to the Dardanelles – A Midshipman's Log.* William Heinemann, London.

Anon. 1981 – *The Register of the Victoria Cross.* This England Books.

Bacon Ad. Sir R. H. 1929 – *The Life of Lord Fisher of Kilverstone.* London.

Bradford S. 1991 – *George VI.* Fontana, London.

Boyce G. D. (ed.) 1990 – *The Crisis of British Power: The Imperial and Naval Papers of the Second Earl of Selborne, 1895-1910.* The Historians' Press, London.

Brassey T. A. (ed.) 1903 – *The Naval Annual.* J. Griffin & Co., Portsmouth.

Britannia Royal Naval College. 1994 – *Encyclopaedia Britannia.* BRNC, Dartmouth.

Bush Capt. E. W. 1963 – *How to Become a Naval Officer.* George, Allen & Unwin, London.

Cherry B. & Pevsner N. 1989 – *The Buildings of England* – Devon. Penguin.

Clare R. & Piska A. 1973 – *The Dartmouth Cadet.* In Watts A. J. (ed.) *Warships and Navies:* Ian Allan, London pp.79-88

Coles A. 1979 – *Three Before Breakfast.* Kenneth Mason, Havant.

Collinson D. 2000 – *Chronicles of Dartmouth* Richard Webb, Dartmouth.

Colville Q. 2003 – *The role of the interior in constructing notions of class and status; a case study of Britannia Royal Naval College, Dartmouth, 1905-1960.* Unpublished PhD thesis.

Cradock C. 1908 – *Whispers from the Fleet.* J. Griffen & Co. Portsmouth.

Davies E. L. & Grove E. J. 1980 – *The Royal Naval College Dartmouth, Seventy Five Years in Pictures. Gieves & Hawkes,* Portsmouth.

Davies E. L. 2003 – The Selborne Scheme: The Education of a Boy. In Hore P. (ed.) 2003 – *Patrick Blackett – Sailor, Scientist and Socialist.* Frank Cass, London.

Dawson Capt. N. 1933 – *Flotillas – A Hard Lying Story.* Rich & Cowan, London.

Dickinson H. W. 1998 – Britannia at Portsmouth and Portland. *Mariner's Mirror* 84 pp.434-43.

Dimbleby J. 1994 – *The Prince of Wales: A Biography.* Warner Books, London.

Donaldson F. 1974 – *Edwards VIII.* Weidenfeld & Nicolson, London.

Fairbairn D. 1929 – *The Narrative of a Naval Nobody.* John Murray, London.

Fellows R. 1995 – *Edwardian Architecture.* Lund Humphries, London.

Fisher, Admiral of the Fleet Lord J. A. 1919 – *Memoirs.* Hodder & Stoughton, London.

Fisher, Admiral of the Fleet Lord J. A. 1919 – *Records.* Hodder & Stoughton, London.

Fletcher M. H. 1989 – *The WRNS A History of the Women's Royal Naval Service.* Naval Institute Press. Annapolis.

Fraser E. & Leyland J. 1898 – *The Story of the Britannias in War and Peace.* The Navy and Army Illustrated.

Freeman R . – *A Wrens-Eye View of Wartime Dartmouth.* Dartmouth History Research Group Paper 12.

Gieves (publishers) – *How to become a Naval Officer (Dartmouth).* Various Editions.

Gieves and Hawkes (publishers) – *Customs and Etiquette of the Royal Navy.* Various Editions.

Hampshire A. C. 1971 – *Royal Sailors.* William Kimber, London.
1979 – *Just an Old Navy Custom.*
William Kimber, London.

Heald T. 1991 – *The Duke: A Portrait of Prince Philip.*
Holder & Stoughton, London.

Holloway A. 1993 – *From Dartmouth to War: A Midshipman's Journal.*
Bucklands Publications Ltd, London.

Hore P. (ed.) 2003 – *Patrick Blackett – Sailor, Scientist and Socialist.*
Frank Cass, London.

Hough R. 1992 – *Edward and Alexandra: Their Private and Public Lives.*
Hodder & Stoughton, London.

Hughes E. A. 1950 – *The Royal Naval College Dartmouth.*
Winchester Publications, London.

Judd D. 1982 – *King George VI 1895-1952.* Michael Joseph, London.

Kalton G. 1966 – *The Public Schools.* Longmans, London.

Kennedy P. 1991 – *The Rise and Fall of British Naval Mastery.*
Fontana Press, London.

Kemp P.K. (ed.) 1960 – *The Papers of Admiral Sir John Fisher Volume 1.*
Spottiswood, Ballantyne & Co., London.

Kemp P.K. (ed.) 1964 – *The Papers of Admiral Sir John Fisher Volume 2.*
Spottiswood, Ballantyne & Co., London.

Lambert N. A. 1999 – *Sir John Fisher's Naval Revolution.*
University of South Carolina Press.

Mackay R. F. 1973 – *Fisher of Kilverstone.* Clarendon Press, Oxford.

Mason U. S. 1977 – *The Wrens 1917-77.* Educational Explorers, Reading.

Marder A. J. 1953 – *Fear God and Dread Nought – The Correspondence of Admiral of The Fleet Lord Fisher of Kilverstone.* Jonathan Cape, London.

Parker J. 1990 – *Prince Philip: A Critical Biography.*
Sidgwick & Jackson, London.

Pack S. W. C. 1966 – *Britannia at Dartmouth.* Alvin Redman, London.

Penn G. 2000 – *Infighting Admirals: Fisher's Feud with Beresford and the Reactionaries.* Lee Cooper, Barnsley.

Perkin H. 1990 – *The Rise of Professional Society; England since 1880.*
Routledge, London.

Perkins R. 1999 – *Military and Naval Silver.* Published privately.

Pevsner N. 1952 – *The Buildings of England – Devon. Vol 2 S. Devon.*
Penguin, London.

Public Record Office, Kew.
Admiralty Papers.

ADM12: 987; 951; 967; 972; (Health of Naval Cadets- 1875-7)
ADM1/6156 Circular 3c. Regarding a Sea going Training Ship after Britannia.(1870)
ADM1/8706/199 Health of Naval Cadets; Dawson Committee Report.(1926)
ADM1/8756/165 Fees for RN Colleges.(1932)
ADM1/8765/314 Entry Regulations for RN Cadets.(1932)
ADM1/8767/98 Board of Education Inspection of BRNC (1933)
ADM1/23410 Noble Committee recommendations. (1946-52)
ADM1/25950 Civilian staff pay & conditions at BRNC (1954-8)
ADM1/26359 BRNC enlarged entry building programme (1954-7)
ADM1/26559 Design for new Badge (1954-7)
ADM1/17264 & 17293 Noble Committee Report (1945)
ADM1/20549 Return from Eaton Hall (1945-7)
ADM1/20918 Revised entry scheme. (1947)
ADM1/21773 Report of Dartmouth Accommodation Committee (1949-50)
ADM1/22463 Candidates from secondary grammar schools (1951)
ADM1/22690 BRNC New system of entry. (1948)
ADM1/778 Director of Naval Education Report (1904)
ADM1/8375/106 Director of Naval Education Report for 1913 (1914)
ADM6/460 List of cadets on *Britannia* and at BRNC.
ADM6/465-7 Selborne Scheme (1903)
ADM7/936 Director of Naval Education Reports (1904-13)
ADM116/1213 Naval cadets committee on training (1913)
ADM116/6360 Entry of cadets to BRNC (1950-1)
ADM178/187 BRNC Examination & passing out results- special entry. (1939)
ADM203 BRNC & RNC Greenwich; correspondence & papers. (1872-1977)

Rodger N. A. M. 1997 – *The Safeguard of the Sea: A Naval History of Britain. Volume One 660-1649.* Harper Collins, London.

Rose K. 1983 – *King George V.* Weidenfeld & Nicolson, London.

Statham E. P. 1904 – *The Story of the 'Britannia'.* Cassell & Co., London.

Watkin D. 1979 – *English Architecture.* Thames & Hudson, London.

Wiener M. 1981 – *English Culture and the Decline of the Industrial Spirit – 1850-1980* Cambridge University Press.

Wheeler-Bennett J. W. 1958 – *King George VI: His Life and Reign.*
Macmillan, London.

Winton J. 1978 – *The Victoria Cross at Sea.* Michael Joseph, London.
1981 – *Captains and Kings.* Bluejacket Books, Clwyd.

Ziegler P. 1985 – *Mountbatten.* Collins, London.
1991 – *King Edward VIII: The Official Biography.* Fontana, London.

Index

Acknowledgements

Anthony Aylmer, Rev John Beadle RN, Lieutenant John Beattie RN (Rtd.), Laura Barlee, Lieutenant Niall Benfell RN, Gary Bodinnar, Lieutenant Tim Boughton RN, Admiral Sir John Brigstocke KCB, Rev Alison Britchfield RN, Rev Kenneth Bromage RN, CPO Nick Carter, Commander M G Chichester RN (Rtd.), Don Collinson, Quintin Colville, Jan Cowling, Dr Harry Dickinson, Sir John Drinkwater QC, Brian Edgington, Lieutenant Commander Carlos Edwards MBE, Michael Floyd, David Gallop, Margo Garcia Almo, Philip Grove, Louise Hardy, Margaret Harrold, Michael Hill, William Hodges, Adrian Holloway, Michael Hunter, Rachael Johnstone-Burt, Craig Keating, Joslin Landell-Mills, Lieutenant F Mauron FN, Lieutenant Gareth Mawdsley RN, Rev David McLean RN, Brian Parker, Karen Peach, Dr Duncan Priestly, Fred Radcliffe, Carol Rampling, Dr Paul Rampling, Dr Ian Roberts, Lieutenant Commander M Rix GN, Rev Peter Scott OBE RN, William Searle, Rear Admiral Robin Shiffner CB, Gillian Smith, Anne Tasker, Gordan Thomas, Martin Thomas, William Thomson, Robert Veale, Robert Wardle, Lieutenant Omar Wheatly USN, Admiral Sir David Williams GCB DL, Captain David Wixon RN (Rtd), Michael Zollo and the staff of the Dartmouth Museum and Cookworthy Museum, Kingsbridge.

Special thanks to Keith Franks for taking and printing many of the photographs, Mandy Shepherd for the cover painting and other drawings in the book, Richard Kennell for his assistance in the library and historic book collection, Michael Pearce for supplying much valuable material, Mark Grove for sharing his historical knowledge, Rear Admiral Roy Clare for his valuable assistance and guidance, Vice Admiral Sir Richard Ibbotson KCB CB DSC, Rear Admiral Martin Alabaster and Commodore Simon Williams for their contributions past and present, Rear Admiral Mark Kerr, Commander Richard Marshall RN, Commander Max Rance RN, Commander David Vaughan RN and our families and colleagues at BRNC for their support during the project.

Dr Jane Harrold and Dr Richard Porter